"Voraciously **CURIOUS,** brilliant, deeply fortifying, hilarious—a heartbreaking adventure. Something like a human heart redesign, a makeover through theater, or an art surgery that hurts, but heals."

– *Barrie Cole* Writer / Playwright

REVIEWS OF: Curious
Plays

"I've been to many **CURIOUS THEATRE** shows over the years. They can be pretty raw, which I like, and are always surprising.

I'd leave FEELING MORE AWAKE & MORE ALIVE, which is exactly what you want when you go see a show."

– *Ira Glass* *"This American Life" Host, NPR*

This book is dedicated to our beloved comrade, Matt Rieger.

Our coach.

"All that matters is – that here I stand. That's enough.
And I know the question. Have had plenty of time to
contemplate it. And yet the question remains.
And yet here I stand. And that is enough."

— *Matt Rieger*

Curious
Plays

curious theatre branch • contemporary theater collection

CURIOUS Playwrights – 1988-2022

Jayita Bhattacharya

Bryn Magnus

Jenny Magnus

Beau O'Reilly

Shawn Reddy

Matt Rieger

Matt Test

Julia Williams

Curious
Plays

Curious Theatre Branch

CURIOUS MEMBERS at a table read / *Prop Thtr, CHICAGO*

Curious
Plays

Jayita Bhattacharya
Bryn Magnus
Jenny Magnus
Beau O'Reilly
Shawn Reddy
Matt Rieger
Matt Test
Julia Williams

Copyright © 2022 by Curious Theatre Branch
Published by JackLeg Press in 2022

ISBN: 978-1-956907-02-5 / Paperback

Library of Congress Cataloging-In-Publication-Data
Library of Congress Control Number: **2022942643**
Playwrights: Bhattacharya, Jayita | Magnus, Bryn |
           Magnus, Jenny | O'Reilly, Beau | Reddy, Shawn |
           Rieger, Matt | Test, Matt | Williams, Julia
     Titles: *Curious Plays, 1988-2022*
           An Introductory Alphabet, essay by Barrie Cole
Description: 8 plays by Curious Theatre Branch playwrights
Publisher: Jennifer Harris | Jackleg Press, Washington D.C.

The Curious Theatre Branch - Contemporary Theater Collection
Curatorial Selection of plays by Beau O'Reilly
Book Editing & Design by Jason Greenberg / Art Works Design
Principal Photography by Jeffrey Bivens

Image Credits:
Cover illustration (Curious Theatre logo) by Jason Greenberg, 2021
Original Curious Theatre logo designed by Colm O'Reilly, 1992
Frontispiece, back cover & internal photography by Jeffrey Bivens

ACKNOWLEDGEMENTS

This book is dedicated to:

The MEMBERS—both past, present, living & dead—
of The Curious Theatre Branch...and the FRIENDS,
our Curious Comrades; Chicago's artists, actors,
musicians, & collaborators who make our theater
community so strong and vibrant; SO CURIOUS!

The work in this book was created & produced by,
with, and for The Curious Theatre Branch

2022 Ensemble Members:
Jayita Bhattacharya, Jeffrey Bivens, Stefan Brün,
Jenny Magnus, T-Roy Martin, Beau O'Reilly, Matt Rieger,
Vicki Walden, & Julia Williams

Alumni Members / Alumni Participants:
Scottie Barsotti, Kristin Basta, John Coyne, Mark Comiskey,
Jennifer Cozzi, Jill Daly, Marianne Fieber, Hallie Gordon,
Paul Leisen, Michael Martin, Bryn Magnus, Guy Massey,
Kat McJimsey, Jennifer Moniz, Colm O'Reilly, Liz Paine,
Kathleen Powers, Shawn Reddy, Adam Rosenberg,
John Starrs, Anita Stenger, Spencer Sundell, Kate
Teichman, Matt Test, H.B. Ward, Teresa Weed, Matt Wilson

We would also like to thank Jennifer Harris & JackLeg Press

General Notes on the Text:

Some dialogues—and the opera—require alternating and simultaneous
line delivery in complex call and response structures or movements.
Where necessary those details are presented in stage directions.
Some texts are structured in opposing left and right columns or
in multi-adjacent columns. See each play's notations indicating
sequencing of lines delivery. Our invitation is that you interpret and
experiment with these structures. Unless otherwise indicated, roles
can be played by performers of any gender, age or ethnicity.

TABLE of CONTENTS

PLAYS / Authors

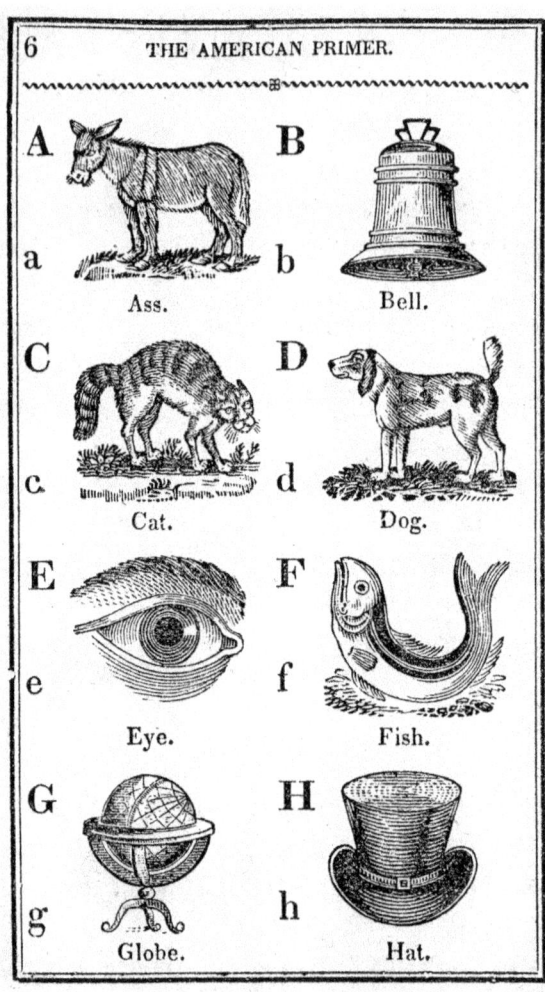

A a   Ass.

B b   Bell.

C c   Cat.

D d   Dog.

E e   Eye.

F f   Fish.

G g   Globe.

H h   Hat.

AN INTRODUCTORY ALPHABET

by **Barrie Cole** / July 4, 2022

A is for **A.** A is for both the letter A and A the word. A is a beginning and by the time Z comes around, well then, the beginning is probably over, unless, unless, unless of course, whatever the "it" is has a very long beginning and if it does, well, then what? A is also for anthology and that is what this book is. *It is an anthology.*

B is for **Book,** this book. This is in an introduction to the book. It is not the beginning of the book, even though it is, at the beginning, near the beginning. The real beginning begins with the first play in the book, the title of which begins with the letter B. And what play is that? Why, it is *Black River Falls* by Bryn Magnus whose name, by the way, also begins with the letter B. And that Reader, certainly is convenient. But perhaps you will read the plays out of order, read Beau O'Reilly's *One Boppa*, or Jayita Bhattachayra's *To End to Seem to End* first and then, well, *you will have made your own beginning.*

C is for **The Curious Theatre Branch** and C is also for Chicago. The branch is the theater company and it is located in the city of Chicago and so the two have a great deal to do with each other, and the branch that is the Curious Theatre Branch is a branch which extends out and out and out some more. The Curious Theatre Branch is a heavy, continually fruit-bearing branch. Some might call it miraculous. It is a branch so replete with branches that the branch of it now has branches extending from its original branch. In fact, it is such a branchy branch that it is practically a tree and it continues to bloom *and fruit continually.*

D is for **Decades;** more than three of them now, since 1988, just blooming and blooming in the form of original plays and performances and doing so *despite countless obstacles.*

E **is for eight.** There are eight of them here, in the book; eight plays from the branch. This book is a place to explore them and in doing so, delve into what the playwrights themselves were exploring when they wrote them, and revised them and also when they were brought to life with actors, and sometimes directors and designers, and stage managers too and all the other elements that go into the experience of making the lived experiences that are *the wonderments called plays.*

F **is for the first time,** here they are together in this form, available to be read because even if you have been a long time audience member of this work, it can be challenging to remember every aspect of them and maybe you want to experience them if only in your mind, or read scenes aloud with friends, or maybe you have heard of the Curious Theatre Branch but live in Wyoming or Brazil or Antarctica, or maybe you do live in Chicago, but were born quite a bit later than 1988 and so you missed out on some of the earlier work. Regardless of your reason, it is fortunate to have these plays all bound together and with photographs too to *fortify your memory and/or imagination.*

G **is for gorgeous** because oh, what a gorgeous thing this book is, this voraciously curious, brilliant, hilarious, *complicated book of plays.*

H **is for the heart of the thing.** It can be hard to get to the heart of a thing in a collection, in an anthology, especially one like this. There are very different plays here, but I think you will find that regardless of straightforwardness or experimentation, regardless of cast size, regardless of structure or the absence of it, the plays that the Curious Theatre Branch produce are plays that deal most of all with being human, with what it means to be a human and what it means to have relationships with other humans. *How do humans decide what matters* and what doesn't? And once they do decide, what do they do then?

I is for the **inherent impossibility** in existing, while existing anyway. That's the "it" of it. And, also, that the audience is always included. It's a shared impossibility project, and it's never resolved, and everyone copes with this together and this book furthers this *inquiry and investigation into this impossibility of existing* project which is constantly underway.

J is for **jellyfish** and, also, for Jason Greenberg who is the editor and designer of this book. Jason writes, "Maybe these plays are evidence of such a wild and disparate creativity that there is not a single spinal thru-line, but rather a condensed sea of jellyfish absorbing/sending out in every direction, spores of creative output in bursts of exploration and experimentations, like theatrical pollen." *I like that.*

K is for **key.** Maybe the key is something kaleidoscopic, remarkably geometric and all over the place, turning and turning, changing and collapsing, filled with colors and responsive to different amounts of light. Maybe there are multiple keys? *There probably are.*

L is for **language.** Yes, L simply must be for language, the hum and thrum of it throughout every play in this book because, after all, language is the medium of writers, and playwrights are no exception. And here, inside this book, inside these plays, you will find whispers, songs, screams, rhymes, repetition, puns, riddles, jokes, poetry, short sentences, long sentences, *and metaphors galore.*

M is for the **meat of it,** the middle. M is the meat and the middle and we are here. M is also for Madison, Wisconsin where the first play, *Black River Falls* by Bryn Magnus is set. The time is 1978. The play has to do with the too muchness of both a time and a place and the too muchness of thinking and growing up and having messed-up parents, and friends and it is about violence and sex and loving and rage and pain too.

And in it, Bryn's character Laurie says: "Mrs. Gurdy, the librarian thought she was helping me, letting me in the special collections, but you read all this special stuff and your head gets so full it knocks you over and there's no one to pick you up. You have to do it yourself." And Colleen, looking at the sky asks Laurie, "Wha'd you call that color?" and Laurie answers: "Don't Know. Skinned knee?"

N **is for next** in the anthology comes a completely different animal entirely, a chamber opera no less by Matt Test called **Down**. Test's character asks/sings "What brings us down more than the ground?" Advisor Three shouts, "Let's go to war against gravity." Matt's fantastical, satirical work revels in the freedom to experiment with multiple styles: from dirge to declaration, from preaching to political speech. The opera is a treatise on metaphor and an exploration of all floating and flying things which should (of course) *NOT* come down and this happens with a chorus no less. And oh, it is both lyrical, cacophonous, and quite surely the only chamber opera about gravity and an election that has ever existed before *or ever will again, ever.*

O **is for the O,** the letter in the middle of the two Joes who are the characters in Matt Rieger's play, **My Dinner With... Joe,** a funny, farcical wonder and even the title is a double joke not only because it references the Wallace Shawn Film, *My Dinner with Andre*, but just like there are two Matts in this book, there are two Joes in Matt's play and they are appropriately named Joe 1 and Joe 2 and Matt sets these two Joes inside a strange restaurant which becomes a landscape to explore class, culture, power, friendship, desire and appetite. Joe 2: "You know what you should do? Put binoculars on all the tables so folks can look at the menu from wherever they are sitting." and Joe #1 responds: "That's not too bad. It would give the place that feeling like you were on a sightseeing tour." And Joe 2 agrees saying, "Like a safari." And later, in the restaurant, life itself becomes the potential diner and Joe 2 says: "That's my problem. I always think everything is always a thing. And what the fuck do I know? I know this. Life ate me up. I could never do what it was that I wanted to do. Because I got caught up thinking everything is a thing. But no thing is a thing. I know that now. And I'm hungry."

P is for **plays.** The next one is by Beau O' Reilly who has written so very many of them. P is also for pretending, a theme in **One Boppa**, a play about family and sisters and the search for, celebration and experience of, beauty and forgiveness. In it, Tip says, "She gave him that amaryllis in a pot once. That's gardening." And Elm says, "That is not gardening...that's fooling around with things." The play asks, how much does the literal truth count and when is fiction truer? Also, what should people practice remembering and what should they do their very hardest to forget? Elm says, "Doesn't the world make you want to fall apart?" And yet, amidst so many bad memories there is a description of magical windows and window makers: "These windows were on a dolly, this impossibly long dolly so everything floated and glistened the workers were all glowy." The color yellow is described as "love" and lilacs as "groaning with purple." And Andi speaks about seeing angels. Andi: "I used to see them all the time when I was a kid. The sky was all these fluttering blob shapes...but now it's like a sludge. Smudging everything—coal dust between your eyes, and heaven. It's very sad to lose a light like that." *It is, It is, I agree Beau, that it is.*

Q is for **quatrain.** Maybe this book of 8 plays could be seen as a set of two quatrains like a lento or a ballad instead, a ballad about longing or a total of four ending couplets at the ends of two sonnets side by side like a double date or maybe this book is two sets of quadruplets conceived by art and all grown up and walking around *asking important questions in stanzas that are only masquerading as plays.*

R is for **reading** and **room.** I like that the *origin of the word STANZA* means stand or a place to stand, a room to stand in. I like the notion of a book as a room. And, if you think about it, a book like this anthology is a standing place, a hangout, a tree house. And not only that, but the etymology of the word *ANTHOLOGY* is a collection of flowers, so maybe it is best, *when reading this book, in whatever way or order that you do,* to think of it like that, like a language bouquet.

S is for **Salvagers,** Jenny Magnus's stellar collection of monologue works which dig into the basements of popular culture, the rich and sometimes shadowy inner life, and especially love in love's many permutations and variations. In a thrillingly long, all-encompassing catalog of love, Jenny's character delivers a list of metaphor after glorious metaphor: "Our love is stinky cheese, wood grain, and flip flops. Our love is a clean desk, the smell of hazelnut syrup, cotton sheets, and the funniest cat video"...it goes on... And in another monologue, Jenny contends with and investigates a familiar, uncanny feeling which she describes as a "petty, unwelcome, vulgar, dull, ghastly boring and unimaginative visitor" and in doing so creates an immediate partnership with the audience/reader, a palpable connection: Whether Jenny is in the role of Jenny or is playing a character, she speaks to the audience directly asking "Am I right?" Am I right about this?" "But here it is," she says. "But here it is, and one may not ignore it, one must acknowledge the feeling, and welcome it." *...and suddenly, somehow, we can.*

T is for **theatre** and **theater.** Both spellings are not only unerring but also interchangeable. You can use one on Tuesdays and the other on Thursdays or use only one or the other. *Personally, I prefer both.*

How about you?

U is for **unravelling** the **unbearable** and Shawn Reddy's, ***The Art of Unbearable Sensations***, deals with this deftly. It is a play featuring circus characters who contend with roles they have been assigned, roles in which they must always pretend to be something they are not. The play explores identity, and the idea of magic and what exactly magic is, what magic can never be and if it is foolish to believe in something like magic at all. The play considers the difference between reality and spectacle as well as what happens when public and private selves collide. When Galvini, for example, who is described as a tinkerer of dead frogs, enters the arena, he does so sobbing, but then, pulls himself together for the audience promising, "Acres and acres of entertainment." Later the feeling of guilt, is smartly described as the "head's Achilles' heel" and his wonderful character Petrovna says: "You want closure in life? Then go get yourself a necklace of bells and sit in the dark."

V is for **vitality** and **vacancy.** This anthology has so much of the former and so little of the latter. And furthermore, a V on its side is of course a *more than* symbol and so when you consider the mathematical vector it looks like this: Vitality > Vacancy. *This is a fact.*

W is for **weeping corners** where people can weep freely whenever they feel the need to which is what Julia Williams dreams up in the penultimate work of the collection. In ***The Near Future/That Sort of Thing*** customers can shop for "a sense of completion" at the grocery store instead of—or including—groceries. They can learn jokes while in line at the bank and behave as if this is the most matter of fact thing ever. Oh, and by the way the the weeping corners are in banks too, because well of course they are. These new worlds are irresistibly captivating. Poison is perfectly described as "nature's hate." Characters can walk down "the mossy hallway that is life." In Julia's worlds one can even be offered (in a fantasy and fear hybrid) a tiny piece of a dead lover "the material self, pollen on the wind." *(Ah, pollen, again!)* All the while, Julia periodically calls attention back to the work itself, the existence of it and the making of it by asking inside the work, as part of the work: "Are you interrupting my personal narrative? Are you advancing the plot? Can something like safety actually exist?"

X is for **X.** X is for all the unknown factors, the mysterious, the ineffable. X is for trying to mark a spot, but not finding a spot to mark. X is for a spot that continually migrates. *X equals theater.*

Y is for **yesterday** and **yonder,** and yes to both yesterday and yonder at once. Simultaneity, ongoingness, time and memory are central themes in the final play of the collection. Jayita Bhattacharya's ***To End to Seem to End*** has us wonder if maybe all endings are contrived, simply made-up things to confront and rearrange. She writes, "Absence ought to matter, so should presence." In Jayita's work, a great deal of attention is paid to the having of a body and the connection of the body to language, to investigating what one has to do with the other without the need or expectation of finality: *Openendedness*. There are explanations of foot fights and invitations to participate in foot fights with feet, delving into definitions and explanations of what everything is and what it is not. Often, there is repetition as if to go at something again to see how or if it changes. Life itself is an experiment. The dialogues are like fortune cookie fortunes, only quite a bit more poetic and they echo and echo and echo: "The universe under my skin. Sadness does not have a weight. My mind changed before I changed it. It feels like we're not here together even though we are. It's baffling and it hurts. Where will we meet? In December or noon?" *I say both.*

Z is for **zippers.** I like zippers. I like the way they sound. I especially like it when they are on large, expandable suitcases because on large expandable suitcases, the zipper goes around and around and around. I like how *zippers join things together.* A wonky zipper made to work once again, after not working, is so satisfying. I like the anatomy of zippers too: the sliders, the pull tabs, the teeth. I feel exactly the same way about zippers as I do about alphabets, and even more so as I do about this anthology of plays. I like it to a zillion ...*and I hope you do too.*

--- --- ---

Chicago writer, monologist and playwright Barrie Cole is a versatile creative artist who has collaborated with Curious Theatre performers and has been an audience and witness to these plays throughout the arc of their development. She has written numerous plays, poems, short stories and essays. To read more of her work, visit: www.barriecole.com

--- --- ---

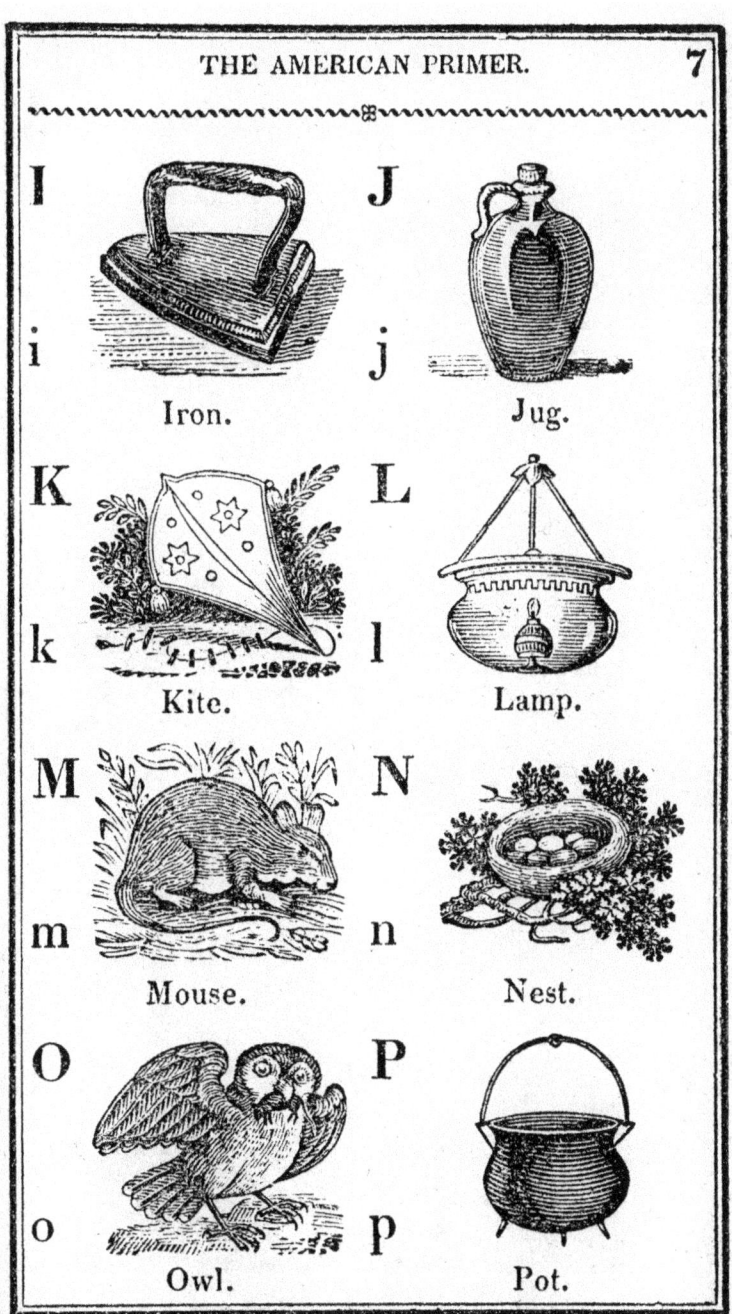

I i — Iron.	J j — Jug.
K k — Kite.	L l — Lamp.
M m — Mouse.	N n — Nest.
O o — Owl.	P p — Pot.

THE
PLAYS

JOHN MACHESKY
STEPHEN WALKER
MAC LOKI **MODEAN**
DIANE MCNULTY
MATT RIEGER
in *Black River Falls*

Black River Falls

Premiered **July 2015**

Prop Thtr / Chicago, IL

written by **BRYN MAGNUS**

directed by **Jenny Magnus**

performed by:

Nick Leininger
Sam Liss
John Machesky
Diane McNulty
Mac Loki Modean
Matt Rieger
Stephen Walker

THE
PLAYS

SETTING

Dousman Wisconsin. 1978.
The long Thanksgiving weekend.

Lights on DAD, 50's, shlumpy, camped out in
his recliner in front of the TV.

GARY, 17, enters carrying a case of beer in one hand
and open beer in the other—a rifle scabbard over his houlder.

Hunter

Dad: Fuckineddy—the hunter?

Gary: Yep.

Dad: Get yer buck?

Gary: Laur's ok?

Dad: What?

Gary: Laur.

Dad: Ok?

Gary: She's ok right?

Dad: Whyn't you go up and ask her?

Gary: Her room?

Dad: Yeah, Gar, where else?

Gary: What's she doin?

Dad: Gar, what's with the—what does Laur always do? What does she only do?

Gary: Readin. What's she readin?

Dad: Jesus! Now you're worryin me with the mental case questions. Have I ever known what she's readin?

Gary: Yeah, no.

Dad: A book she got at the libarry or rummage this fat and full of crap I don't understand. Geez.

Gary: Right.

Dad: What are you doin back?

Gary: Just came back.

Dad:	Get your buck then?
Gary:	Nah.
Dad:	By Monday ain't it?
Gary:	Yeah.
Dad:	Buck by Monday.
Gary:	Came back early.
Dad:	Whad'ya do that for?
Gary:	Just came back.

Gary turns the case of beer toward Dad.

Dad: Didn't ya?

Dad grabs a beer and is distracted by the football game.

Dad: Ya lousy cows!

Gary: Who's playin?

Dad: Who's playin?

Gary: Who's playin?

Dad: Use the eyes in yer head why don't ya? Jez-zus! Most anticipated game of th'season.

Gary: Packers and Vikes. Good game?

Dad: GOOD GAME? Will you look a second? Pack down 7, clock tickin. Whitehurst to Lofton, Whitehurst to Lofton, Whitehurst to Lofton 'cept Lofton's got no hands. Boyd Dowler—he had hands. And Bart Starr—arm a gold.

Gary: Five years they'll come around.

Dad: Really, you tell the future?

Gary: Probably—SuperBowl-what?

Dad: Superbowl?

Gary: What Twelve, thirteen in 5 years?

Dad: SUPERBOWL? What is with you?

Gary: Nothin.

Dad: Where's your brother?

Gary: He stayed.

Dad: What?

Gary: Him and Shawn and Porty.

Dad: What now?

Gary: They stayed.

Dad: Yeah, 'they stayed'.

Gary: They stayed.

Dad: Yeah, but you came back.

Gary: Yeah.

Dad: And you drive back?

Gary: Yeah.

Dad: How are they gonna get back?

Gary: Gonna go get em.

Dad: Gonna drive back up there?

Gary: Yeah.

Dad: Six fuckin hours.

Gary: Five only, or.

Dad: Three up and three back?

Gary: Yeah.

Dad:	In my truck?
Gary:	Said we could.
Dad:	For a buck.
Gary:	Donnie.
Dad:	What is wrong with you? Why'd you come back?
Gary:	I don't know.
Dad:	You know the Packers are goin to Superbowl Twelve but you don't know why you came back?
Gary:	Yeah, don't know.
Dad:	You get too cold?
Gary:	Not really.
Dad:	Was it cold?
Gary:	Not so bad.
Dad:	Food?
Gary:	Laurie made that ton of chili.
Dad:	The cabin?
Gary:	Good.
Dad:	That, uh, Mrs. Soolo—
Gary:	Sewell—
Dad:	Propane and water and all?
Gary:	Yeah. All there.
Dad:	Wood?
Gary:	Plenty of wood.
Dad:	So why'd you come back?
Gary:	Don't know.

Dad: Didn't run out of beer.

Gary: See that tackle? Think when a guy like that lands on top of you knocks your farts out?

Dad: What?

Gary: You get slammed down like that has to knock your farts out.

Dad: Now you're talkin farts?

Gary: No.

Dad: Gary. The fuck, Gar?

Gary: What?

Dad: What's with you?

Gary: What?

Dad: You see the KING of tackles and you think farts.

Gary: What should I think of?

Dad: Willie Buchanon squarin his body, wrappin his arms, and nailin the guy to the ground.

Gary: Yeah. Probably knocks the wind out of you. Both ways.

Dad: What a goof. Fight with your brother?

Gary: No.

Dad: You didn't fight?

Gary: No.

Dad: You always fight.

Gary: Just came back.

Dad: Cause he pissed you off?

Gary: No.

Dad: He didn't piss you off?

Gary: Yeah.

Dad: He always pisses you off.

Gary: He's a fuckin dewee, but I just came back.

Dad: Let me get this. You're sittin in the woods in a blind.
        Got your sights on baggin a buck. 'This year,' you said.
        You made the big speech to Donnie and me,
        'This year, will not get cold, will not get hungry...'
        Socks won't give out or beer or Donnie pissin you off.

Gary: He took a shot.

Dad: Yeah?

Gary: At a buck.

Dad: Yeah?

Gary: Like half a mile away.

Dad: Ok.

Gary: And he hit it. And it ran off. So.

Dad: Oh, god, so.

Gary: Yeah. They went trackin.

Dad: For chriesakes—trackin!

Gary: Told him it was a stupid shot so.

Dad: You just drove home?

Gary: Like to drive.

Dad: Fuckin-eddy.

Gary: Had beer for the ride.

Dad: Beer.

Gary: And weed.

Dad: Don't tell me that.

Gary: Makes the time pass.

Dad: You drink purple cool-aid too?

Gary: No.

Dad: You didn't stay to help track that poor deer?

Gary: No.

Dad: The fuck, Gar.

Gary: Wanted to come back.

Dad: You're back. Here you are. How is it?

Gary: Decent.

Dad: You were cold, must'a been.

Gary: Just came back.

Dad: Gimme another. (beer)

Gary: But Laurie's okay, right?

Dad: What?

Gary: She's–there's nothin goin on with her?

Dad: How would I know?

Gary: Yeah, no.

Dad: She came down for a soda like three hours ago.

Gary: But—

Dad: Go up and ask her.

Gary: Nah, if she's okay. I just...

Dad: Just?

Gary: Nothin.

Dad: Gar?

Gary: I got a feelin.

Dad: You got a feeling?

Gary: Yeah, spooky, heard the shot, you know, Donnie all stoked
         he hit it. Then it takes off and he's like, 'Fuuck' and Laurie
         popped into my head. That Jonestown thing really bugged
         her out, ain't it?

Dad: Bugged you out.

Gary: Yeah. But Laur?

Dad: Didn't notice.

Gary: No. Well yeah. You didn't want to see the game
         at the Lighthouse?

Dad: Went there to see the game.

Gary: But you came back.

Dad: Tom Dabney was runnin off about White Rabbit.

Gary: *(sarcastic)* He wrote White Rabbit?

Dad: With Grace Slick and Marty Balin in Milwaukee and—

Gary: —no lawyers will touch his case cause the record companies
         have a contract with the Hell's Angels to settle all scores.

Dad: Yeah. Big mouth. Big man. And Bob, stupid, wipes the
         bar down then stands in front of Dabney and pushes
         up his glasses like he's gonna say somethin—
         Dabney tips his cap back like yeah? What?
         Out comes another beer for Dabney. So 'prick.'
         And I must've been louder than I thought because
         Dabney asks what's my problem and could he help me
         swallow my teeth if I want. Fuck him.
         So, yeah, I came back here to watch.

Gary: Anything to eat?

Dad: No venison.

Gary: I know. Any leftovers from last night?

Dad: Laur fixed TV turkey. Was good.

Gary:	Any left?
Dad:	I don't know. You weren't supposed to be back till Monday. With your buck. You think Donnie's gonna find that one?
Gary:	He says.
Dad:	You gonna drive back up there, then?
Gary:	Told em I'd be back Monday to get em.
Dad:	Look at that pass...he's at the 40, he's at the 30, he's at...the 30.
Gary:	Gonna look in the freezer.
Dad:	Call her down, she'll fix for you.
Gary:	No need if she's readin.

Gary exits to the kitchen leaving the case of beer. Dad gets up and grabs a couple and sits back down. Gary reenters.

Gary:	There's nothin. Going to the Lighthouse for a burger.
Dad:	Gonna drink your beer.
Gary:	Yeah. Ok. Many as you like.
Dad:	Tell Dabney to shut his big mouth.

Gary stops at the door.

Gary:	Anything-news on the cool-aid drinkers?
Dad:	What'ya mean?
Gary:	Stopped for gas and some truckers said now they're sayin some of the people—the kids—were forced to drink the cool-aid. I don't know, man. Force your kid drink it?
Dad:	Do anything that madman said.
Gary:	Make your kid drink poison.

Dad:	They were high on the grass.
Gary:	No.
Dad:	Ain't it?
Gary:	You ever smoke weed?
Dad:	Are you out of your fuckin mind?
Gary:	Doesn't make you...force your kid. Purple cool-aid.
Dad:	Okay Jim Jones.
Gary:	They say that on the news?
Dad:	Had to be the grass.
Gary:	Goin to the Lighthouse for a burger.

> *He exits.*
> *Dad watches the Packers play the Vikes.*
>
> *Craig comes down the stairs from Laurie's room.*
> *He's 15, big, trouble.*

Dad:	The fuck are you now!?
Craig:	Craig. You know me. Donnie's friend.
Dad:	Fuck you doin up there?
Craig:	Hangin out with Laurie.
Dad:	What are you talkin about?
Craig:	Laurie.
Dad:	Yeah?
Craig:	Laurie.
Dad:	No one hangs out with her.
Craig:	No, I was. She called me.
Dad:	She called you over here?

Craig:	Donnie gave me your number.
Dad:	When was this?
Craig:	Few days ago.
Dad:	No, when did you call?
Craig:	Oh, don't know. Like a hour ago or about.
Dad:	She told you come over?
Craig:	Yeah.
Dad:	I don't fuckin believe it.
Craig:	What? No. She told me come over. We have class together. She told me come over and we could go over class stuff.
Dad:	On Thanksgiving break? Fuckin egg head girl.
Craig:	Yeah.
Dad:	She help you?
Craig:	What?
Dad:	With school stuff.
Craig:	Oh, yeah.
Dad:	What like?
Craig:	What?
Dad:	What are you working on?
Craig:	I don't know—Moby Dick.
Dad:	Never got through that either.
Craig:	No.
Dad:	Who's your old man? I know your old man?
Craig:	Don't know. He works Plasticon— third shift, floor supervisor.

Dad: What's he drive?

Craig: Duster.

Dad: Oh, yeah, I think I know'm.
          Plays left field for Nashotah Inn. Brundage, right?

Craig: Yeah. Gotta get goin.

Dad: Alright. Well, tell your old man I say hey.

Craig: Sure. Later, Mr. Titslaugh.

Dad: Tetzloff ya little shit.

                    Craig exits. Dad watches TV and drinks beer.

                    Laurie enters.
                    She's an extremely uncomfortable 15 year old.

Laurie: He gone?

Dad: Craig? Yeah. Laur, I gotta say—

Laurie: He gone?

Dad: Yeah, Laur, take a look.

Laurie: I don't see him.

Dad: You didn't tell me he was comin over.

Laurie: I didn't know.

Dad: Alright. Just. Didn't know he was here.

Laurie: You weren't here.

Dad: Well, I was here. What?

Laurie: Nothin. Just, he's gone.

Dad: Yeah, just took off.

Laurie: He's gone.

Dad: Yeah. You help him with his homework?

Laurie: What?

Dad: He said you helped him with Moby Dick.

Laurie: He said that?

Dad: Yeah, kid's got a smart mouth too.

Laurie: I hate his fuckin guts.

Dad: Whoa. Well. Laur, why'd you call him over?

Laurie: I didn't.

Dad: He said you told him come over.

Laurie: He just called and came over.

Dad: Alright. But. He's a smartass.

Laurie: You weren't here.

Dad: Was at the Lighthouse like two minutes.

Laurie: Two minutes.

Dad: Yeah.

Laurie: Sure.

Dad: His old man plays softball for Nashotah Inn. Not too good. Drives a Duster.

Laurie: I don't care.

Dad: Gary came back.

Laurie: What?

Dad: Drove back by himself.

Laurie: Why?

Dad: Doesn't know.

Laurie: No?

Dad: Says he doesn't know. But he uh wondered how you were doing cause of the Jonestown thing.

Laurie:	That's why he came back?
Dad:	Says he doesn't know.
Laurie:	Donnie stayed up there?
Dad:	Donnie hit a buck, I guess. It ran. Has to track it.
Laurie:	Donnie.
Dad:	Yeah. But Gar drove back, out to lunch, right?
Laurie:	I don't know.
Dad:	Big speech he was gonna finally get a buck this year.
Laurie:	Made all that chili.
Dad:	He's gonna drive back up and get them on Monday.
Laurie:	What? You're kidding.
Dad:	No. Says. Came back, he says, cause he had a feeling.
Laurie:	Gary had a feeling?
Dad:	He says.
Laurie:	He must have come back for the party.
Dad:	There's a party?
Laurie:	At the Speigle's. Tomorrow night.
Dad:	You're goin to a party?!
Laurie:	No.
Dad:	Was gonna have a heart attack.
Laurie:	Everybody was talking about it.
Dad:	That Craig?
Laurie:	NO.
Dad:	You could go.

Laurie: Wasn't invited.

Dad: Alright. But you think Gary's gonna go?

Laurie: Forsure. Colleen'll be there.

Dad: The Buska?

Laurie: Yeah.

Dad: Her old man croaked ain't it?

Laurie: Stomach cancer.

Dad: Probably didn't help that what's-her divorced him right
          when he was sick after he built that big house for them.

Laurie: I don't know.

Dad: He built that thing with his own hands. That's really
          somethin. The wiring and everything. Don't you think
          that's somethin? Head grounds keeper at St. Johns and
          Fire Chief too. That's—when do you have time to build a
          house with your own hands? And she divorces him.

Laurie: I don't know. He broke Colleen's collar bone when
          he caught her tryin to sneak out that one time to go
          to the Who concert. Gar told me. And the mother
          was always wearin sunglasses at church to cover
          the black eyes.

Dad: Well, that's, over.

Laurie: Saw her at McAdam's when I was gettin stuff for the chili.
          Buying wine.

Dad: Wonder if she got that awesome truck of his?

Laurie: Don't know.

Dad: Beautiful Silverado. How'd she look?

Laurie: Didn't see a truck.

Dad: No, her.

Laurie:	Don't know. Tired.
Dad:	No, I mean she puff back up? She really dropped em after the divorce.
Laurie:	No.
Dad:	No Cheryl Tiegs, but...
Laurie:	No.
Dad:	What was she wearing?
Laurie:	Dad.
Dad:	What? Just wonder what she was wearin.
Laurie:	Go buy some wine and find out!

Laurie exits.

Dad:	Hey! Hey! Laur, the hell I step in this time... *(more under breath.)*

Lights fade.

Lighthouse Inn

Lights. Dingy little lakeside Inn with pool table and jukebox.
Gary sits at the bar. Empty plate in front of him—scrunched napkin.
A beer. Football on the TV.

Tom Dabney plays pool. He's 30's, greasy jeans and big mouth.
His cue is fancy.

Bob:	*(while tending bar)* That okay, Gar?
Gary:	Yeah. Good. Can I get another? *(beer)*
Dabney:	Not of-age, Bob.
Bob:	Shut up Dabney.
Dabney:	Ask him if he's even of age.

Gary: I'm not.

Bob: Just say yeah, ok? Always just say yeah.

Gary: Then, yeah.

Dabney: Shouldn't serve underage, Bob.

Bob: You got plenty of beers from me when you
           were a bedwetter, Dabney, so shut up.

Dabney: Who's gonna play me?

Bob: Ya chased everyone out, now, already,
           so no one's gonna play you.

Dabney: Shut up Bob, PBR and fuck you.

Bob: Not cool, Dabney, not cool.

Dabney: Cool. Oh, Cool?! You wouldn't know
           cool if it fucked you in the eyes.

Bob: Oh, Here it comes.

Dabney: No you wouldn't cause I been fucked in the eyes before.

Bob: 1968, Wolski's, Dabney, we know—

Dabney: *(to Gary)* Wolski's 68. Shootin eights and this chick
           nails me across the bar—eyes...it was like lookin at
           two lighting bolts. She looked familiar, but I humped
           a lot of chicks so...then this little guy comes over
           to the table and drops a stack of quarters to play me.
           He looks familiar too.

Gary: Marty Balin?

Dabney: Martin-fuckineddy-Balin and Grace Slick.
           Jefferson Airplane. Eights at Wolskis.
           Eyes like shotgun blasts across the bar.
           Balin says do I know where to get some speed.
           He'll play me for speed. Forsure, I say, Mukwonago,
           White Rabbit. Balin says If he wins, I get him the
           White Rabbit. If I win, I get him the White Rabbit, and,
           AND I get to fuck Grace Slick.

Bob: Right, Dabney, Grace Slick.

Dabney: Yeah, it was my rack. Knocked a stripe.
           Didn't stop till that 8 ball fell. Fuckin Grace Slick
           in the ass in the can at Wolski's. With Marty Balin grateful!
           Grateful to give his pecker a rest.
           'She's a maniac nympho, man, and I can't keep up!'
           That's what he said, Bob. Guess who kept up?

Bob: Dabney give it a rest.

Dabney: Not what she said, Bob, she was SINGIN
           cause I kept up, Bob. She loved it. And that ass,
           that ASS, primo DY-NO-MITE...Yeah, I scored the
           White Rabbit. They hit town for the show at the
           auditorium and they were so fuckin grateful that
           Milwaukee was cool. Milwaukee was cool because of me.

BOB   This is Dousman, Dabney and—

Dabney: Where's my PBR!

Bob: Here. Take a look. PBR. Bob's 78.

           Bob lands a PBR for Dabney.

           Dabney waves his cue around knowing
           Gary is watching—a fine piece of equipment.

Dabney: Play, kid?

Gary: No.

Dabney: Man would.

Gary: No.

Dabney: Who is that? Titslaff? Know what? Your old man is a twat.
           What? What? You say somethin? I didn't hear you. Yeah.
           He's another one don't know what cool is. Come on,
           play ya for beers.

Gary: No thanks.

Dabney: Ya scared?

Gary: No.

Dabney: Why don't you want to play then?

Gary: Don't know.

Dabney: You're scared, ain't it?

Gary: No.

Dabney: Yeah? Just say yeah.

Gary: Yeah. I said no.

Dabney: Then get your ass over here and shut the fuck up.

Bob: Dabney, he doesn't want to play.

Dabney: Shut up Bob. No one's talkin to you. Titzlaff, you break.

Gary: No thanks.

Dabney: Everyone else's off stuffin the family turkey.
          You just gonna watch?
          Just gonna sit there and watch?

Gary: Gotta go in a minute.

Bob: You went up north, I thought, Gar.

Dabney: Won't hustle ya. Just for beers. Play for quarters?

Bob: Dabney.

Dabney: Quarters, Bob. What's the big deal? Know what?
          I played quarters against Marty Balin for speed
          when Airplane was here. He said he wins I get the
          speed and Grace Slick's ass, I win I get speed and
          Grace Slick's ass. I know where to get some speed?
          Did I know? I drove all the way out to Mukwonago
          cause I knew a guy worked with Owsley in Berkeley
          had to move his operation when the feds got hot.
          You know Owsley?

Bob: Yep. Yep. We do.

Dabney: Bob you don't know shit. Shut the fuck up. This guy I knew made White Rabbit speed. Took my whole week's pay and bought 500 hits. Brought em back to the Airplane at Wolski's. All of em thought it was the cleanest best shit they had. 'White Rabbit' I said, 'one pill makes you larger and one pill makes you small.' I said that shit. My dick was in Grace Slick's ass when I said that shit and she looked back at me with those shotgun eyes and said 'After this let's jam.' And we did. Went back to the Pfister penthouse and Balin gave me his guitar and we jammed for four fuckin hours on the song. One point hotel security knocked on the door complaining that we were too loud and I open the door and fuckin BOOM. BLAM. Titzlaff you ever just haul off and punch someone's head?

Gary: No.

Dabney: Bob either, right Bob? Well, heads are hard. Lot of bone. Teeth. Here. *(holds out his fist)* See that on my knuckle? Where his tooth broke off. Security. I flicked it back at him. He begged me to keep jammin after that. Begged me to write a hit song. We did. Kanter swallowed a handful of White Rabbits and was humping this huge pillow in the hotel room. Grace Slick sucking my dick with her eyes. Then. Year later. Surrealistic Pillow comes out. Suprize! This monster hit, White Rabbit.
'One pill makes you larger...' just like I said.
I'm workin Tool and Die and they're flyin in a private jet on my song! But I didn't sue.

Gary: Cause the record company has a contract with the Hell's Angels?

Dabney: Fuckin-eddy! Everybody knows I put anything on paper get a Harley up my ass.

Gary: You should write another song.

Dabney: Got a thousand songs. Come on Titzlaff, rack em and I'll beat your ass for beers. Played Balin for quarters, Airplane, 68 Grace Slick, Wolski's—

Gary: Want a beer? I'll get ya a beer. And a shot of Jager. Bob, two Jagers, three, one for you too, and a PBR for him. It's Thanksgiving.

Bob: *(low to Gary)* Yeah and you're out a here in a minute.

Dabney: The fuck you say, Bob? I'll fuckin knock your nose over ya faggot.

Bob: Not kiddin, Dabney, two seconds I call Ardent.

Dabney: Call the fuckin 5-o, see if I care, I'll kick his nuts back in for him. Tell him you serve Titzlaff here—underage.

Bob: Ok big stuff. Have your drink. But shut up, ok?

Pours the shots and cracks the beer. They lift.

Gary: To Thanksgiving.

Bob: Thanksgiving.

Dabney: To Grace Slick's ass.

They drink. Gary pays.

Bob: Didn't you go up north, Gar, I thought?

Gary: Yeah.

Bob: With Porty and Shawn?

Gary: Donnie too.

Bob: Back already?

Gary: Came back.

Bob: Why?

Gary: Don't know.

Dabney: Cause you're a fuckin pussy.

Gary: Yeah.

Dabney: *(finding it hilarious)* You just said you were a pussy.

Gary: Yeah. Just say yeah.

Dabney: Hear that, Bob? Titzlaff is a fuckin pussy. How bout
           another one (jager) pussy? Or are you too fuckin pussy.

Gary: No. Too broke.

                    Exits to piss.

Dabney: When you're pussy, you go through the door with the 'L'.

                    Gary goes into the Ladies room.

Dabney: You see that? That kid's fuckin fruit. He's in the ladies.

Bob: Bought you a round.

Dabney: You know how much money I'd have by now if I sued Airplane?
           I could buy this place and everyone drinks for free.

Bob: Ok. Yeah, sure.

                    Gary returns from the john.

Dabney: Piss sittin down?

Gary: Yeah.

Dabney: Can show you how to hang a nut, you ever want to see.

Gary: That's ok.

Dabney: Man would.

Gary: See ya Bob.

Bob: Later Gar.

                    He exits.

Dabney: What is it with that guy?

Bob: What?

Dabney: He's fruit, right?

Bob:	Not really. Don't think so.
	He's got the hots for Colleen Buska.
Dabney:	She fucks like a fullback.
Bob:	Dabney.
Dabney:	If a fullback was a hot chick, what?

Lights fade.

Transporter

*Lights. Gary crosses paths with Colleen at the transporter—
the buttress of an old bridge crossing over abandoned railroad tracks.*

Gary:	Hey.
Colleen:	Hey.
Gary:	What's up?
Colleen:	Nuthin.
Gary:	Yeah? Me either.
Colleen:	Was gonna transport.

Colleen holds up her bowl.

Gary:	At the Transporter?
Colleen:	Uh. Yeah.

Gary sits next to Colleen.

*Colleen pulls out her weed and takes
time loading her bowl.*

Colleen:	Thought you were hunting?
Gary:	Came back.

Colleen:	Why?
Gary:	Don't know. Donnie took a stupid shot, winged a buck and him and Porty and Shawn went trackin. Didn't want to be there for that.
Colleen:	Don't blame ya. With stupid Porty.
Gary:	You went out with him.
Colleen:	That's how I know he's stupid.
Gary:	He said.
Colleen:	What?
Gary:	Nuthin.
Colleen:	What?
Gary:	He said—
Colleen:	Porty?
Gary:	Can't say.
Colleen:	Tell me.
Gary:	Can't.
Colleen:	Fuckin tell me!
Gary:	It was stupid.
Colleen:	Yeah?
Gary:	Yeah.
Colleen:	So?
Gary:	Uh…
Colleen:	YEAH?
Gary:	Can't it was stupid.
Colleen:	He's stupid—don't tell me…TELL ME.

Gary: You tasted.

Colleen: Tasted?

Gary: You tasted—

Colleen: Wha'd'I taste?!

Gary: He said you tasted like slut.

Colleen: Like that duckdick would know.

                    Beat.

Colleen: They're never gonna find that deer.

Gary: No.

Colleen: No.

Gary: No. Forest was beautiful tho. Quiet.
          You know that kind of quiet? The trees.

Colleen: But you didn't want to stay?

Gary: Don't know. Had a buggy feeling about my sister.
          Like this Jonestown shit was, I don't know. Wait.
          You're out. It's like late and your mom let you out?

Colleen: Noooo. Got a good system now. Say I'm goin to read,
          lock my door and put the radio low, climb out the
          window. Ma just thinks I fell asleep with the radio on.

Gary: "Parents: DO YOU KNOW WHERE YOUR CHILDREN ARE?"

Colleen: No way! Here.

                    *She hands him the bowl and
                    holds her lighter over it.*

Gary: *(taking a big hit)* These are the voyages of the Starship
          Enterprize whose five year mission is to seek out new life,
          new worlds, to boldly go where no man has gone before.
          (singy) Dooo Weeee Doodoodoo Doo Weeee…

Colleen:	*(laughing—moving like Startrek bridge turbulence)* Scotty. Scotty. This planet sucks. Beam me up, beam me UP, Scotty, beam me—
Gary:	Scotty, Scotty, the force fields are down and 5-o is closin in—bring me the bowl and a light, Scotty.
Colleen:	Beam me outta Dousman. Scotty! SCOTTY!? —Nope, still here.
Gary:	Cool that you can get out now.
Colleen:	Yeah.
Gary:	Different when your Dad was.
Colleen:	Yeah.
Gary:	Can't put a cast on a collar bone, can ya?
Colleen:	No. It healed. Not my 4-H riding trophy, tho.
Gary:	No, huh.
Colleen:	No. Keep the pieces on the shelf by the window right where it was when he grabbed it to smash me.
Gary:	Yeah.
Colleen:	Yeah. Wanted to see the Who so bad.
Gary:	What a mean fucker.
Colleen:	Not when he died. Shrank. All grey.

Silence.

Colleen:	Fuckin bummer about Keith Moon.
Gary:	Yeah. Forsure.
Colleen:	The Who's gonna break up now. They have to.
Gary:	Forsure.
Colleen:	Without him.
Gary:	Yeah.

Colleen: Was all set to go to Madison with you guys.
Had my totabota and everything. He nailed me.
Probably good though, cause if I went with
and been gone up to St. Paul three days?
I don't know man.

Gary: Obituary.

Colleen: Yeah, yeah. Porty wouldn't shut up about it bein
'so fuckin Epic hunderd percent gravy to the max!'

Gary: Yeah, it was ok.
Three encores in Madison and four in St. Paul.

Colleen: Wanted to go so bad.

Gary: Be cool if you'd a gone.

Colleen: You saw cid three days straight I heard.

Gary: Yeah, but forward, never straight.

Colleen: Right, right. And you had to drive
cause Porty and Steve couldn't see.

Gary: They were seeing dinosaurs and shit.
Everything was melting.

Colleen: You weren't seeing that?

Gary: I was, but the road was comin through
like the most beautiful thing I ever saw.

Colleen: Yeah?

Gary: Yeah.

Colleen: What car?

Gary: Shawn's mom's.

Colleen: She let you?

Gary: Kinda.

Colleen: You even have your license?

Gary: Kinda. He died in the same room as Cass Eliot.

Colleen: Who?

Gary: Momma Cass.

Colleen: Who died?

Gary: Keith Moon.

Colleen: No fuckin way.

Gary: Yes way.

Colleen: The same room?

Gary: Yeah.

Colleen: What room?

Gary: Don't know. In London. Their friend's house.

Colleen: Don't die in your friend's house.

Gary: What are friends for?

Colleen: Whatever way, I just don't want to see it comin.

Gary: Think either of them saw it comin?

Colleen: Yeah, no. Just, fucked up, close your eyes. Transport.

Gary: Can you believe all those people drinking killer cool-aid?

Colleen: That's what I mean, man, to know it's coming.

Gary: Standing in line for it.

Colleen: Seriously, not me.

Gary: Maybe if, like it's, you make something better.

Colleen: Better?

Gary: Yeah, I don't know.

Colleen: No way. My mom can't watch the news anymore.
           She cries.

Gary:	Jonestown.
Colleen:	Yeah. They forced it down the kid's throats.
Gary:	Yeah, man.
Colleen:	She's been talking about going back to church.
Gary:	Not St. John's?
Colleen:	Yeah.
Gary:	Totally treated her like shit though.
Colleen:	Totally. Father Smith called her a whore.
Gary:	Heard that.
Colleen:	Said she gave my dad cancer.
Gary:	Fuck Father Smith.
Colleen:	You were part of his work team.
Gary:	Only to rip down the old summer camp. When he started inviting us over to his place—
Colleen:	Sweaty face freak.
Gary:	They called it 'Revolutionary Suicide.'
Colleen:	Who?
Gary:	Jim Jones. Said it was against tyranny.
Colleen:	What?
Gary:	The—Jonestown. A paradise against tyranny. You know Ghandi?
Colleen:	I, yeah, Ghandi?
Gary:	That's what they were saying. That they were against tyranny like Ghandi. Willing to die. But it wasn't like Ghandi. Those people sat down ready to die if they had to. These people lined up to drink cool-aid cause he said so. I could never die for someone who wore glasses like Jim Jones.

Colleen: That's what I mean. You can see him comin a mile away.

Gary: You believe in reincarnation?

Colleen: Don't know. Not like in Heaven you mean?

Gary: No. I mean coming back in another life.

Colleen: Probably I don't.

Gary: Buddhists. You know?

Colleen: Yeah, no.

Gary: Some of them believe that you can reach this level of... reach this level where you can choose to come back as like a fly. A bee. A fuckin slug. Anything. To help people.

Colleen: A slug that helps people?

Gary: Yeah. Bodhisattva.

Colleen: You are fucked up.

Gary: Not really. Well, yeah, but I'm not makin it up about the buddhists. I want to come back as a tick or something and attach myself to someone who's fucked up and help them.

Colleen: How would you help them?

Gary: Don't know. When I'm a tick, I'll let you know.

Colleen: A tick that helps people...three days of cid, man.

Gary: No. No. Fuck it. Don't believe me. I'll show you the book. Alan Watts. Ever hear of him?

Colleen: No.

Gary: Yeah. I'll show you the book.

Colleen: Who would you help?

Gary: Don't know.

Colleen: You're stoned.

Gary: Good weed.

Colleen: Steve's got the line.

Gary: How come you're not hanging with him?

Colleen: He's hunting with his dad.

Gary: It's the season.

Colleen: Broke up with him, you know.

Gary: Oh yeah?

Colleen: Yeah.

Gary: Recently.

Colleen: Yeah. Just don't think he's that into chicks.

Gary: No?

Colleen: Don't think so.

Gary: Not into chicks?

Colleen: Don't think so.

Gary: No.

Colleen: Yeah.

Gary: How could you tell?

Colleen: Was pretty obvious...

Gary: You gonna tell me or...

Colleen: *(laughing)* I can't tell you.

Gary: Alright. Yeah you can.

Colleen: No. I better not.

Gary: You better now.

Colleen: Shouldn't have said.

Gary: Ok. Don't. I don't want to know.

Colleen: Ok.

Gary: Yes I do.

Colleen: Forget I said it.

Gary: No.

Colleen: Forget I said it.

Gary: No way. Seriously.

Colleen: You tell anyone and...I can't tell you.

Gary: Why not?

Colleen: Just think it's better if I don't.

Gary: I think it's better if you do.

Colleen: Swear you keep this a secret.

Gary: Yeah. I swear.

Colleen: Saw him with Greg Vock.

Gary: Saw him.

Colleen: In his bedroom. Opened the door.
           Steve screamed 'We're wrestling!' Greg started crying.
           They weren't wrestling tho.
           They begged me not to tell anyone.

Gary: Really? Greg Vock?

Colleen: He was scared shitless, hand over his crotch.
           Steve, you know, laughing.
           That was a couple of weeks ago.
           Guess I know why he had those magazines now too.

Gary: Greg and Steve? You pissed?

Colleen: Not really. I'm glad we broke up.
           He has the biggest cock ever. Always hurt.

Gary: Oh.

Colleen: I'm cold.

Gary: Totally.

Colleen: Put your arm around me.

He hesitates.

Colleen: Put your arm around me, I'm cold.

He does.

Colleen: Want to smoke another bowl?

Gary: Not really.

Silence. Gary's looking at the moon.

Colleen: What's'a matter?

Gary: Nothing.

Colleen: Look at me.

Gary: The moon.

Points.

Colleen: Look at me.

He can't.

Colleen: What's the matter?

Gary: The moon.

Colleen: Can't you even look at me?

He can't.

Gary: Got to get goin.

Colleen: Now?

Gary: Got to go.

Colleen: Gary?

Gary: Later.

Colleen: Not even gonna give me a ride even?

> *He leaves.*
> *Fade lights on Colleen.*

Laurie and Gary

Lights up on livingroom. Dad's chair is empty.
Laurie sits on the couch with a beer watching TV. Gary enters.

Gary: Laur?

Laurie: Yeah.

Gary: What are you doin?

Laurie: Watchin TV.

Gary: TV?

Laurie: Stupid movie.

Gary: And beer?

Laurie: Yeah.

Gary: The fuck you doin Laur?

Laurie: What?

Gary: What the fuck?

Laurie: What?

Gary: You don't watch TV or drink beer.

Laurie: No big deal.

Gary: No?

Laurie: No big deal.

Gary: Alright.

Laurie: Why'd you come back?

Gary: Don't know.

Laurie: Dad said you didn't know.

Gary: Yeah, don't know.

Laurie: I think you came back for the party.

Gary: Party?

Laurie: The party to see Colleen.

Gary: No.

Laurie: You like her.

Gary: Not why I came back.

Laurie: You like her.

Gary: How many beers you have?

Laurie: 3.

Gary: He know you're drinking beer?

Laurie: Went on a run for more.

Gary: Now?

Laurie: No one has to get up in the morning.

Gary: Ok. Want another?

Laurie: Sure.

> *Gary gets them. Keeps one, hands one to her.*

Gary: *(offering)* Some weed?

Laurie:	Took an aspirin.
Gary:	Aspirin and beer, Laur, way to go.

They watch tv.

Gary:	Thanks for the chili.
Laurie:	You like it?
Gary:	Yeah. Was good. Hot.
Laurie:	You're welcome. You goin to Speigle's party?
Gary:	No.
Laurie:	Yeah you are.
Gary:	No. I'm not.
Laurie:	Colleeeeeeennnzzzz gonna be there.
Gary:	No, Laur, come on.
Laurie:	You like her.
Gary:	Laur.
Laurie:	Don't you?
Gary:	I don't know.
Laurie:	How can you not know?
Gary:	Just don't.
Laurie:	You should go over to her house.
Gary:	What?
Laurie:	Just go to her house.
Gary:	Whad'you mean?
Laurie:	Go to her house.
Gary:	I don't want to.
Laurie:	You should go to her house.

Gary: Don't want to go to her house.

Laurie: Go to her house when her mom's not there.

Gary: No.

Laurie: Chicken.

Gary: What?

Laurie: Chicken. Bawk. Bawk!

Gary: Shut up!

Laurie: Bawk. Bawk. Bawk.

Gary: What's your problem? Drink your beer.

Laurie: No. You're a chicken. How long you like Colleen for?

Gary: Go to bed Laurie.

Laurie: No.

Gary: Go to bed.

Laurie: No. How long you like her for?

Gary: Shit, Laur.

Laurie: 3 years or somethin and you let Porty go out with her, and then Farley, and now Steve.

Gary: She broke up with Steve.

Laurie: Call her and go over there.

Gary: Too late.

Laurie: Go over there and wake her up.

Gary: Laurie. No. You don't know what you're talkin about. You're drunk.

Laurie: I know what I'm talking about.

Gary: I was just with her.

Laurie: At her house?

Gary:	No. The transporter.
Laurie:	Whad'you do?
Gary:	Smoked a bowl. Looked at the moon.
Laurie:	Romantic.
Gary:	Not really.
Laurie:	Were you chicken?
Gary:	Man. You must of…I don't know. You read something?
Laurie:	No. I didn't read something.
Gary:	No Hunter S. Thompson, or Helter Skelter for like the tenth time?
Laurie:	*(bitterly)* Moby Dick!
Gary:	Go to bed. Sleep it off.
Laurie:	You fuckin sleep it off chicken shit.
Gary:	GO!

Gary pushes her off the couch.
She lands on the floor and stays.

Gary:	Get up.
Laurie:	No.
Gary:	GET UP!
Laurie:	Not scared of you.
Gary:	Not tryin to scare you, Laur.
Laurie:	Oh no?
Gary:	No.
Laurie:	What are you tryin to do?
Gary:	To get you off the floor and up to bed.
Laurie:	Why?

Gary: You're drunk and actin stupid.

Laurie: Of everything, of everything I am not stupid.

Gary: No. So go to bed.

*With Gary's help Laurie gets to her feet.
She falls back on the couch.*

Laurie: Not stupid. You're chicken. Bawk...

Gary: What's this movie?

Laurie: Bawk. Virgin.

Gary: What?

Laurie: You're a virgin bawk.

Gary: Hey, you have that Alan Watts you showed me?

Laurie: Yeah. Why?

Gary: Wanna see it again.

Laurie: Because?

Gary: Get it for me will ya.

Laurie: Right now?

Gary: Yeah.

Laurie: In my room

Gary: Yeah, so?

Laurie: Upstairs.

Gary: Too drunk?

Laurie: Yeah.

Gary: Where?

Laurie: On my desk under the Thorn Birds.

Gary goes.

Blackout.

Colleen's Bedroom

Lights up on Gary at Colleen's window knocking softly.
Colleen gets up and opens the window.

Gary: You up?

Colleen: Shhhh. Gary. Shhh.

Gary: Looked for you at the transporter.

Colleen: You went back for me?

Gary: Yeah.

Colleen: Wasn't there, was I?

Gary: No. Your bed is like right under the window.

Colleen: So I can sneak out.

Gary: I don't have to sneak out.

Colleen: I know, but I do, so shhhh.

Gary: There are cows out here.

Colleen: It's a field.

Gary: Can I come in?

Colleen: Quiet.

She motions him in. They sit on Colleen's bed.

Gary: Can't sleep.

Colleen: No?

Gary: Brought you that book.

Colleen: What?

Gary: Alan Watts.

Colleen: That's not a book.

Gary: Yeah. It's a lecture.

Colleen: You brought me a lecture?

Gary: It's from a lecture he gave at a college. Look, look...
           I want to show you. See read this, this part.

Colleen reads.

Colleen: Wow.

Gary: Right?

Colleen: Where'd you get this?

Gary: My sister.

Colleen: Yeah?

Gary: She, you know, she's almost a librarian.

Colleen: Alan Watts. I don't know, man, pretty freaky.

Gary: No, it's cool.

Colleen: I don't want to be a bug that helps people.

Gary: You wouldn't have to. You could be anything.

Colleen: Don't want to be anything.

Gary: No?

Colleen: I don't know.

Gary: Think'd be cool. Like a dragonfly.
           It would be so cool to ba dragonfly.

Colleen: Get smashed on a windshield? Not cool.

Gary: No. That would be a bummer. But. Unless. What if, yeah,
           what if because you got smashed on the windshield,
           you were a big SPLAT on the windshield and the driver
           can't see anything so he pulls over to wipe you off and
           because of that he avoids hitting a kid who's running
           across the street or something.

Colleen: Yeah but what if you're the splat on the windshield and
           the driver can't see and because of that he hits the kid?

Gary: That would be a different dragonfly than me.

Colleen: You are so weird right now.

Gary: Not really.

Colleen: Gary?

Gary: Yeah?

> *She takes his chin and turns his head*
> *to look at her. It is intense.*
> *They look at each other.*
>
> *Very slowly she leans to him and kisses him.*
> *They kiss deeply.*

Colleen: Wow.

Gary: Man.

Colleen: Wow.

Gary: Man.

Colleen: That. Felt.

Gary: Yeah?

> *Gary gets up from the bed.*

Colleen: What?

> *He takes her hand and puts it on his heart.*

Colleen: Wow.

Gary: Crazy.

Colleen: Come here. Sit here.

Gary: Can't.

Colleen: Why not?

Gary: No, it's just.

Colleen: What?

Gary: Just.

Colleen: Did I do something wrong?

Gary: No. No.

Colleen: Sit here. Come here.

Gary: Can't.

Colleen: Why?

Gary: Don't know.

Colleen: Come on.

Gary: No.

Colleen: Ugh. God, you're like a smashed dragonfly right now.

Gary: Yeah.

Colleen: Maybe you're not that into chicks either. Is it true, what Dabney said?

Gary: What?

Colleen: Tom Dabney.

Gary: Yeah?

Colleen: He said you were a pussy.

Gary: Yeah. When?

Colleen: He said he called you a pussy to your face at the Lighthouse and you pissed in the ladies sittin down.

Gary: Yeah, when did he say this?

Colleen: After you left me at the transporter. He showed up. We smoked a bowl. Got to hear all about White Rabbit, cause you know he wrote that shit.

Gary: You tell him you broke up with Steve?

Colleen: What?

Gary: Nuthin.

Colleen: You're not goin again?

Gary: Yeah.

Blackout as Gary climbs out her window.

Where's He At?

Dad and Laurie watch TV. After a long pause.

Dad: This is too weird, Laur.

Laurie: No it's not.

Dad: No?

Laurie: Gettin a beer.

Dad: You've had a real lot, Laur.

Laurie: Havin another.

She gets up unsteadily and goes to the kitchen.

Dad: Are you out of your fuckin mind now?
            Laur?! Laur?! Get me one.

*Laurie returns with two beers—
hands one to Dad.*

Dad: I don't know about this.

Laurie: No?

Dad: You're gonna still read aren't ya?

Laurie: Don't want to be in my room right now.

Dad: No? You-you're always in there.

Dabney kicks in the door.

Dabney: Where's he at?!

Dad: What the fuck?!

Dabney: Where's he at?!

Dad: What the FUCK?

Dabney: Where's that pussy son of yours?

Dad: Get the hell out of here!

Dabney: Where's he at?!

Dad: What the hell do I know! Get off a me!

Dabney: You know where your pussy brother is at?

Laurie: Leave me alone.

Dabney: You fucking know where your brother is at?!

Dad: Dabney, leave her—

Laurie: NO.

Dabney: Tell me!

Laurie: I told you.

Dad: Hey now leave her alone!

Dabney: Where's he at?

Laurie: Fuck you.

Dad: Leave her alone.

Dabney: Tell you what. When I find pussy Gary I'm gonna crush his nuts with a bat.

Dad: What the fuck Dabney?!

Dabney: He broke into my truck and stole my pool cue! He stole my fuckin pool cue!

Dad: I'm callin Jack Ardent.

Dabney: Call'im.

Dad: I'm callin.

Dabney: Just tell me where my cue is at!

Laurie: You want it back?

Dabney: Yeah.

Laurie: You want your cue back?!

Dabney: Yeah, know where it's at?

Laurie: Yeah!

Laurie exits to the kitchen.

Dad: Callin Jack Ardent!

Dabney: Callim! He can put his pussy cuffs on
          your pussy kid—Grand Larceny.

Dad: What?

Dabney: That's a $5,000 cue.

Dad: NO WAY.

Dabney: Yes way and I'm still gonna smash Gary's nuts.

Laurie returns with Gary's hunting rifle.

Dabney: ..That's not it.

She takes aim at Dabney. Dad is freaked out.

Dad: Jesus, Laur, Jesus, now, careful.

Laurie: You want your cue?

Dabney: Jesus, alls I want is my cue...

Dad: Laur, now, think it through, Laur...

Dabney: Alls I want...

Laurie: Craig Brundage.

Dabney: What?

Laurie: Craig Brundage has your cue.

Dabney: No way—I saw your brother at the Lighthouse and
          called him a pussy and he broke the window
          out of my truck and stole my cue.

Laurie: Craig Brundage told me he stole it. He said he wanted
          to see the look on your big mouth face.

Dabney: Craig Brundage?

Dad: Laur?

Laurie: He has your cue.

Dabney: Craig Brundage?

Laurie: He said you have the stupidest face in
          this whole stupidface town.

Dabney: That little motherfucking piece of shit!

Laurie: He said he was gonna sell it at Wolski's.

Dabney: That motherfucker! He is DEAD. Oh he is so dead.
          I'm gonna smash his nuts flat to baloney. Wolski's?!
          He knows I fucked Grace Slick's ass at Wolski's...

          Dabney exits.

Dad: Laur? Laur?

          *She sits with the rifle across her lap
          watching TV and drinking her beer.*

Dad: Laur? Think we should call over to Brundage? Laur?
          Tell em, tell em Dabney's on the way?

Laurie: NO.

Dad: You don't think we should?

Laurie: No. No. No.

Dad: Well, Laur...Wanna go catch a burger? Later maybe?
            Wait, what time is it? Laur? Know what?
            We could catch a burger maybe before it closes—
            or I could run by the Lighthouse and pick some up?
            Before it closes. Laur? You want? We could watch
            something different. What's tonight? Dallas.
            You ever see that? No. You never did. Pretty good tho,
            Laur. But. What time is it? Maybe might be over.
            There's this new show too, WKRP Cinncinati,
            you might like. That's probably over too. You pick tho.
            Two good ones. Know what? I'm goin to the Lighthouse
            get you a burg with cheese. Be right back.
            Hey, no more beers, okay?

                        Dad exits.
                        Laurie watches tv with the rifle in her lap.

                        Beat.
                        Gary Enters.

Gary: That is so weird, Laur?

Laurie: Tom Dabney came here looking for his pool cue.
            He called you a pussy.

Gary: You didn't shoot him?

Laurie: Chased him off.

Gary: Dad's not back yet?

Laurie: Getting burgers now.

Gary: Here, give me that.

Laurie: No—

Gary: It's okay. He won't come back.

Laurie: How do you know?

Gary: I'll give him his cue back.

Laurie: You have it?

Gary: Yeah.

Laurie: Said he was gonna smash your balls.

Gary: For sure.

Takes rifle and puts it away.
Gary starts to leave.

Laurie: Just wait.

Gary: Wait?

Laurie: Don't go right now, okay.

Gary: It's okay, Laur. He's not gonna come back and
           he's not gonna smash my balls.

Laurie: No. That's not...just wait with me awhile, okay?

Gary: Okay.

They sit on the couch.

Laurie: Why'd you come back early?

Gary: Was so weird. In the blind, you know, Donnie took a
           stupid shot hit this deer like a thousand yards away
           and it ran off, you know, and right then I had a feelin
           about you.

Laurie: You did?

Gary: Yeah.

Laurie: That's why you came back early?

Gary: I guess. So?

Laurie: What?

Gary: I don't know. You believe that Alan Watts Buddhist stuff?
           Comin back as a dragonfly, to help people?

Laurie: Help people.

Gary: Yeah.

Laurie: No. No help.

Gary: You don't believe it?

Laurie: No one helps. No one helped the Purple Coolaid people,
           none of the bugs in that jungle helped. And they were all
           there cause they thought that guy was helping them,
           you know, make paradise. What a joke. People, maybe,
           open the door for ya, carry your groceries. But that's
           not really helping. That's easy. Some people even really
           try to help. Try to do something, but it's too late or
           doesn't matter. Doctors can't really help. Couldn't help
           mom. Mrs. Gundy, the librarian thought she was
           helping me. Letting me in the 'special collections' but
           you read all this special stuff and your head gets so full
           it knocks you over and there's no one to pick you up.
           You have to do it yourself.

Gary: I don't know, Laur.

Laurie: Who? Who's gonna help? Dad?

Gary: I'll help you.

Laurie: You came back.

Gary: I think I can do this, you know, after I die,
         come back as like a—

Laurie: If I had to come back, I'd come back as a rock. Don't
           need water, or food, or sunlight, or heat, or even air.
           Don't need help, or even need other rocks. Might be
           at the bottom of the ocean or the top of a mountain
           and it wouldn't matter cause you don't need to know—
           you're a rock. This world was made for rocks.

Gary: Laur. You're waaay better than a rock.

           Lights out.

Burgers

Lighthouse Inn. Lights find Bob behind the bar.
Dad waiting on burgers with a beer in front of him.

Dad: You put cheese on, right?

Bob: Cheese goes on.

Dad: Laurie like em with cheese.

Bob: She's what now? 14?

Dad: Don't know. Yeah. 14 or 15.

Bob: Growin up.

Dad: She's a reader.

Bob: Yeah?

Dad: Books this thick.

Bob: Sure. Good.

Dad: Ain't it?

Bob: So Gary came back early.

Dad: Yeah. But he's goin back up to get Donnie.

Bob: Really?

Dad: He likes to drive he says.

Bob: I don't like to drive that much.

Dad: No kiddin. Gar likes to drive, Laur likes to read, fuckin Donnie's the only regular kid I got. Maybe. Winged a buck at like a half mile. Trackin it. Probably get it. But Laur started watchin TV now.

Bob: Yeah?

Dad: Yeah, comin out of her room.
         Know that Craig Brundage kid?

Bob: He's bad news.

Dad: I guess Laur was helpin him.

Bob: No, really? Helpin him what?

Dad: Read. I don't know.

Bob: Wouldn't let that kid near my daughter.

Dad: No?

Bob: There's talk he forced himself on Juniper Farrell.

Dad: The 'tard?

Bob: That's what I mean, yeah.

Dad: No shit? She's really filled out.
         Saw her at McAdams other day.

Bob: Grown up body but five years old
         in the brain department.

Dad: Huh.

Dad starts to realize about Craig and Laurie.

Bob: That crazy idiot Brundage might do something
         real stupid one day. I'd keep Laurie away from him.

*Bob can see that something bad
has already happened.*

Dad: Yeah. Yeah. God. Okay. Right. Keep him away.

Bob: The Pack, huh? Tie game. What a dud.

Dad: Right? Tied. Even.

Bob: Shouldn't be ties allowed in the NFL.

Dad: I know. Keep going overtime till someone scores.

Bob: Someone has to score at some point.

Dad: Just keep going till one of ya scores.

Bob: A fumble or—

Dad: Plus it's like, what does it mean?
          Tie. It's like nothing happened.

Bob: They get a half out of it.

Dad: A half?

Bob: Yeah, half win.

Dad: What the hell is a half win?

Bob: Opposite of a half loss.

Dad: That's the stupidest rule in the NFL. Half win.

Bob: Yeah, they should rethink that.

Black out.

Craig Gets Rocked

Lights, Craig dashes across the stage.
Then Dabney with a bat in pursuit.
Then Craig again. Dabney closer. Craig.
Dabney closing, swings the bat and takes Craig's feet out.

Dabney: Where's it AT!

Craig: STOP! STOP! YOU CRAZY FUCKER!

Dabney: Where's it at?

Craig: What?

Dabney: WHERE'S IT AT?

Craig: What?! What?!

Dabney: My cue!

Slams him with the bat.

Craig: Stop. What? Your cue?

Dabney: Gimme back my cue!

Craig: Your cue?

Dabney: Where's it at?

Craig: I don't know!

Dabney: Laurie Tetzloff says you have it.

Craig: NO!

Dabney: Last chance. Where's it at?

Craig: I DON'T KNOW!

Dabney: Sell it at Wolski's already?

Craig: No. No. Shit! We have the same boots!

Dabney swings on his nuts.
Craig screams into blackout.

Gary Returns the Cue

Lights. Dabney sits at the bar in the Lighthouse bitterly
drinking a beer.

Dabney: No shit. That little Brundage kid is tough. Beat the shit
           out a him and he still wouldn't give up my cue.

Bob: You beat the shit out of him?

Dabney: With a bat. So what? My cue is gone.

Bob: You did it this time.

Dabney: Had the same boots as me. So what.

Bob: You tellin me you beat Craig Brundage
            with a baseball bat?

Dabney: He stole my cue and probably already sold it at Wolski's.

Bob: Probably already has Ardent lookin for you.
            Man, that's assault.

Dabney: Fuck you. What is it he stole my cue, Bob?
            —Grand Larceny.

Bob: Grand Larceny?

Dabney: $5,000 for that cue, Bob.

Bob: No cue is worth $5,000.

Dabney: Szamboti, Bob, bird's-eye maple forearm,
            with rosewood butt sleeve and brass joint—ah, fuck you.
            No way he narcs on me.

Bob: He's 15, you're like what?

Gary enters with Dabney's cue.

Dabney: THFUCK?! That's my cue!

Gary: Aint it.

Dabney takes his cue and looks it over.

Dabney: This is my cue. What the FUCKINEDDY!?

Gary: Yeah, broke the window out of your truck and took it.

Dabney: I FUCKIN KNEW IT! I FUCKING KNEW IT! You're dead.
            You are so dead. I fucked up Craig Brundage cause your
            bitch sister told me he took it.

Gary: She told you he took it?

Dabney: Yeah!

Gary: But I took it.

Dabney: She was savin your ass!

Gary: But she didn't know I took it.

Bob: I'm calling Jack Ardent.

Dabney: *(laughing)* Oh my god, that Craig kid—
            thought he was a hard case cause he wouldn't give it up,
            and he didn't even have it.

Gary: Here.

Handing Dabney money.

Gary: For your window.

Dabney: Still gonna smash your balls flat.

Gary: Yeah.

Dabney: Your ass is grass.

Bob: Dabney, I am calling Ardent right now.

Dabney: Call'im, I'll pound that pussy too!

Bob: Your bullshit did it this time—

Dabney: Now I gotta pound you too.

Bob: Dabney. It's ringing.

Gary: It's okay, Bob.

Bob: He already assaulted Craig Brundage over that stupid cue.

Dabney pushes off from the bar. Makes a big show.

Dabney: You're dead ya fruit.

Gary: Yeah. Just say yeah.

Dabney: Fight me back and it'll be worse for ya.

Gary: Yeah.

Dabney: Better take it like a man.

Gary: Yeah, Dabney, man would.

Dabney: Try hittin me and I'm gonna smash your balls double flat.

Bob: I'm a witness Dabney—testify at your fuckin trial.

Gary: Bob. He can't hurt me.

Dabney: Whad'you say!?

Gary: There's really nothin you can do to me worse than hearing your pathetic story again.

Dabney: Whad'you say?!

Gary: That sad, that boast, tha Wolski's, White Rabbit shit never happened Dabney.

Dabney: WHAT THE FUCK DID YOU JUST SAY?!

Gary: Ever look at the album cover, Dabney? Surrealistic Pillow came out in 67. 1967.

Dabney: Oh yeah? OH YEAH? You are dead!

> *Dabney swings at Gary but stops. It's a test
> to see if Gary's gonna block him or fight back.
> Dabney's fist stops inches from Gary,
> but Gary doesn't flinch.*

Dabney: Pussy! I knew it was you.
Why'd your sister tell me Craig Brundage took it?

Gary: I don't know.

Dabney: I flattened that kid bad.

Bob: Ardent's on his way, Dabney.

Dabney: Got my cue and my money.

> *He chugs what's left of his beer.*

Dabney:	Know what Titzlaff? Fuck you and your stupid sister and your worthless old man.

Dabney exits.

Bob:	You believe that guy?
Gary:	I know.
Bob:	Wasn't gonna let him hurt you. No way.
Gary:	Thanks, Bob.
Bob:	You weren't gonna fight back?
Gary:	Don't know. Don't think so.
Bob:	I'd have stopped his ass.
Gary:	Thanks, Bob. Guess I should go before Ardent—
Bob:	It's okay, he never picked up.
Gary:	Oh, yeah. Jaeger?
Bob:	Sure. So. Really, 67?
Gary:	Yeah. Played the album the other day and just, you know, saw it on the cover.
Bob:	Dabney killed that album for me.

Lights fade.

Going To Pick Up Donnie

Lights warm on Gary knocking on Colleen's window.

Colleen:	What? Who's that?
Gary:	Gary.
Colleen:	Man. What do you want now man? You are one frustrating dude.

Gary:	Want to go with me to pick up Donnie tomorrow?
Colleen:	It is tomorrow.
Gary:	Wanna go with?
Colleen:	You mean drive up to the cabin and back?
Gary:	Yeah.
Colleen:	Come in here.

Gary climbs into her bedroom.

Colleen:	First you gotto tell me, you into me or not?
Gary:	I'm into you.
Colleen:	Then why can't you even look at me?
Gary:	Don't know.
Colleen:	Tetzloff the freak. Sit here.

He does. They kiss.

Colleen:	Lay down.

He does.

Colleen:	Be here with me.

She lays next to him and they kiss.
They look one another in the eye.

Lights fade.

MAC MODEAN as Laurie / *DOWNTOWN, Black River Falls*

– ACT TWO –

Believe Me

Night. Tetzloff house. Laur on the couch reading. TV on low.
Dabney Enters.

Dabney: Saw your old man leave.

Laurie is freaked and frozen.

Laurie: Gar's—

Dabney: Lighthouse. Saw him too. Give a shit where Donnie is—
not here. You heard Brundage's old man dimed me?

Laurie nods.

Dabney: Ardent put out the APB. Why I'm in Hurley at the Aunt's
place. Ever been to Hurley? Colder'n icicle dick.

Laurie: Iron River.

Dabney: Why?

Laurie: *(sarcastic)* The awesome snow.

Dabney: Yeah, well usually Hurley chicks you can have for like a
couple smirny and sevens. So now I go up to one,
lean against my cue—finger her with my eyes.
She looks at me and says "Suck my dick." Her DICK?
That's not natural. Now gotta make her cough up a turd.
Say somethin. But. Nothin. Walked out. I never walk out.
I walked out. And I'm outside this stupid bar in coldass
Hurley. And I was like—you owe me.
You told me it was Brundage.

Laurie: Yeah.

Dabney: You said—

Laurie: So what?

Dabney: You said—

Laurie: Shouldnt have believed me.

Dabney: I knew it was Gary.

Laurie: Why'd you believe me?

Dabney: Well, the 30 ott six.

Laurie: Shouldnt have believed me.

Dabney: You made me.

Laurie: Made you.

Dabney: Yeah, now you owe me. Tell old man Brundage
            and Ardent it was you. Get this APB offa me.

Laurie: Make them believe me?

Dabney: Fuckin Eddy! Like how you did me when I knew! Convince
            old man Brundage and Ardent to drop the APB. Call'm.

Laurie: No.

Dabney: What?

Laurie: No.

Dabney: Call'm.

Laurie: No.

Dabney: Call'm now.

Laurie: No.

Dabney: You OWE me.

Laurie: No, I don't.

Dabney: You know you owe me.

Laurie: No. I don't.

Dabney: You don't think you owe me?

Dabney looms.

Laurie: No.

Dabney: You know Brundage kid will never have kids. Cant.

Laurie: ...Oh?

Dabney: Didn't hear that? Yeah. I mean. Never.
          Hit his balls hard. Bunch a times. With the bat.
          But. No kids. Why his old man dimed me.
          Ya gotta wanna have kids if you're a dude.
          Be able to. Ya know?

Laurie: No.

Dabney: Well ya do.

Laurie: Yeah?

Dabney: It's a dude's fuckin prerogative.

Laurie: To have kids?

Dabney: Swimmers. At least. Now Brundage can't. You—

Laurie: Good.

Dabney: WHAT?! Not good. Not good. Kid's fifteen.

Laurie: I'm fifteen.

Dabney: Just get this APB offa me!

Laurie: Get out of here.

Dabney: Get this offa me!

Laurie: Get out.

Dabney: You owe me.

Laurie: I'll call'em and make it worse. Tell'em you threatened me,
          convince'em to double the APBs.

Dabney: You'd.

Laurie: GET OUT OF HERE!

> *Laurie slams her book closed.*
> *She stands to Dabney.*
> *Dabney does not know what to do.*
> *He is full of rage and fear.*
> *He exits.*

Someone To Talk To

Lighthouse Inn. Low effort Christmas and New Years decorations.
Bob behind the bar. Helen, 40's, strong, dressed up a bit,
more makeup than necessary, enters.

Bob: Well, well, look at the cat draggin in.

Helen: Hey Bob.

Bob: Helen. Been a while. After the service for Al, I think.

Helen: Yeah, really tied one on that night.

Bob: Yeah, yep, 'member. Still go with wine coolers?

Helen: Still do.

> *Bob makes one.*

Bob: What, uh, brings ya out?

Helen: Frankly Bob, goin stir crazy.

Bob: Sure. Good to get out. See folks.

Helen: Hard, though. After.

Bob: Right. Father Smith sayin.

Helen: Just awful. In front of everyone.

Bob: How do you stand before your congregation,
         open the Bible, and say somethin like that?
         A man of the cloth.

Helen: You were there?

Bob: No. No. Heard, tho.

Helen: Al's folks really ate it up.

Bob: Well. That's. Their only son.

Helen: No. He drives by.

Bob: Who?

Helen: Dad Buska.

Bob: Drives by?

Helen: In the Sliverado.

Bob: Al's truck?

Helen: Yeah.

Bob: The house?

Helen: Yeah. Slows down.

Bob: Grief I would think.

Helen: Not the look on his face, Bob.

Bob: Well that's just. Maybe he's, maybe he wants you
         to renew your policy.

Helen: Bob.

Bob: I know.

Helen: Has everyone in town by the ears.

Bob: Insurance. It's a people business.

Helen: McAdams for wine, the looks I get.

Bob: What I think, Helen, couple years. Chentiss,
         new Fire Chief, it's all be water under the bridge.

Helen: Couple years.

Bob: Sure. You'll see, town'll. Like nothin. Couple parades.
         Chentiss tappin beer from the back of the 150.
         Couple soft ball tourneys. No one's gonna remember
         what Father Smith or Don Buska said.

Helen: Bob?

Bob: Yeah?

Helen: What have you been drinkin?

Bob: You don't think?

Helen: Donald Torrence Buska?

Bob: Well.

Helen: Yeah.

Bob: How come you didn't go back to the maiden name?

Helen: Want to. Cant just yet.
         The house and the deed. You know.

Bob: Sure. Another?

Helen: Sure.

Bob: How's, uh, Colleen?

Helen: Don't know, not talkin to me these days.

Bob: Teenagers.

Helen: Yeah.

Bob: In a galaxy far far away.

Helen: No kidding. She's—

         Bob makes another wine cooler.
         Dan enters.

Bob: Hey Dan.

Dad: Hey.

Bob: You know Helen?

Dad: Sure.

Helen: Mr. Tetzloff.

Dad: Ok, whoa, that's Dan. Dan.

Helen: Dan. Helen.

           They shake.

Dad: Hey. Great, to officially—uh

           Dan sits at the bar.
           Nervous beat. Dad chuckles a bit and
           fields a beer from Bob.

Dad: So.

Helen: Yeah, so...

Bob: Just talkin how difficult teenagers can be.

Dad: Fersure. Mine are.

Helen: Short tempered. Tired all the time. Fallin asleep with the
         radio on. Colleen. Since Al passed—you knew Al?

Dad: Sure, built that house with his own hands.

Helen: That burns me alive! Hearing that just burns me up!

Dad: Oh. Didn't'he?

Helen: Everybody says, everybody thinks but know what?
         I put in way more hours on that house then he ever did.
         And Colleen too. We worked day and night till it was built.
         Who talked everyday to the architect? I did.
         To the contractor? Me. Built the frame, hung the
         dry wall, lot of the wiring, plumbing, painting, fixtures—
         I was right there the whole time.
         Bout the only thing I didn't do was pour the foundation.

Dad: Oh, yeah, no, didn't mean to—

Helen: That picture of him. Mr. Fire Chief. Wavin from his truck. Mr. do-it-all head grounds keeper. Buildin a home for his family with his own two hands. What sickening bullshit. His smug parents down the block sittin in their picture window glarin at me. Cruel. You know what? Al had a brother. Did you know that?

Dad: No.

Helen: Bob, you know that? Al had a brother?

Bob: No. Really? That's news.

Helen: Well he was mental and they kept him in a locked room in the basement for 30 years! That's Don and Karen Buska for ya. Al never told me. I found out cause his brother got loose one day—all hell, chasin him down the street. What kind of people. 30 years in a single room in the basement! Then they put him in a home and they'd visit at like 4 in the morning and get home by 6 and pretend to wake up and start their day. Pretend. So the neighbors wouldn't—we'd go over there and they'd have put their pajamas back on so Al's old man could step out the front door and grab the paper in full view of the nosey neighbors. Oh god. That's who raised Al. No wonder he never mentioned how much pain he must have been in for years while that tumor grew in his gut to the size of a football. And that greasy Father Smith—at the service fawning over the passing of a great son, a great dad, one of Dousman's leading lights. All those confessions— didn't think I could stand Al one more minute. Know what? Glory Be's and Our Father's—even a Hail Mary—which he never, but none of it really takes the punch out of a black eye. And he sided with Al's folks to try and force us out of the house. So. You maybe have a sense of why that infuriates me when people say that about that house and Al.

Dad: No, yeah, I can see—

Helen: It's okay. Just, in the past. All in the past.

Dad: Yeah, yeah, of course.

Bob: Over and done. Good to move on.

Helen: No need to drag up the past. Al croaked.
            Just glad to be able to talk.

Dad: It's a real nice house anyway.

> *Dad and Helen down their drinks.*
> *Bob lands two more.*

Dad: Saw old man Buska in the Silverado other day.

Helen: Oh yeah. He drives by all the time. That look on his face.
            Not enough he got the Life Insurance and the pension.
            He wants the house.

Dad: What for?

Helen: All the marbles. He got a lawyer but so did I.

Dad: Al really punched you right in the face?

Bob: Dan.

Helen: Al was never more vicious than when the house was
            almost done. Me and Col like eager dogs, lining up the
            trim, sconces, caulking. He would come home look at us
            and yeah, we didn't do it the way he said maybe but we
            did it the way it worked...and he'd—pow. He had—
            he installed a Garbage disposal in the kitchen sink to
            show us the way things should be done and he called me
            and Col in for a great demonstration. His prized finishing
            touch. Turned it on, held up an old chicken bone.
            'Even this' he said and threw it in. There was a terrible
            scream and that bone shot out and stuck in the ceiling
            like a knife. And I felt it. I felt it like it stuck in me.
            That was it. Filed the next day. But no need to drag it
            all up again.

Dad: No. Ok. Yeah, no. Sounds bad.

Helen: No need to haul it back up out of the crypt.

Bob: That is. Ancient history.

Helen: What's past is past.

Dad: My wife, you heard—stupid Leukemia—
           but married what 12-17 years, whole time,
           don't think she ever liked me.
           Do something not too stupid, but not smart—
           really tick her off–the look she'd give me.
           Like I left a fat crap floatin.

Helen: Uh-huh.

Dad: We were young.

Helen: Yeah, we were too. Lost those years. But no more.

Dad: No?

Helen: Not gonna lose any more time.

Dad: No?

Helen: No.

Bob: Gonna—?

Helen: One day, just—

Bob: What?

Helen: Like.

Dad: Yeah? Like.

Helen: Nothin. Forget it.

Dad: No, like?

Helen: Like, soon just.

Dad: Just soon?

Helen: Just. Do not repeat this to anyone, either a you, promise.

Dad: Ok.

Helen: Promise.

Bob:	You have my word, Helen.
Dad:	Oh, yeah, mine too.
Helen:	Selling the house and moving out a here.
Dad:	Yeah?
Helen:	Me an Col, yeah. Maybe Myrtle Beach, maybe Atlanta, maybe I don't even know, but gone.
Bob:	Good on you, Helen, new start, that's how to do it.
Helen:	One way or another. However it settles. Lawyers or bust. Off we go.
Bob:	No lookin back, huh?
Helen:	Nope. Already halfway packed up. Some people comin for a last looksee. But. BUT. Just. *(zips her lip and tosses the key.)*
Bob:	You got it.
Dad:	Mm-hm.
Helen:	Put it all behind. No more vultures chewin on my heart. But.

Again, indicates silence.
They drink. Sit.

Dad:	Colleen gonna do that flag, the marching flag thing, this year?
Helen:	No, Dan. Flag thing?
Dad:	Doesn't she do the, uh, what's—Color Guard?
Helen:	No.
Dad:	Huh. I thought she did—was real good. For St. Johns?
Helen:	Never.
Dad:	No?
Helen:	No.

Dad:	Then who was that girl looks just like Colleen in Color Guard?
Helen:	I don't know.
Dad:	What does Colleen look like?
Bob:	Jesus, Dan.
Dad:	What?...I guess Gar's liked Colleen a bunch of years.
Helen:	Gar?
Dad:	Gary, my middle, and, but, she was goin out with those other guys.
Helen:	What guys?
Dad:	Uh.
Helen:	What guys?
Dad:	Uh.
Helen:	What guys?
Dad:	Porty, Farley, Steve...I mean, Gary said.
Helen:	...Colleen?
Dad:	Maybe I don't know what I'm talkin about.
Helen:	Colleen?
Bob:	Hey, now, hey, hey. Here, let's toast. What's over is done. To the New Year—to new beginnings. To gettin while the gettins good.

Helen breaks down.

Bob:	Whoa, whoa there.

Hands her some napkins.

Helen:	Sorry. Sorry. It's just.
Dad:	I don't know what I'm talkin about. Just never do.

Helen: Just, used to be no secrets between me and Col.
Used to be a team. I thought, now is our time.
We're finally free, no one holding us back and now,
and now it's like living with a Coyote.

Dad: Got to admit. Bout my kids. There's a lot I don't know.
But then there's alot I don't want to know.

Bob: Wow Dan.

Dad: I mean. They got to have their own lives, yeah?

Helen pulls herself together.

Helen: You gotta wanta know if they're doin stupid stuff.

Dad: Well. Maybe they'll learn from their mistakes.

Bob: I don't know. I'm a confirmed bartender so I know more
about raisin a toast then raisin kids, but dont some
mistakes last a lifetime. Oh, jeez. Ok. Yeah.
Another round. *(to Helen)* You?

Helen: Sure.

Bob whips them up.

Helen: No one wants their kid to pay a lifetime for a mistake.

Dad: Yeah. Yeah, I guess that's true.

Landing the drinks.

Bob: These are on me folks. Let me join you in a toast to the
New Year. This is my favorite, I think
from Teddy Roosevelt...
Here's to doing the best you can with what you got.

Dad: With what you got.

Helen: Cheers.

They drink.

Love

Radio playing softly. Gary and Colleen in her bed getting down.
Their rapturous climax is long and loud. After, they snuggle.

Colleen: Ummmm.

Gary: Unreal.

Colleen: Fuckin-eddy.

Gary: Whose fuckin eddy?

Colleen: Not me.

Gary: Not Eddy.

Colleen: Keeps gettin better. Never thought. Man!

> *Gary starts to kiss her going for seconds.*

Colleen: Know what? Maybe, maybe just let's...

Gary: Oh.

Colleen: And I wanna just, so intense and maybe just be—

> *Helen enters with a shotgun.*
> *Colleen's door is locked.*
> *She stands outside knocking.*
> *Gary and Col freeze.*

Helen: Col? Col? Col?

Colleen: Ma?

Helen: Hear that?

Colleen: What?

Helen: Heard somethin.

Colleen: No, Ma.

Helen: Yeah.

Colleen: What?

Helen: Don't know.

Colleen: Probably the radio.

Helen: Not th'radio.

Colleen: Probably the cows.

Helen: No. Not cows.

Colleen: Thought you went out.

Helen: I'm back.

Colleen: Tryin to sleep ma.

Helen: Lemme in.

Colleen: No, what? Tryin to sleep.

Helen: Open the door, Col. I heard somethin.

Colleen: Super tired.

Helen: Let me in, Col. Now, Col.
            I mean it—open th'door now. Colleen.

> *Colleen and Gary don't know what to do.*
> *They cover him up with blankets and pillows.*
> *Colleen puts on a bathrobe and flicks open the door.*
> *She stands in the door. Sees the gun.*

Colleen: This is crazy. Ma. Wha'd you hear?

Helen: Don't know. Not like somethin I heard before.

> *They listen.*

Colleen: Nothin, come on, go back to bed.

Helen: Col—are you sexually active?

Colleen: Ma?!

Helen:	Col, are you?
Colleen:	Come on.
Helen:	Jus answer. Answer th'question.
Colleen:	Go away. Yer drunk!
Helen:	A lil tight, but don think you can pull crap on me.
Colleen:	Jesus. Not talkin to you.
Helen:	You are. Col. Cause jus had a super intersting talk with Dan Tetzloff about you and Gary.
Colleen:	Ma, get out!
Helen:	Are you having sex with Gary Tezloff?
Colleen:	Ahhhhahhhhh!!!
Helen:	You want kids?
Colleen:	MA! FUCK!!
Helen:	Col! SEROUSLY. You want kids?
Colleen:	No. Ma. No. That's not it. You don't know ANYTHING!!!
Helen:	Oh no? Dont know? You dont know. He use protection?
Colleen:	Ma.
Helen:	Jus, does he wear rubbers?
Colleen:	MA!
Helen:	You have your friend this month yet, Col?
Colleen:	None a your business, Ma.
Helen:	You get pregnant and your life is over Col.
Colleen:	Ma. God, you are so. Ma. Get out. Get out.
Helen:	Tomorrow we're goin to the clinic.
Colleen:	I'M NOT PREGNANT!

Helen: The pill. Col, no way you're gettin get pregnant.

Colleen: Ma. I been fuckin since I was 13.

Helen: ...Oh God, Col, no. That's—when did you have time?

Colleen: Made time, believe me.

Helen: Oh Col.

Colleen: You don't know anything. I been to the clinic.

Helen: Oh jesus. Col!

Colleen: Get out of here. OUT NOW.

> *Colleen shoves Helen out the door.*
> *Helen comes back in.*

Helen: Oh jesus, Col, you been to the clinic?

Colleen: OUT!

> *They struggle.*

Helen: For the pill?

Colleen: Ma-

Helen: For the pill, Col?

Colleen: No. Not the pill.

> *They stop struggling.*

Helen: Oh. Col. Oh. Oh dear.

Colleen: I can take care of myself.

Helen: Oh Col. Oh.

> *Helen tries to hug Colleen. It is awkward.*

Colleen: Ma. Go to bed.

Helen:	We're gettin outta here, Col. Soon. We're gonna get somewhere else. I'm so sorry.
Colleen:	Yeah, yeah, ok. Talk tomorrow.
Helen:	Folks are comin to look at the place tomorrow. Prolly make an offer. You gotta clean this room, smells like last Friday's fish fry in here.
Colleen:	MA!

> *Helen exits. Colleen locks the door.*
> *Gary pops up breathing hard.*
> *Gary and Colleen sit on her bed.*
> *Gary slowly and quietly gets dressed.*
> *The spell is broken. He sneaks out the*
> *window super slow and quiet.*
> *Colleen sinks back and looks at the ceiling.*

Pan Toast

Laurie sleeps on the couch. Her book is on the coffee table.
TV is on. Something wakes her. She smells something.
Dad enters from the kitchen with a cookie sheet of toast
and stands at the stairs calling up.

Dad:	Pan toast! Getcher pan toast here!

> *Laur sits up.*

Laurie:	You made—
Dad:	Jesus! Scared the crap outta me. Sleep on the couch again?
Laurie:	Yeah.
Dad:	Geez.

Laurie: You made pan toast?

Dad: Yeah Laur. What's this?

Laurie: ...Pan toast.

Dad: Aint it.

Laurie: You don't cook.

Dad: Yeah, well. Wanted some.

Laurie: I'd a.

Dad: I know, Laur, but.

> *Laurie cautiously lifts a piece of toast,*
> *it's soggy with butter.*

Dad: From memory, maybe less butter.
           Lemmie get papertowels.

> *Exits to get papertowels.*

Laurie: And cinnamon.

Dad: *(os)* Crap. Cinnamon! Hold on.

> *Returning with cinnamon and papertowels.*

Dad: Here we go.

Laurie: Lemme.

> *She carefully sprinkles cinnamon on the toast.*
> *Dad grabs a piece, swabs the bottom with a*
> *papertowel and takes a big bite.*

Dad: Hmmm.

Laurie: Buttery.

Dad: Didn't she used to use a couple sticks?

Laurie: Half a stick.

Dad:	No.
Laurie:	Half a stick soft, rub each piece. Then sugar, cinnamon.
Dad:	Not too toasty this way.
Laurie:	No.
Dad:	No crunch.
Laurie:	No.
Dad:	Man that crunch. Toast and sugar. She could. It would snap. Nothin like that.
Laurie:	No.
Dad:	More uh, like fry bread more.
Laurie:	More like dough.
Dad:	Still good.
Laurie:	Yeah. It's.
Dad:	Hey, well you know. Happy New Year, Laur. But more than anything, just wanted. God, used to be able to put away two whole loaves. Member? Just, she'd land em and we'd.
Laurie:	Yeah.
Dad:	Donnie could eat a whole loaf himself. Still can. Probably more. *(calling)* Pan Toast Donnie!
Laurie:	Milwaukee.
Dad:	Milwaukee?
Laurie:	Waiting for tickets. Uriah Heap, Slade, and Blue Oyster Cult at the Arena.
Dad:	Blue Oyster Cult?
Laurie:	The band. *(singing)* Don't Fear the Reaper. Took a tent.
Dad:	Took a tent to buy concert tickets.

Laurie: Said he wanted no worse than third in line.

Dad: Gods. Donnie, goin for bronze.

                    Beat

Dad: Why you think that is?

Laurie: Donnie?

Dad: Yeah, like that deer. That was—how could he do that?

Laurie: No idea.

Dad: How could'ee?

Laurie: What you think happened to it?

Dad: Nothing good. Wolves maybe, or coyotes. Or just bled to
            death. Stupid. Why would you shoot at a deer like a
            thousand yards away? There's a tradition. You know,
            do it right takes a lot of skill—

Laurie: Catch a deer with your bare hands, get it to lay down,
            whisper to it till it falls asleep, then cut its throat.

Dad: Jesus, Laur.

Laurie: That would be skill.

Dad: Two days trackin—can't find a wounded deer?

Laurie: If they did even bother trackin.

Dad: Oh. You think. Gar woulda. But. He came back.
            Should get him up for—

Laurie: Colleen.

Dad: Colleen?

Laurie: With her.

Dad: Yeah?

Laurie: Yeah.

Dad:	Whad'they have a date to see the sunrise?
Laurie:	Went last night.
Dad:	Last night?
Laurie:	To see her, yeah.
Dad:	But. Oh. No. That's. Does Helen know?
Laurie:	Helen?
Dad:	Kind of a dynamite lady.
Laurie:	Helen?
Dad:	She was at the Lighthouse last night.
Laurie:	Call over.
Dad:	No.
Laurie:	Go over. Just go over.
Dad:	Laur. Laur. Come on. Crisesakes. That's. Gar would. And...
Laurie:	And?
Dad:	Gar seems so happy, aint it.
Laurie:	Sure.

TV catches his attention.

Dad:	Yeah, he's—look this's classic.
Laurie:	Classic?
Dad:	Yeah.
Laurie:	Know what's classic?
Dad:	Hm?
Laurie:	Classic, know what's super classic?
Dad:	*(mimes something) (mouth sound of a big explosion)*

Laurie: Like the most classic—

Dad: *(mimes dizzy Coyote) (laughs)* Meep-meep. What, Laur?

Laurie: Nothin.

Dad: No, what?

Laurie: Nothin.

Dad: All ears.

Laurie: Okay.

Dad: What?

Laurie: Nothin.

                    Beat.

Dad: What you readin?

Laurie: What?

Dad: What's the book?

Laurie: Uh. The Stand, Stephen King.

Dad: Don't know how you do it.

Laurie: What, read?

Dad: Fat as a car battery.

Laurie: Goes fast.

Dad: We'd be sittin here till next year, had to read that.

Laurie: Don't.

Dad: ...What's it about?

Laurie: I don't know, civilization gets wiped out by flu—I don't know. I'm losin interest.

Dad: Laur?

                    Gary enters.

Dad: There you are.

Gary: Yeah.

Dad: Aint it like morning?

Gary: Yeah?

Dad: Well. Gar. It's morning.

Gary: Yeah?

Laurie: How's Colleen.

Gary: I don't know.

Laurie: No? How's her ma?

Gary: Laur.

Dad: Jesus, Gar, ya stayed over right under Helen's nose?

Gary: Helen?

Dad: Yeah.

Gary: No.

Dad: Well. It's mornin Gar.

Gary: Spent the night at, in one a those, up on 18, the Clovercrests.

Dad: The development?

Gary: Yeah. In a empty one a those.

Dad: Uh. That's breakin and enterin Gar.

Gary: Was open. Didn't break anythin.

Laurie: Why'd you go there?

Gary: The carpet.

Dad: Carpet?

Gary: Yeah, drag your feet on that new carpet and these really trippy green sparks jump out—but, but—pan toast?

Laurie:	Dad made it.
Gary:	Wait, you made this?
Dad:	Yeah, Gar, what's it look like? For New Years.

Gary takes a slice.

Gary:	God, you made this.
Dad:	No big deal. From memory.
Gary:	Flavor's right. No crunch tho.
Dad:	Half a stick next time. Gar. Just don't think you should be at Buska's when Helen don't know.
Gary:	Yeah, well. Probably won't anymore.
Dad:	Cause they're movin?
Gary:	What?
Dad:	Helen said they're movin like to Myrtle Beach.
Gary:	She said that?
Dad:	Or Atlanta, or something. Yeah, she was sayin new beginnings and her and Colleen but that we should I promise to...maybe don't know what I'm talkin about.

They eat pan toast.

Dad:	Just, dont get caught draggin your feet in the Clovercrests.
Gary:	No. Hey, tell Harshaw it's okay I go full time at the plant.
Dad:	Sure. Full time?
Gary:	Yeah.
Dad:	Like second shift?
GAR	No, first.
Dad:	Yeah, and school?

Gary: No.

Dad: What?

Gary: School.

Dad: Yeah, school.

Gary: Quit.

Dad: What'dyou mean, Gar?

Gary: Quit goin.

Dad: Gar?

Gary: Miss Sher tried to call, she said.

Dad: No.

Laurie: You never answer the phone.

Dad: You either.

Gary: Told her it wouldn't make a difference.
Said she'd send a letter.

Dad: Gar, you gotta finish school!

Gary: No.

Dad: But your education.

Gary: Not there. Stupid school.

Dad: Stupid? It's school!

Laurie: Football coach teaches S-pain-nool,
because he doesn't even speak Espanol.

Dad: Sidin with him?!

Gary: It's, I mean, Porty and Shawn and Donnie, everyday,
dunce patrol. How many smoke bombs you throw into
the teacher's lounge before it's pathetic?

Dad: But smoke bombs, Gar, that's, don't drop out from that.

Gary: No, just. Coach Schmidt caught me tokin, grabbed me by the throat, put me against the wall, said, 'Wrestling and Bible Study—straighten you out.' Like that was it. Looked right at him and said, 'Forward, never straight.' He called me a faggot, told me pray to St. Jude.

Dad: But what about prom?

Gary: Prom?

Dad: Got to take the Buska.

Gary: No.

Dad: No?

Gary: What's the big deal about prom?

Dad: Prom is the big deal!

Gary: There's more in one kiss from Colleen than every single prom dance ever in the history of any school.

Dad: Uh.

Gary: Kissing her is like reading the most incredible book, a whole library of the most incredible books, touching her is like—

Dad: Okay, okay, get the picture.

Gary: She is like—

Laurie: WE GET IT!

Gary: ...something great. Laur?

Laurie: Not great when the rabbit dies.

Gary: Laur.

Dad: Oh geez. Did it?

Gary: No. I don't know.

Dad: Well, Gar?

Gary: She can take care of herself.

Laurie: How'dyou know?

Gary: She's gettin the pill.

Laurie: The pill?

Gary: At the clinic, yeah.

Laurie: What clinic?

Gary: Don't know. Her ma's takin her. Waukesha.

They eat pan toast.

Dad: Full time at the plant tho—

Gary: Only till summer.

Dad: Yeah?

Gary: Yeah.

Dad: Okay.

Gary: Yeah, buy Kangas's old blue Galaxy and hit the road.

Dad: Hit the road?...This is shapin up, Gar, for ya. Great, right, Laur? 'Hit the road'. Good. Okay, you're droppin out to work full time at the plant so you can hit the road.

Gary: Yeah. Boldly go.

Dad: Good plan. Good plan, yeah. Way to be Gar. Good stuff. Man. I can rest easy now. Knowing you're droppin out to work at the plant so you can boldly go. Wow. That's just. I'm, am I? What am I? Stoked.

Gary: Ok.

Dad: Just. So stoked for ya.

Gary: Well, time I learn from the world, you know.

Dad: Gods, wow, what time? Not noon. If it was noon we'd all go down t'th Lighthouse toast your new teacher—the world. Goin back to bed. Get me at noon!

Dad exits.

Gary: Jesus.

Laurie: Well. He's stoked.

Gary: Learn from the world, Laur, what's wrong with that?

Laurie: Never goin back to school?

Gary: Doesn't matter. None of it—couldnt care.
           Miss Sher begged me to write a catch up paper.

Laurie: One paper.

Gary: That's what I mean. She begged and I was like.

Laurie: Colleen.

Gary: Yeah.

Laurie: You should write a paper about Colleen.

Gary: I could write an encyclopedia about Colleen.
           No. I couldn't exactly cause I don't know.
           She's more than an encyclopedia.

Laurie: Sure. So. She's gettin the pill?

Gary: Yeah. Laur.

Laurie: At the clinic in Waukesha?

Gary: Takes care of herself.

Dad enters.

Dad: Can't sleep! Too excited for your trip Gar. My heart, so full
           of joy, like fourth of July, my heart is sparks Gar. Could be
           dyin though, could be havin—could be my heart—let's
           look at a map!

Gary: Chill out. Jesus. Gotta shower.
           Covered in butter all of a sudden.

Gary exits upstairs.

Dad: Good god, always knew Gar was weird, but I thought he was, you know, smart weird. And Donnie, well, goin for bronze. Laur, just.

Laurie: What?

Dad: You're smart.

Laurie: Shootin for best grades in the history of KM. 'A' plus plus plus plus plus plus. Kettle Moraine High. Go Lazers!

Dad: Egghead. If there's anything I can do to help.

Beat.

Laurie: Help?!

Dad: Uh. Yeah.

Laurie: HELP?!

Dad: Ok. I know. But, yeah.

Laurie: Help me?

Dad: Yeah, I don't mean like with your homework or anythin, Laur, but I could cook more or—

Laurie: No.

Dad: I could, I don't know—

Laurie: That's right, you don't know. You cant help. That's what you can't do. Just meep-meep *(explosion noise)*.

Beat.

Dad: ...Shouldn't a got up.

Dad sinks back into the couch and closes his eyes. Laurie glares at the TV.

Suffering

Gary at the Lighthouse slumped over the bar.
Empty beer bottles around him.

Bob: Awful quiet tonight, Gar.

Gary: Yeah.

                 Bob tinkers around, cleans up.

Gary: Know what I realized? I'm a baby.

Bob: Baby?

Gary: Yeah, man, a fuckin baby.

Bob: Like, a baby?

Gary: Yeah. Like. I know nothing.

Bob: Oh, innocent.

Gary: Stupid.

Bob: Oh.

Gary: A stupid baby, man, who—what do I know?

Bob: I don't know, Gar.

Gary: Man, Buddha knew. Really pegged it.

Bob: Buddha?

Gary: The Buddha.

Bob: Like, the Buddha?

Gary: Yeah, know what he said?

Bob: Nope.

Gary: There is suffering.

Bob:	He said that?
Gary:	There is suffering!
Bob:	Well, yeah.
Gary:	Yeah there is!
Bob:	He said that.
Gary:	Two thousand years ago. He said, there is suffering. First Noble Truth.
Bob:	Suffering is the first noble truth?
Gary:	Yeah.
Bob:	Why?
Gary:	Don't know, what he called it.
Bob:	Huh. Be interesting to know why he called it Noble. Suffering.
Gary:	Yeah. Maybe so people would feel better doin it.
Bob:	You think?
Gary:	Don't know. Anyway, I don't feel better doin it knowin that.
Bob:	Suffering like, breaking your arm?
Gary:	Yeah, but your heart.
Bob:	Ah.
Gary:	Do a Jaeger with me?
Bob:	Sure. Sure.

They do Jaeger shots.

Gary:	Don't mean to chew your ear off.
Bob:	No, hey.
Gary:	Just. Now I know how much I don't know.

Bob: Yeah?

Gary: You ever in love?

Bob: Share a times.

Gary: Like really in love?

Bob: Once. Real near miss, but just, got all the way to
          Clearwater/St. Pete together, before, on the beach, you
          know, a couple diaquiris into it, looked each other in the
          eyes and it was like holy shit 'who are you'.
          Hitched back alone.

Gary: Man.

Bob: It was okay. Except for the scary kid outside Birmingham
          wanted to stab me cause, but I ditched him and time
          I got back I, you know, figured it out.

Gary: Yeah, what?

Bob: Figured next time I felt like throwin everything over for
          lookin someone in the eyes in Florida—don't.

Gary: That's what I mean, now you know.
          You lived enough to know.

Bob: I guess. Plus, I had the bar to come back to.
          This bar is like.

Gary: Yeah?

Bob: My home. It feels. Yeah.

Gary: Colleen and me, it's incredible. Bob. Epic. Nothing like it.

Bob: Yeah?

Gary: Except.

Bob: Suffering?

Gary: Yeah. The most amazing ever, I mean, intense, heart just.
          Makes everythin else seem stupid.
          But that one fuckin feelin.

Bob:	Yeah?
Gary:	Will not go away.
Bob:	No?
Gary:	She's, you know, done stuff, felt stuff.
Bob:	Gar, stuff? Whad'you mean?
Gary:	I don't know. But it's that I don't know, and cant know. It hurts so bad.
Bob:	Right. Right. Heavy.

> *Bob and Gary sit on opposite sides of the bar.*
> *Holiday decorations blink wanly.*

Stuff

Night. Gary gently taps on Colleen'swindow.
She talks through the window.

Colleen:	Shhhh. You can't be here.
Gary:	Saw your ma goin into Bob's.
Colleen:	She's…she'll be back in like two wine coolers.
Gary:	Lemme in.

> *Colleen reluctantly lets Gary in.*
> *Her radio is playing softly.*

Gary:	You go to the clinic?
Colleen:	Yeah.
Gary:	Wish I coulda gone with.
Colleen:	What? Why?

Gary: Be with you.

Colleen: At the clinic?

Gary: Yeah.

Colleen: No.

Gary: Get the pill?

Colleen show Gary her pills.

Gary: That's them, huh?

Colleen: Yeah.

Gary: So. You horny?

Colleen: Come on. No. Had the doctor all down there and...
            ma all over me all day.

Gary: Okay. Okay. Just.

Beat.

Gary: Your ma said people were comin over
            to look at the house. They make an offer?

Colleen: You say somethin to someone?!

Gary: What?

Colleen: About that?

Gary: No.

Colleen: Don't. Just forget you heard it.

Gary: Ok. Geez.

Colleen: You don't know.

Gary: Oh. I know I don't.

*Some heavy rocker song comes on like
Don't Fear the Reaper by BOC.*

Colleen: Love this one.

Gary: Yeah.

> *They listen.*

Colleen: Hey you ever comin back to school?

Gary: Nope.

Colleen: Dude?

Gary: Nothin there for me.

Colleen: Come on.

Gary: Listen to Schmidt try and teach? Watch Porty make
            Miss Johnson cry and tear out her hair—
            just cant anymore.

Colleen: But droppin out.

Gary: No. Just. Look. I'm goin full time at the plant
            and by summer. Thinkin. You know,
            a chunk a change and hit the road.

Colleen: Gar.

Gary: Be great. With you.

Colleen: Come on.

Gary: Serious.

Colleen: Seriously, no.

Gary: Kangas will sell me the old blue Galaxy for two fifty.

Colleen: No.

Gary: We could—

Colleen: No.

Gary: Why not?

Colleen: Go where? Do what?

Gary: Don't know. Let the world tell us.

Colleen: Shut up.

Gary: Gotta transport outta here.

Colleen looks out the window at the stars.

Gary: Col?

Colleen: Gar. Here.

She wraps her arms around him.

Gary: Bein with you is it. Man. All I want.

Colleen: Then shut up.

Gary: Let's go. Let's get outta here.

Colleen: Shhh. Just.

Gary: Sleep in the Galaxy till we find a place.

Colleen: Man. Gar. You. You gotta go.

Gary: Alright, I'll shut up.

Colleen: You gotta go.

Gary: Just got here.

Colleen: Before ma gets back. Or Granpa Don.

Gary: Granpa Don?

Colleen: Cruises by in pop's Silverado. He sees you and—

Gary: Yeah?

Colleen: Yeah. Fuck those people who say shit and look at ma.

Gary: Yeah.

Colleen: You cannot say anythin to anyone about people comin to look at the house.

Gary:	Got it. Ok.
Colleen:	You gotta go. I mean it. Go.
Gary:	Can I kiss you?

> *Colleen doesn't say no so GARY leans in for one.*
> *He tries to make it epic,*
> *but the feeling is not there.*
> *Gary climbs out the window.*
> *Colleen listens to the radio.*

Seen Laurie

GARY's on the couch, beer, brooding. DAD enters.

Dad:	Gar, the long face all day and all night. And now again all day?
Gary:	You seen Laur?
Dad:	Come on Gar, you been sittin there—
Gary:	Just, seen Laur?
Dad:	Whad'you mean Gar?
Gary:	Have you seen Laur?
Dad:	Seen her?
Gary:	Yeah. *(Motions to the otherwise empty couch)*
Dad:	She was gone to school, I thought, when I got up.
Gary:	School's, it's after school now.
Dad:	Oh. Oh. Yeah. No. Shopping maybe?
Gary:	Called McAdams, haven't seen her.

Dad: You called McAdams?

Gary: Yeah, the Library too.

Dad: Jesus. Well. Where would she go?

Gary: Yeah.

Dad: The Lighthouse maybe?

Gary: You think she went to the Lighthouse?

Dad: I don't know. It's a place to go if you're goin someplace around here.

Gary: Yeah. She wouldn't just go there, tho, would she?

Dad: Doesn't seem like it.

Gary: Where?

Dad: Was she, there was nothin goin on with her?

Gary: I don't know.

Dad: Yeah.

Gary: You don't think.

Dad: What?

Gary: We should call Ardent?

Dad: God. Now you're freakin me out.

Gary: So we should?

Dad: I don't know. She's not in her room, right?

Gary: No. Her book's here too she was readin.

Dad: Oh man. Think she went with Donnie to Iron River snowmobilin?

Gary: No. I don't think that.

Dad: Uh.

Gary: Yeah?

Dad: Probably I should put some TV dinners in the stove.

Gary: What?

Dad: Maybe she'll be home by the time they're hot?

Gary: I'm callin Ardent.

Dad: He never answers the phone.

DAD goes to the kitchen.

Laur and Colleen

Laurie and Colleen at the transporter.
Colleen has her totabota. They drink.

Colleen: Cold?

Laurie: No.

Colleen: Me either.

Laurie: Sorry about today.

Colleen: No. No. Hey. Come on. I'm glad you called.
           Didn't have to be alone.

She pulls out the totabota.

Colleen: Hate white wine. But.

Takes a big swig and hands it to Laur
who also swigs.

Laurie: Sweet.

Colleen: Ma drinks it with 7-Up.

Laurie: Why?

Colleen: Yeah.

They watch the clouds.

Colleen: Umm. 'Ludes. Creamy. Creamy as the clouds.

Laurie: Yeah.

Colleen: No pain, right?

Laurie: Nope.

Colleen: Yeah, ya gotta, I mean.

Laurie: No. Feel—I mean. Like rubber. In the oven.

Colleen: Yeah. Here, here.

Colleen digs pills out of her bag and
hands them to Laurie.

Laurie: No. No.

Colleen: Not for now.
           For when what the doc gave ya doesnt cut it.

Laurie: Ok.

Colleen: No more'n two a day. See how you feel in a week.

Laurie: Yeah?

Colleen: Or two.

Laurie: Ok.

Colleen: If you feel anythin. Call me.

Laurie: Ok. Thanks.

Colleen: Or. Know what? No. I won't. Look, if you feel any pain
           just up the dose to three. But you'll be fine.

Laurie: Yeah?

Colleen: Forsure. I can tell.

Laurie: Thanks for takin me today.

Colleen: Doc Angela is good, right?

Laurie: Yeah. I like her.

Colleen: Gotta kinda keep it to ourselves. What she does.

Laurie: Yeah. Got that. She said.

Colleen: Hey know what? By the time Aunt Flo comes back in town, you'll be good as new.

Laurie: I don't know.

Colleen: Yeah you will. You'll see. Like nuthin happened.

Laurie: Nuthin?

Colleen: Yeah.

Laurie: You never think about it?

Colleen: I think about if I didn't do it.

Laurie: Yeah.

Colleen: Hey, don't worry. Like when you're 20, 23 have a kid then. When you're ready. When you want to.

They look at the evening sky.

Colleen: Sky's like...whad'you call that color?

Laurie: Don't know. Skinned knee?

Colleen: *(cracking up)* Yeah. Yeah.

Laurie: Look tho.

Colleen: Huh.

Laurie: Fire, yeah?

Colleen: Yeah, could be. Where there's smoke...my old man would smell like smoke for weeks after a fire.

Laurie: Yeah?

Colleen: Yeah. Smell him comin and, you know, hide the evidence. Ma too. But with her it's Charlie.

Laurie: Your ma wears Charlie?

Colleen: Buckets of it.

Laurie: My ma wore Jean Nate.

Colleen: Oooo.

Laurie: Yeah. And once a year they'd go out, Jean Nate and English Leather all decked. Kept her bottle. Probably never wear it, but sometimes I open it up for the smell. From when I'd sit on her lap, when I was little. Be so warm.

Colleen: Got some Babe.

Digs it out of her bag. Gives Laur a whiff.

Laurie: Yeah, nice.

Dabs Laur's wrist with it.

Colleen: Man that smoke's gettin thick. Guess this'll be Chentiss's first.

Sound of sirens in the distance.
Colleen and Laur sit and watch the smoke.

Colleen: Know what? Maybe I should. You ok to walk you think?

Laurie: Sure. Yeah.

Colleen: Maybe I should get goin.

Laurie: Ok. Yeah.

They rise to exit.
Black out.

TV Dinners

Lights up. GARY and Dad sit with empty TV dinner trays.
Laur enters—moving thickly.

Gary:	Laur!
Dad:	Where you been?
Gary:	You okay Laur?
Dad:	Laur?
Laurie:	I'm fine.
Dad:	Well Laur, where you been?
Laurie:	Transporter.
Gary:	Really?
Laurie:	I'm fine. You made TV dinners?
Dad:	Yeah Laur. There's one for you. Thought you'd be home before. In the oven, warm.

Laur pours herself onto the couch between them.

Dad:	Lemme get it.
Laurie:	Not too hungry right now.
Dad:	I'll get it. Meatloaf.
Laurie:	No. That's okay. I'll grab somethin later.
Gary:	You smell like?
Laurie:	Babe.
Gary:	Yeah, like Colleen.

Laurie:	We were hangin.
Gary:	You were hangin with Colleen?
Laurie:	Yeah she put some Babe on me at the Transporter. Sky was amazing. Skinned knee.
Gary:	What?
Laurie:	Saw a fire.
Dad:	You saw the fire?
Laurie:	Saw smoke anyway.
Gary:	We heard the sirens.
Dad:	Chentiss's first, I guess. Laur?
Gary:	You ok?
Laurie:	I'm fine.
Dad:	Don't seem fine.
Laurie:	Really. Feelin no pain.
Dad:	Yeah I get that.
Gary:	You smoke a bowl or somethin?
Dad:	Jesus not the weed.
Laurie:	No. No. The sky was amazing though.
Dad:	Ok. You said that a couple times now.
Laurie:	Well it was.

Dabney enters.

Dad:	THFUCK!

Gary's on his feet.

Dabney: *(no bluster)* ...Know what's horrible? The Aunt's Pinto—
any Pinto. Know what happens when you tromp the gas
in a Pinto? NOT MUCH. And they all saw me drivin it.
All of em. Headin to the fire. Chentiss in the 150,
Sommerfeldt the C/K, even Duzz Lowery in the
Riceburner rippin down the road, cherries screamin.
All of em lookin at me douffin along in the PINTO.
Ardent last, sees me, cranks the wheel on the Fury
and tromps the gas and. I'd'a laughed if it wasn't so
pathetic. Bout 255 too many horses for'im and it just
whips around, tires smokin right off the road into
Charlie Bechtal's swamp. So now. Double APBs on me.
What am I gonna do?

The Tetzloffs are stunned.

Gary: You should turn yourself in.

Dabney: Forsure that has to be the pussiest thing
ever been said by anybody ever.

Gary: Maybe but. Then it would be over.

Dabney: I'm up for assault and swampin the Fury.
(to Laur) You did it, didn't ya? Dimed me to them.

Laurie: No. Never called.

Dad: Called?

Dabney: Old man Brundage and Ardent—to get
the APBs offa me cause she owes me.

Dad: Owes?

Gary: Laur?

Laurie: Think about—

Dabney: You know you owe me.

Gary: Owes you?

Laurie: Think about it.

Dabney:	What? What? Think about what?
Laurie:	Already gave you an amaaaaaazing gift.
Gary:	Whad'you give him, Laur?
Laurie:	Like.
Dad:	Like?
Dabney:	Yeah, like?
Laurie:	Like. You will always think twice before believing someone. Want to sit down?
Dabney:	Uh?
Laurie:	Sit down.
Dabney:	You mean sit down?
Laurie:	Yeah, sit. SIT.

Dabney sits awkwardly on the couch.

Dad:	Laur?
Laurie:	He looks hungry.
Dabney:	What?
Laurie:	Hungry.
Dabney:	Uh.
Laurie:	Doesn't he look hungry?
Gary:	Uh.
Laurie:	Are you hungry?
Dabney:	I could eat.
Laurie:	Dad, get the Meatloaf for him.
Dad:	For him, Laur?
Laurie:	Yeah.

Dad: Laur?

Laurie: He's hungry. I'm not. Do it. Come on.

> *Dad goes for the kitchen. Gary hovers*
> *watching Dabney and Laurie on the couch.*

Laurie: He looks thirsty too.

Dabney: I do?

Laurie: Doesn't he look thirsty?

Gary: Thirsty?

Laurie: You thirsty?

Dabney: Uh.

Laurie: Wanna beer?

Dabney: Uh.

Laurie: I'll take one too. Gar?

Gary: Laur?

Laurie: Two beers, Gar.

> *GARY exits to get beers. Laurie digs*
> *all the ludes out of her pocket.*

Laurie: Here.

Dabney: Whatter these?

Laurie: Ludes.

> *Dabney pockets the ludes.*
> *Gary returns with a beer for Dabney and Laur.*

Dabney: Ok. I. This. What in the fuckineddy is goin on in here?

> *Dad returns with the TV dinner and a*
> *tray which he puts in front of Dabney.*

Dad: Meatloaf. Decent.

Dabney is super confused.

Laurie: You don't have to think twice about this.

Dabney: No? Cause. Like. Every. You said.
          And my brain is, thinks I do.

Laurie: No you don't.

Dabney: Why not? Cause.

Laurie: Cause, tonight is, what's on tonight, Dad?

Dad: Uh. Lessee. TV? What's tonight?
          Barnaby Jones. Or. Charles Angels.

Laurie: *(to Dabney)* Cause tonight, you pick.

Dabney: Pick?

Laurie: Charlies Angels or Barnaby Jones?

Dabney: Uh. Well. Both good, right? But I mean. Chicks in shorts,
          or the Beverly Hillbilly drinkin milk? But both good.

Laurie: Sounds like a Charlie's Angels kind of night.

Dad: Laur?

Laurie: Charlie's Angels.

Dad puts on the show. Dabney starts eating.

Laurie: That ok?

Dabney: Yeah. Really good. Guess I was hungry.

Laurie: And thirsty.

*Dabney raises his beer to the Tetzloffs
and takes a long swig.*

*Dad returns to his chair. Gary slowly
sinks to the couch next to Dabney.*

Laurie: After this you wanna shoot some eights?

Dabney: Eights?

Dad: Laur, now...eights now?

Laurie: You got your cue?

Dabney: Trunk of the Pinto.

Laurie: Eights then, later.

> *They watch TV and drink beer as Dabney eats.*
> *Lights.*

Laurie and Craig

Laurie at transporter. Craig enters, slight limp. He holds an open beer and has anther dangling from a six pack holder.

Laurie: Stay down there.

Craig: Can't climb anyway.

Laurie: Ok.

> *He holds the unopened beer up to her.*
> *She declines.*

Craig: You wanted to see me?

Laurie: Yeah. For you.

> *Laurie throws Dabney's cue down to Craig.*

Craig: What's this?

Laurie: Dabney's cue.

Craig: Are you fuckin crazy??

Laurie: He gave it to me.

Craig: Gave it to you?

Laurie: Yeah.

Craig: Just gave it to you?

Laurie: Yeah. I'm giving it to you.

Craig: No.

Laurie: Yeah, it's yours.

Craig: No.

Laurie: Yes.

Craig: He just gave it to you?

Laurie: Well, yeah, convinced him.

Craig: Yeah?

Laurie: Yeah.

Craig: I dont know.

Laurie: It's okay. Keep it.

Craig: Don't want it.

Laurie: Sell it at Wolskis.

Beat

Craig: I liked you.

Laurie: No.

Craig: Yeah.

Laurie: Impossible.

Craig: No.

Laurie: What is wrong with you?

Craig: Nuthin.

Laurie:	Juniper Farell?
Craig:	What?
Laurie:	Is that true?
Craig:	I don't know.
Laurie:	You see what's left of Buska's?
Craig:	Drove past with my old man.
Laurie:	Burned to the ground.
Craig:	Bad wiring.
Laurie:	Not true.
Craig:	What?
Laurie:	Bad wiring.
Craig:	No? That's what Chentiss said.
Laurie:	Yeah. Well. Don Buska cancelled the insurance two days before.
Craig:	No way.
Laurie:	Yeah. Colleen said. They found out. After. So. Not bad wiring.
Craig:	But. Chentiss said—
Laurie:	Don't believe it.
Craig:	But. He's the Fire Chief.
Laurie:	Sure...You ever dream?
Craig:	What?
Laurie:	You ever dream?
Craig:	Like?
Laurie:	Dream. Have a dream.

Craig: Not really.

Laurie: You've never had a dream?

Craig: I don't know. Like?

Laurie: Last night I dreamed I was flying along a path in the woods. It was dark. Trees hanging over. Wasn't flying up in the air, but like 6 inches or a foot off the ground and had to work at it, flap my arms like crazy to keep up, slack even a little, dip down and slam into a root or rock on the path. Was banging along up a hill working hard, sweating, sweat in my eyes and at the top of the hill was a little clearing and I just fell flat. When I stood up Kojak was there.

Craig: Kojak?

Laurie: Yeah. And was like, like he shifted the lollipop in his mouth one side to the other looking at me.
            Could see myself in his sunglasses. Then he pointed off down the path on the other side of the hill at a little girl who was running. Kojak *(mimes flapping arms and chucking chin)* so I threw myself over flapping like crazy after her. Zooming down the path. She ran into a big house at the end of the path. I stopped outside.
            Could feel the house. Knew it. Knew it was my house. Walked in. Anywhere I put my eyes, I remembered building—how it was built. The way the wall met the ceiling or the floor met the wall. I knew it.
            Could hear giggling. Giggling. Followed the sound to the library. Library was huge, sunny, thousands and thousands of books. There were two big leather chairs and a little table between with snacks. And the giggling was coming from behind one of the chairs. Her voice, saying, 'You can't find me mom.' But I found her.
            And she jumped into my arms and, 'Snack time.'
            And we sat in the chairs and we had cookies and milk. And she said, 'Mom?' 'Yes Petal.'

Craig: Petal?

Laurie: Yeah. Her name. 'You build this house?' 'I did.'
'I want to build a house.' And I was like, 'I'll help you.'

Beat.

Craig: You're stoned.

Laurie: No.

Craig: You dreamed that?

Laurie: Yeah, I did.

Craig: Don't believe you.

Laurie: It's the truth.

*Craig can tell she is done with him
and he slowly leaves.
Laurie watches him go.*

Lights.

—The End—

MAT RIEGER as Dad in *Black River Falls*

ROGER BABSON, *Temperance Party Presidential Candidate,* 1940

DOWN: A CHAMBER OPERA

Premiered **February 2015**

Prop Thtr / Chicago, IL

written by **MATT TEST**

performed by:

Jennifer Colburn
Casey Cunningham
Jeff Garceau
Rob Grabowski
Jenny Magnus
T-Roy Martin
Lucía Mier Y Terán Romero
Briavael O'Reilly
Taran O'Reilly
Allison Shoemaker
Vicki Walden
Charles Worth

THE
PLAYS

SETTING

*Roger Babson—Temperance Party Presidential Candidate—
makes a last ditch plea for War.*

CAST of CHARACTERS:

*ROGER BABSON
Baritone. Age is between 30-50 years old.
A clean cut, corporate type.*

*CHORUS of ADVISORS (7 total):
Soprano, Mezzo Soprano, Alto, Tenor, Bass.
Ages range from 20-60 yrs. old.
Advisors are a little sycophant-ish.*

TIME

Election night, 1940

NOTE

All text is sung unless otherwise noted.

Darkness. Silence. From far upstage we begin to make out the forms of people, either suspended by wires or on silks about 6 feet off the ground, configured in a horseshoe arrangement.

These are The CHORUS of ADVISORS. They sing something like a funeral dirge or threnody as the lights fade up.

ADVISORS:
Down
Down
Down
Always further
Down

What goes up
Won't drown
Without the
Down

Sudden shift of focus to the middle of the stage, where ROGER BABSON is also either suspended by wire or silks, but less high up than the advisors. He is dressed in a tasteful suit and is conspicuously pantsless. He addresses the audience as though it were a stump speech.

ROGER:
Now friends
'Tis true
That in eighteen minutes
The polls will close

And it's reasonable
To suppose
Each ballot
Does have
Their man
Their woman
Their proposal
Sewn to them
By now

Some men will win
Some women will win
Some proposals will pass
And some will go

Quick return to the dirge feeling

ROGER:	ADVISORS:
Down	Down
Down	Down
Down	Down
Down	Down
Down	Down
Down	Down

And now a return to the stump speech feel

But friends
I wouldn't be
A proper candidate
If i did not fight

                                                Fight!

Until

                                                Fight!

The end

Sometimes that end
Is a ribbon
Snapped across
Our running breast

And sometimes that end
Is the ground

Depending on
Our starting spot
And
If
We
Can
Slow

ROGER:		ADVISORS:
Down		Down
Down		Down
Down		Down
Down		Down
Down		Down
Down		Down

ROGER:
Now friends
I came
From nothing
And i brake
For nothing
As my lack of bumper stickers
Will atest

I am always moving forward
Never giving over to the idle lark
Because i am an American
And

Roger seems to lose his place in the speech.
The advisors attempt to urge him forward.

ROGER:		ADVISORS:
And		and?
And		and?
		And?

ROGER:
And
I am a shark

The advisors breathe a sigh of relief

ADVISORS:
Whew!

It's true
He's a real
Shark-American

And where i come from

The prodigal son
of everyone

That is still worth
A tidy some

Here here!

Now friends
I speak in metaphor

All sharks are
Metaphors

As i often will
But what is not metaphor

All sharks are
Metaphors

Is in these moments
Just before
And still
While i have been
Speaking
I have also been

Thematic change in the music.

Falling
Quickly
And from a great height

Suddenly, the orientation of the stage rotates abruptly, as though the entire space was attached to a rickety crankshaft or pinwheel. Now the audience is angled facing up at about 150 degrees, reminiscent of the seating arrangement in a planetarium, with both Roger and the Advisors hanging almost directly above. During the rest of the scene, they slowly move closer to the audience, as though in slow motion freefall.

ROGER:
Now friends
While yes
The height
Is great

The height is not
Um
Eighteen minutes
Worth of
Great

So uh
I will be
Um
Brief

My advisors

The advisors introduce themselves in a slightly dissonant barbershop sounding harmony.

ADVISOR 1:
Communication

ADVISOR 2:
Treasury

ADVISOR 3:
Homeland security and
foreign policy

ADVISOR 4:
Education

ADVISOR 5:
Campaign strategy and
miscellaneous obstruction

ADVISOR 6:
Specified obstructions and
general maleficence

ADVISOR 7:
Alcohol, tobacco and firearms
minus tobacco and firearms

ROGER:
Those who serve
To brief me
On the goings
Of the day

ADVISORS ALL:
War!

And unlike some
Did not quickly
Abandon my campaign

ADVISORS 2 & 4:
Bye!

*Advisors 2 and 4 disappear with the feeling of falling, as if standing
on a trapdoor that opens or a support rope snapping.
They join the pit orchestra.*

When the polling numbers
Went from
Climbing
To declined

Are falling as well

ADVISORS:
We're falling as well...

ROGER:
Somewhere
Around
Um
Here

*Roger gestures to the general location of
the remaining advisors.*

Above me
And at
Different rates

None of them
Have yet to taste
The great
And grating cake
That is
Terminal velocity

Not like me

Terminal velocity
Is for leaders
Only

You also
Might notice
I'm missing my
Pants

They're falling as well

Somewhere
Down there

ROGER:
If i requested
I could make myself
Torpedo-esque
Bounding down
To reunite before
Well

> *Gestures to the ground.*
> *Roger and the advisors all clap hands.*

The ground

But that would take away
From my time
With you

So i will leave the meeting
Of me and my pants
To friendly winds
And gravity's chance

Where was i?

Ah yes

In these measured
Moments left
Before the polls close
And-
Well
You know

> *All clap hands.*

—That SPLAT—

ROGER:
I thought it might
Be best
To review
My platform
One more time
For those
Yet to make up
Their mind

And for you
Who have
Missed
My speeches

                                 ADVISOR 3:
                                 Like me

My debates

                                 ADVISOR 7:
                                 Guilty

That unfortunate commercial

                                 ADVISOR 6:
                                 Which one?

You know the one

                                 ADVISOR 5:
                                 It tested so well

The one with a sash
Saying
'Miss USA'

                                 ADVISOR 1:
                                 But no one got it

Draped over
A shipping crate

                                 ADVISOR 7:
                                 I miss when politics
                                 Was a sellers market

Brief pause to catch our breath.

ROGER:
But friends
It comes down
To this:

War

                                        ADVISORS:
                                            War!

A stucky thorn
To be sure
That no one wants
To address head on

The abscess born
From a lovers' stroll
Through the briar patch

I get it

                                        ADVISOR 1:
                                          I wrote that

I get it

Even war drums
Hum Pete Seeger tones
When they think
That they're alone

But friends
Who among us
Would truly choose
Or pay good money
To hear a drum
Sing?

Roger looks out over the audience, as if to take a poll. Advisor 6 raises a hand, but is quickly shamed by the others into lowering it.

Ok
That's more
Than i was
Expecting

But my point remains
No matter what
The masses say
And my point remains:

War

But when i say
War
What i mean is
Temperance

ADVISOR 7:
Whoo!

In all things

In spirits
And schemes

In death
And dreams

In all the things
That bring us down

ADVISORS ALL:
Down
Down
Down

ROGER:
And friends
The war to which
I speak
Is none of these things

The war to which
I speak
Is not a war
Against
A country
Or a sheik
Or a hollywood villain
With diplomatic
Immunity
Or the opposing
Party
Or you

ADVISOR 3:
Or me!

Friends
I say:

Music change to an upbeat, soft-shoe feel.

Let's go to war
Against gravity
The kind that start
Properly

The kind with
A capital
G

Let's go to war
Against the things
That bring us down
And what brings us
Down
More than
The ground

Let's go to war
Against
Gravity
The kind you wage
Endlessly
With a faceless
Enemy

*The feel of a crooner talking to the audience
over an instrumental break.*

Now friends
Don't mistake me
For taking
A page from
The flat Earthers tomb
The disckies have had
Their day
In the oft
 Revolving sun

Add in the feeling of a revival preacher.

This is America
And we don't care
About ancient dreams
Of a firmament dome

ROGER:
The only domes
We pray to are

Half Dome
The Astrodome

That Stephen King
TV show
That made us all
Groan

Heaving bosoms
And sno cones

ADVISOR 6:
Fuck sure of it!

This is America
And we don't care

Referring to advisor 6's interjection.

For that kind of
Language

Or novelty
Or dreams
Or anything
That brings us down

And what brings us
Down?

As though a testimonial.

ADVISOR 7:
A spirit imbibed
Flattens the mind

As easy as
A cartoon cat
Shakes off
20 Stories
Of falling to
Splat
To climb and to fall
For the amusement
Of all
Again
And again
And again
And again

ROGER:
Gravity flattens us
Without metaphor

Return to softshoe style music.

A vote for me
Is a vote repealing
All the things that
Bring us down

And what brings us down
More than
The ground?

Change in musical tone.

But friends
I've heard
The talk

And for those who
With a softened stare
Expound:

ADVISOR 5:
Why don't we just
Go to war with
The ground?

ROGER:
To those friends
I say:

I am not swayed
My stance remains:

Without the ground
Where will we stand
Friends?

Where
Will
We
Stand?

The ground is no threat
Without the threat
Of approaching it
Unfavorably

I hope this puts an end
To that kind of
Anti-landism

And let us return
To the heart
Of the plan
That still beats
In our hand

Behold friends
Alphabetized
For your order
And pleasing

ROGER:
Behold
The weapons
Of war!

> *Dramatic swell. Roger gestures toward advisor 1.*

A parachute

> *Advisor 1 holds out an army man with a parachute and freezes. Roger gestures to advisor 3.*

A periscope

> *Advisor 3 holds out a toy submarine and freezes, mimicking advisor 1. Roger gestures to advisor 5.*

A plane

> *Advisor 5 presents a toy plane. Roger gestures to advisor 6.*

A telescope

> *Advisor 6 presents a telescope. Roger gestures to advisor 7.*

A zoo

> *Advisor 7 presents something meant to represent a zoo. All advisors frozen in tableau.*

You know what
Theses rapturous
Things and
Righteous places
Do

They prove a healing balm
But no cure
A shiny gun

But not the bomb
To end our
War

Let us take them
One by one:

Advisor 1 unfreezes. During the following, each advisor's section has its own distinct musical arrangement, theme, and melody.

ADVISOR 1:
THE PARACHUTE

The great
Procrastinator

The one that makes us
Last among our peers
But first in the true-hearts
Of our cause

But what does
A parachute
Do
When removed
From
'Up'?

The drowning
Go down
More quickly
Tis' true

Becoming food
For hungry crabs
And sea mews

The standing
Get plucked
At the first
Friendly breeze

ROGER:
(Interjecting)
Mother said
While bouncing me
On her knee

ADVISOR 1:
"A man
Standing with a parachute
On his back
Will soon
Need it"

ROGER:
I knew exactly
What she
Meant

Advisor 1 freezes. Advisor 3 unfreezes.

ADVISOR 3:
THE PERISCOPE

The it
That lets us go
Down
While still looking
Up

A swiveling freedom
From tyranny
Of direction

But only
An illusion

It's unnatural
To look from
Above where
You are

ROGER:
(Interrupting)
It's unnatural
And it makes
No sense

ADVISOR 3:
No amount of staring
At the air
Will remove reality
If reality
Dines with the tides
And fills our lungs
With brine

Advisor 3 freezes. Advisor 5 unfreezes.

ADVISOR 5:
THE PLANE

So close
So close
So close

Just like the butter
To the bun

ROGER:
(Clarifying)
If it wasn't for gas prices
We just might have won

Advisor 5 freezes. Advisor 6 unfreezes.

ADVISOR 6:
THE TELESCOPE

See: PERISCOPE

Long pause, as though done.

ROGER:
(Elaborating)
But see it
In reverse
And look toward
The lack of air
Instead of
From it

Advisor 6 freezes. Advisor 7 unfreezes.

ADVISOR 7:
THE ZOO

The elephant
And the rhinoceros
Has no use to us
In our cause

But the aviary
With the
Weary wary
Bowerbird
And peregrine
Interned

Who know
That they could
Fly off forever
In their cleverest
Of fashioned cares
Without that netted dome
That sits in place
And taunts them
With further air

ROGER:
(Mimicking)
'No fair'
They squawk
'No fair'

ADVISOR 7:
The arc of their
Stunted flight
A sullen mascot
For our plight

*Roger regains the focus, and during the following
there is a level of earnestness that is almost jarring.*

Now friends
Know
That i know
That those who go
To war
Against a dragon
With mascots
Air
And rattle
Don't so much win
As tattle-tell
To a friendly
Uncaring wind

Who nods
But thinks
It knows
Where character
Grows

But friends
I am no longer
A child
In need of
A playground

Trouncing
To know what
'Good' is

I slayed stock markets!

I dined on dry-aired peaks!

I lost days to weeping
For family lost
To the bottom of lakes
And creeks!

All for
A simple decree

ROGER:	ADVISORS:
"What goes up	"What goes up
won't drown	won't drown
without the	without the
down"	down"

The remaining advisors repeat this sung cadence over the following:

And friends
My critics
Have said
That the downfall
Of my campaign
Was a certain
Lack of urgency

And I do not
Entirely
Disagree

I recognize
That temperance
Is often code
For bland

People like to drink
People like to stand

So standing on the cliff
Of a grand abyss below
Watching my pants fall
To read
The wind's
The speed
And tow

Addressing those
Who would have filled
My embassies
And cabinets

To all my friends
A final call!

ADVISORS:
Step

ROGER:
Be it aggregate

Step

Or deficit

Step

Urgency

Fall

Is what you
Make of
It

Down

They all fall down.

– The End –

HISTORICAL ENDNOTE:

BABSON used his presidential campaign to champion high-minded moral values and a church affiliated religious agenda.

Impressed with Isaac Newton's studies of gravity, Babson founded the non-profit Gravity Research Foundation in 1948 believing it was possible to develop and build a conductor for harnessing gravity waves as they occur in nature.

MATT RIEGER, NICK LEININGER & MICHAEL MCKUNE
as Joe #1, Waiter, Joe #2 in *My Dinner With... JOE*

My Dinner With ...JOE

Premiered **February 2019**

Prop Thtr / Chicago, IL

written by **MATT RIEGER**

directed by **Stefan Brün**

performed by:

Nick Leininger
Michael McKune
Matt Rieger

CAST of CHARACTERS–

Joe #1
Joe #2
Waiter (Gregory)

STAGE–

Minimal furniture, cafe tables & chairs
to suggest an upscale restaurant.

They sit at a table for two in a presumably upscale restaurant.

Joe #1: I don't know.

Joe #2: You don't.

Joe #1: I know.

Joe #2: Or you don't. Nobody knows. You don't know. I don't know. My dad don't know. That's just how it goes. It eats you up. Everybody wants to live forever, trying to figure it all out. But you never figure it all out. I never figure it all out. My dad never figures it all out. I never could do what it was I wanted to do. I got my reasons. Same with you. You got yours. Same with my dad. He got his.

Joe #1: So, quit trying?

Joe #2: What?

Joe #1: To figure it all out?

Joe #2: No. What is there to figure out? You have one of those days. You're driving down the street. And all of a sudden, it seems like the world isn't such a bad place after all.

Joe #1: Yeah. Sure.

Joe #2: You know what's even better than that?

Joe #1: What?

Joe #2: Nothing. That's it. That's the best we get.

Joe #1: I'm okay with that. But then you roll down the exit ramp, and there's some guy standing there. Little cup in his hand. Maybe a sign. Advertising his woes. Spilling it out. Trying to guilt me into something.

Joe #2: I never done nothing out of guilt.

Joe #1: Never?

Joe #2: Not once.

Joe #1: You never gave a broke guy a dime?

Joe #2: Eh, once in a while, I'll throw the guy a buck. If I'm in a good mood. Like I got it real good that day. And look at this poor bastard in comparison.

Joe #1: That's not guilt?

Joe #2: No. That's pity. And pity born from arrogance at that.

Joe #1: The thing of it. I don't want to look. You know. At them.

Joe #2: They say they don't like that, but I'm not convinced they really feel that way. Probably some bullshit from the righteous. Dignity is... .... outdated.

Joe #1: Not revolted. Not frightened. I have empathy.

Joe #2: You do have that.

Joe #1: I just get all hung up wondering what happened?

Joe #2: To who?

Joe #1: The guy or whatever. The bum. I can't look at some guy begging for change, all filthed up like that, and not wonder. What the hell happened to that guy? What was the train of events that led this poor bastard to this particular moment? And then I start making up stories in my head.

Joe #2: Same. Same.

Joe #1: Yeah?

Joe #2: How can't you?

Joe #1:	And then I'm stuck thinking for the next hour. Thinking? Hell, I'm making it up. Inventing it. All the fucked up ways you could mistreat a person so he ends up like that. So. I'm speculating about... torture, I guess. And then I have to wear that around the rest of the day. I don't want that on me.
Joe #2:	It's different with me.
Joe #1:	How?
Joe #2:	I still wonder. You know. What happened. But I always think it's something stupid. Guy lost a bet. This is the debt he must pay. His pals are fucking with him.
Joe #1:	A bet?
Joe #2:	Or... a practical joke. Like a TV show. Or one of them internets. His buddy is probably hiding across the street with a camera.
Joe #1:	That's what you think?
Joe #2:	I guess you get to think what you want to think.
Joe #1:	But you don't. I don't want to think about all the fucked up shit that could have happened to the guy. But I do.
Joe #2:	It's a job though. Bum is the wrong word. Those fuckers are out there ten, twelve hours a day. Snowstorm. Hundred degree heat. They don't take days off. There's a whole crew of them. They mix up corners every so often. Probably to put the swerve on the customer.
Joe #1:	Customer?
Joe #2:	There's customers and there's hustlers. That's all. Guy's trying to sell you something.
Joe #1:	What?
Joe #2:	Hard to say. But it's something. This much I know. Ever see them all congregating under the bridge? I always

wondered if they were pooling their cash. Could they be that organized? Could they give enough of a fuck about each other? Wouldn't that be something? The panhandlers forming a socialist, underground network. The rest of us wouldn't spare a dime to a stranger at the grocery store cash register.

Joe #1:   Another story for the Pastor to tell. Get the congregation all revved up. Guilt tripping them on the generosity of the poor.

Joe #2:   And then hit them up for their wallets. That's shitty. But... I ain't convinced they're poor. I asked this one guy. Stood out in front of the plaza all winter. Setting up shop. Like it was his camp ground. I stopped. I asked him. I was curious. I said, "What's the most you ever made in a day?" He tells me he pulled in three hundred Christmas Eve.

Joe #1:   But that can't be the norm. It's Christmas. Jesus and all. Even if it is the norm. Is it worth it?

Joe #2:   At three hundred a day? Five days a week, that's seventy-five dimes a year. And that's with two weeks factored in there for vacation or... funerals. I'm guessing the IRS don't get a cut neither. Besides, there's people make a lot less for a lot more degrading shit. What's so bad about it? Outside all day. Get to meet new people. And you don't have to get all up in each other's shit. That's the best part. Your longest interaction with anyone is... how long is the average red light?

Joe #1:   But the shame of it.

Joe #2:   I don't know many folks who shouldn't be ashamed of what they do for their day to day. Even more, they should be ashamed for being proud of what they do. The only downside as I see it, for me, is that I don't want everybody looking at me all the time. But then again, seems like a lot of folks want to be looked at. Seen. They eat that shit up.

Joe #1: Look at me! Look at me!

Joe #2: Most people I know would let you hit them in the head with a two by four if it made a name for them. Think about it. How many assholes you know got a job but have convinced themselves that they're just buying time until they ride that fame wave straight into hell. Teacher/writers, waiter/actors, dogwalker/dancers, landscaper/singers. For a normal guy, being on the local news would be embarrassing. For them, it's a big breakthrough.

Joe #1: I don't watch the local news. It depresses me.

Joe #2: Lot of bad shit these days.

Joe #1: Not because that. Hundred or so people get shot fourth of July weekend. Ah salud. Live and let live.

Joe #2: Makes you not want to go out.

Joe #1: What the fuck you want me to do?

Joe #2: Duck.

Joe #1: Play a violin?

Joe #2: Wait. You play?

Joe #1: Not a lick.

Joe #2: So why you not like the local news?

Joe #1: The anchors. They disgust me. And then by association the whole institution of the local news disgusts me. Who behaves like that? The makeup? The fake laughs? The fake concern? The fake reverence? Who acts like that? Is there some focus group somewhere that has determined that this is the best way to speak to us? Bunch of phonies laughing hysterically at cats dressed up in people clothes at some fashion show? That's not funny. That's not funny to no one—nowhere—never. Thirty seconds later, they're acting like they give two fucks because some lowlife got hit by a bus. Is that what they think of us? That we want people like that? People who act like that? People who look like that? No. Local news. It's like a soap opera without the sex or the plot. What's the point? You know, Benny Rubin used to tend bar where all those local news folks would hobnob. He said they were all a bunch of raging drunks. Every night playing a game to see who could garner the most attention. Hey! Check me out! It's sad. You ask me.

Joe #2:   Half want to be seen. The other half want to be heard.

Joe #1:   I like that. Fuckin Benny Rubin...

Joe #2:   I thought about it one time.

Joe #1:   TV news?

Joe #2:   No. Bumming.

Joe #1:   Begging people at the red light?

Joe #2:   Why not?

Joe #1:   What's stopping you?

Joe #2:   Ah, god damn panhandling laws.
            Who knows where it ends?
            I don't need the hassle.

Joe #1:   That ain't right. Cracking some guy for begging.
            He already got it bad. That's low.

Joe #2:   I get it though.
            Some folks feel like they're being harassed.

Joe #1:   Doesn't matter. The deal with free speech is you can't regulate the content of what a guy says. But you can regulate the time, place and manner of it. Like some guy might get busted if he goes into a residential neighborhood at four a.m. and starts screaming like the bombs were coming in.

Joe #2:   What if they were?

Joe #1:   You can see why.

Joe #2:   Yeah. The prick would wake everyone up.

Joe #1:   Exactly. But the same guy has every right to walk through the neighborhood at a reasonable time and at a reasonable volume and discuss any god damn thing he pleases with random strangers. The weather, traffic, sports, his family, polar bears, rainbows... the death of god. So, these panhandling laws are out to regulate not the where, the when, the how the guy says something. They're after what the guy says.

Joe #2:   How's that?

Joe #1:   They're saying I can walk up to a perfect stranger and ask him for directions. But I can't ask him for a quarter.

Joe #2:   Both are helpful.

Joe #1:   Indeed they are.

Joe #2:   So, you think maybe I should re-consider, you know... like a career?

Joe #1:   I....

Waiter enters.

Waiter: Good evening. My name is Gregory and I will be—

Joe #2:   Gregory. I'm Joe. Nice to meet you.

They shake.

Waiter: Nice to meet you.

Joe #2:   And this is my friend, the Mayor.

Waiter: Oh... well.

Joe #2:   I'm just fucking with you. I like playing games like that. Like tell people that someone is someone they should know, but then they don't know. And then they feel like a dumb shit about it. Or I sit on the bus all day and whenever some schmuck gets off. I tell the one next to me it was someone famous. They fall for it every time. The world is full of shit heels I tell you. 'Hey that was Bill Murray.' 'What? No. Really?' 'Bet my life on it.' That's all you got to do. Bet your life. People think that means serious. No one ever considers that your life might not be worth a shit. But, 'Hey, look. That's Beyonce.' That shit gets their attention. That's funny to me. But you seem like a good guy, Gregory. Got good energy. I don't want to put you through any of that for my amusement. I like the way you come over, introduce yourself. Spoken like a gentleman.

Joe #1:   Uh, Joe.

          They shake.

Waiter: Hello, Joe. Wait, Joe and... Joe?

Joe #2:   Just Joe.

Waiter: But no ordinary Joe.

Joe #2:   Good one, Gregory. See. He gets it.

Waiter: Do you have any questions about the menu?

Joe #1:   Just one. Where do you keep them?

Waiter: Oh, it's on the wall when you come in. We're paperless.

Joe #1:   So, I can't read the menu, and I can't read the paper in this place?

Joe #2:   What's with you and reading?

Waiter: It's okay. I can go over tonight's offerings.

Joe #2:   You know what you should do? Put binoculars on all the tables so folks can look at the menu from wherever they're sitting.

Joe #1:   That's not bad. It would give the place that feeling like
          you were on a sightseeing tour.

Joe #2:   Like a Safari.

Joe #1:   Yes.

Joe #2:   And you were picking out what prey was going on your
          plate.

Joe #1:   I wouldn't go that far.

Joe #2:   No different than the lobster tank.

Joe #1:   It's different.

Joe #2:   Pick your own steakhouse?

Joe #1:   That's already dead.

                    Joe #2 ponders this.

Waiter: Well, for the appetizer this evening,
          we have a lemon-butter sautéed oyster—

Joe #1:   No no no no! Don't!

Waiter: I'm sorry.

Joe #1:   No. It's fine. I just don't like when people read to me.

Joe #2:   Again with the reading?

Joe #1:   It's demeaning. Makes me feel like a little kid.

Waiter: I wasn't reading.

Joe #2:   He's right. He wasn't. He had all that committed to memory.
          He was more like an actor there.

Waiter: Actually. I am auditioning currently -

Joe #2:   See. What did I say? *(Beat)* It's like watching a movie.
          Just instead of following the plot, he's talking about food.

Joe #1:   Like a salesman?

Waiter: Maybe. Sort of.

Joe #1:   It's okay. I'll go over there, have a look at the menu.

Waiter: Fair enough.

Joe #2:   Let me ask you something, Gregory. You shook our hands when we met. Does that mean before you can go back to handling food that you have to wash up?

Waiter: Of course.

Joe #1:   Why? We look like scuzzballs? Do I strike you as the type of guy who goes around picking his ass all day? Maybe, I'm the germophobe.

Waiter: Then you wouldn't have shaken my hand.

Joe #2:   That's right. You wouldn't. I like you, Gregory.
          You're not like the other people. Here. In the world.

Joe #1:   I get it. I get it. You got to do what you got to do.
          Your job can't be sizing people up all the time.

Waiter: Of course. It cannot.

Joe #2:   You are one charming motherfucker, Gregory.

Waiter: Thank you. Can I get you something to drink?

Joe #2:   Water.

Joe #1:   And Scotch.

Joe #2:   Scotch and water. Yes.

Waiter: And for you?

Joe #1:   What did we say?

Waiter: Scotch.

Joe #1:   And...

Waiter:	Water?
Joe #1:	Yes.
Waiter:	So, two scotch and waters? Or two scotches and two waters?
Joe #2:	Both for both.
Waiter:	Both what?
Joe #2:	Scotches... and waters.
Waiter:	That's what I'm asking. Do you want a scotch and a water? Or do you want them mixed together?
Joe #1:	I hadn't thought of that.
Joe #2:	I see the problem now.
Waiter:	Yes. You see?
Joe #1:	How about this? A bottle of scotch and a pitcher of water. And then we can figure it out from there.
Waiter:	No problem.
Joe #1:	Splendid.
Waiter:	Wait. Two glasses or four?
Joe #2:	Gregory, you think of everything.
Waiter:	Or six? Could be six? One glass each for water. One glass each for scotch. And one glass each for scotch and water.
Joe #1:	This is more complicated than it seems.
Waiter:	I'll bring six. Just in case.
Joe #2:	I agree. That would be best.
Waiter:	It would.
Joe #1:	Then it's settled. And we'll take a look at that menu while you're away.

Waiter:	Perfect.
Joe #1:	And Gregory, I might think about washing your hands if I was you.
Waiter:	I will.

Waiter exits.

Joe #2:	Shall we?
Joe #1:	What?
Joe #2:	Go look at the menu?
Joe #1:	What if he brings the scotch back while we're gone? The whole bottle? That's probably expensive. I don't like the idea of leaving it here on the table unattended.
Joe #2:	Want me to go look at the menu and come back and give you the rundown?
Joe #1:	Then we'd be back in the same boat we were with the waiter.
Joe #2:	Right. The reading of stuff. You want to go and come back and give me the rundown?
Joe #1:	Somehow, I feel like that would be worse.
Joe #2:	It would.
Joe #1:	What the hell does that mean?
Joe #2:	Just....
Joe #1:	How about this? Let's leave a note.
Joe #2:	A note?
Joe #1:	Yeah. We'll write a little note. It'll say—Dear Gregory, can you stay and keep an eye on the scotch until we return from viewing the menu?

Joe #2:	How do you sign off on something like that?
Joe #1:	What?
Joe #2:	You know, how do you wrap it up? Your clients comma? But we're not really clients. I don't know. Regards comma? Best wishes comma? Love comma? Love seems a little forward.
Joe #1:	Thank you. We'll close it – Thank you comma. Joe and Joe.
Joe #2:	Fantastic.
Joe #1:	Do you have a pen?
Joe #2:	I...

Waiter returns with the drinks.

Joe #1:	Wow. Great timing, Gregory.
Waiter:	Are you ready to order?
Joe #1:	We didn't even look at the menu yet.
Waiter:	Oh, well there's no rush.
Joe #1:	That's the thing of it. Do you think you can wait here for a minute and keep an eye on the scotch while we go look at the menu?
Waiter:	Keep an eye on the scotch?
Joe #2:	Well yeah.
Waiter:	I don't understand.
Joe #1:	Say we get up to look at the menu. Some lowlife comes by the table and pockets the scotch. I'm already into you for the bottle.
Waiter:	I don't think that would happen. This is a pretty upscale place.
Joe #2:	It is nice.
Joe #1:	You don't think it would happen. But do we know for sure?

Waiter:	I tell you what. If someone takes the scotch, I will replace it at no charge.
Joe #2:	That's a scotch guarantee. You can't do any better than that. You'll get a handsome tip up behind that, Gregory. The old scotch guarantee. This fucking guy.
Waiter:	Thank you.
Joe #1:	I get it. I get it. Just. I would feel better if you just kept an eye on this bottle. I mean this is the scotch that you selected for us. I'm sure it's the best.
Joe #2:	I've got nothing but the best from you thus far, Gregory.
Waiter:	I do aim to please.
Joe #1:	Then please. Watch the fucking scotch. We won't be long.
Joe #2:	No. I get it. He can't watch the scotch.
Joe #1:	Why not?
Joe #2:	Say the manager comes by. He's supposed to be working. Not standing in front of an empty table watching a bottle of scotch. Guaranteed scotch at that. But still. He could get shit canned over this.
Joe #1:	You know this would be a whole lot easier if you just had menus like normal places.
Waiter:	We're paperless.
Joe #1:	You said that. Then put them on wood. I don't care. Put a frickin etch-a-sketch on every table with the menu on it.
Joe #2:	You can't put an etch-a-sketch out as a menu.
Joe #1:	Why not?
Joe #2:	Because –
Waiter:	Because some asshole would inevitably shake it up and ruin it for the next guy.

Joe #2:   He would.

Joe #1:   Fucking pricks ruin everything.

Waiter: Look. It will be fine. You guys go have a look at the menu, and I will stay here and keep an eye on the scotch.

Joe #1:   Are you sure? We don't want to get you in trouble.

Waiter: It will be fine. If my manager asks, I will tell him that you requested that I watch your drinks while you went to look at the menu. He certainly can't be angry about that. I am serving the customer. That's my job.

Joe #1:   I like you, Gregory. You're not like the other people. Here. In the world.

Joe #2:   Of course, that assumes that we back up your story.

Waiter: What?

Joe #2:   Say your manager comes by and you tell him all that. That you're doing us a solid. Watching the scotch and all. And then we tell him that we don't know what the fuck you're talking about. That we found it kind of creepy that you were hanging around the table when we came back from looking at the menu. Made us suspect that you were trying to put something in our drinks. When you think about it, our story is a little easier to buy. I mean, who insists that somebody keep an eye on their drinks because they're worried someone will steal them? At an upscale place like this? You said so yourself.

Waiter: Why would you do that?

Joe #2:   I wouldn't. I'm just saying. You're a nice guy, Gregory. You're not like the other people. Here. In the world. But you're trusting. Which is good. But be careful with that. Lot of assholes out there. Everyone is looking to get over.

Waiter: But you're not.

Joe #2:   I am not.

Joe #1:   He's not. I can vouch for that.
          He's thinking of becoming a panhandler.

Waiter: I hear they make good money.
          Especially around the holidays.

Joe #2:   Starting salary is seventy-five K a year.

Waiter: That can't be. Then why isn't everyone out on the street,
          begging?

Joe #2:   When was the last time you were outside?
          It's a confederacy of whores.

Joe #1:   Gregory, do you have a pen?

Joe #2:   And paper? A pen and paper? And can you just leave them
          on the table. We ran into this problem before. So. In case
          we need to not be here for a minute and you come around.
          We'll leave you a note letting you know what the deal is.

Waiter: I think. It's a small place. You could easily find me.

Joe #2:   But we don't want to make a scene. Like, if you're with
          another table. You don't want one of us poking our head
          in saying– "Hey Gregory, I'm going to take a shit. Can you
          keep an eye on the scotch?"

Waiter: Got it. Okay. Here's what we're going to do. I'm going to
          keep an eye on the scotch while you look at the menu. And
          when you come back. I am going to take your order. And
          then, I am going to put your order in and return right away
          with a pen and paper for future communications any of us
          might deem important.

Joe #2:   That's fucking amazing. You got a military background,
          Gregory?

Waiter: No.

Joe #2:   Because that's fucking sharp.

Waiter: So, what do we think? Time to check out the menu?

Joe #2:   It is.

Joe #1:   Say, Gregory. Did you wash your hands?

Waiter: I did.

Joe #1:   Good. Good.

Joe #1 and Joe #2 exit. Joe #1 returns.

Joe #1:   Did you shake anybody else's hand since?

Waiter: No.

Joe #1:   You sure?

Waiter: I'm not much of a hand shaker.

Joe #1:   But you shook mine.

Waiter: That's different. I like you.

Joe #1:   Thank you, Gregory.

Joe #1 exits. After a long silence –

Waiter: *(At Audience)*   The question. Always comes down to the question. And that question is, like it always has been. Should we or should we not sucker punch the waiter? It's on your mind. At least now it is. But it always is. Whether you realize it or not. That's always been the question. And here I stand. And you can easily say that either makes me a fool or a sage. It's a fair question. But all that's irrelevant. All that matters is - that here I stand. That's enough. And I know the question. Have had plenty of time to contemplate it. And yet the question remains. And yet here I stand. And that is enough. Should we or should we not sucker punch the waiter? And here I stand. So, certainly I play a part in the resolution of this issue. But which part I play is not entirely up to me. Because there remains a question to which I do not have the answer. Possible responses to an affirmative answer to this query: 1. Why? 2. Please don't. 3. Just run, man. Split. 4. Wanna test? 5. Go fuck yourself. And if the answer is no: 1. Why not? 2. Go ahead. Do it. 3. Just run, man. Split. 4. Pussy. 5. Go fuck yourself. *(Beat)* I believe in manners. I believe in etiquette. I believe in decorum. But still. The question remains. Should we or should we not sucker punch the waiter?

Joe #2 enters.

Joe #2:   Let me ask you. This one plate says Balsamic reduction. What the hell is that? Is that like only half a plate?

Waiter: No.

Joe #2:   Is the plate smaller or something? Because I'm hungry.

Waiter: No. The balsamic reduction is a sauce.

Joe #2:   Half a sauce?

Waiter: Well, no. They cook balsamic vinegar and a lot of the liquid evaporates. It's thicker. Sweeter. It's good.

Joe #2:   Oh. Okay.

Joe #2 exits. Joe #2 returns.

Joe #2:   Cornish game hen? That's like the tiny chicken, right?

Waiter: Correct.

Joe #2:   Just checking. Thanks.

Joe #2 exits. Joe #2 returns.

Joe #2:   What the hell is frisee?

Waiter: It's a type of lettuce.

Joe #2:   Is it Good?

Waiter: If you like lettuce, I guess.

Joe #2:   Yeah, I hear you.

Joe #2 exits. Joe #2 returns.

Joe #2:   What the fuck is Tzatziki sauce?

Waiter: It's like a Greek cucumber sauce. Yogurt.

Joe #2:   Yogurt? For dinner?

Waiter: Yeah. It's the stuff they put on a Gyro *(Yee-Ro)*.

Joe #2:   Yee-roll?

Waiter: No. The Greek sandwich. With the lamb and the pita. Gyro *(Ji-Ro)*.

Joe #2:   Oh, those are good. I had one at the fair.

Waiter: Nice.

Joe #2 exits. Joe #2 returns.

Joe #2:   Cedar plank salmon? Is that salmon that tastes like a cedar plank. Or a cedar plank that tastes like salmon?

Waiter: It's salmon. They cook it on a cedar plank.

Joe #2:   Why?

Waiter: Makes it taste better.

Joe #2:   My ass it does.

Joe #2 exits. Joe #2 returns.

Joe #2:   What the fuck are capers?

Waiter: To tell you the truth, I don't know
what the fuck those things are.
I stay away from them.

Joe #2:   I'll do that then. Thanks.

Joe #2 exits. Waiter takes a pull off the scotch.

After a moment, Joe #1 returns.

Joe #1: I'll have the number three. Extra slaw and tater tots instead of fries. And some Heinz 57 sauce.

Waiter: Oh.

Joe #1: I'm just fucking with you.

Waiter: That's not bad.

Joe #1: You like that?

Waiter: I do.

Joe #1: You're a good guy, Gregory. Don't get me wrong.

Waiter: Why would I do that?

Joe #1: I didn't mean it like that. I'm sorry. I'm not always so good with words. It's just. I got to thinking. I'm up there looking at the menu. And I was standing. That was probably it. I think better when I'm standing. Do you think better when your standing, Gregory?

Waiter: I want to say yes. But I don't know. There's a part of me that, yeah, I'm up on my feet, I'm moving, I'm living, I'm breathing. So sure, the mind is functioning at its highest level. But I am telling you. I have come up with a ton of intensely cool shit just laying on the couch watching 'Saved by the Bell' reruns.

Joe #1: Is that right?

Waiter: It is. But that's a non-sequitur. You were saying? You were at the menu, thinking...?

Joe #1: In your line of business, do you believe that the customer is always right?

Waiter: Are you asking if I believe that?

Joe #1: Well yeah.

Waiter: I don't know. Who fucking cares what I think?

Joe #1: That's what I think.

Waiter: Yeah?

Joe #1: Not about you. About me, I mean.

Waiter: I got you. People pay with credit cards, man. You know why? Pfft. Me neither. It's the modern version of the dine and dash I suppose. Once they leave here, they're the bank's problem. I mean fuck, man, you stand here, you smile, you bring some asshole a salad, maybe he throws you a few bucks. Maybe not. So now I stand here and watch the scotch for a minute. Part of me thinks that's a better way to spend my time. At least I'm helping someone. Yeah yeah yeah, you could say the same. That I am feeding people. But it's different. They were gonna eat anyway. In this instance. Right here tonight. I am the protector of another's property. There's value in that. Is there not? But this is not in my job description. Watch the scotch. Watch the scotch. Watch the scotch. That has never been in anyone's job description. But I take to the task at hand. And I have done right by you, Joe. Not because you are a customer. You are not. Nothing could be further from the truth. I take to the task at hand because I, like you, am a good man.

Joe #1: No truer words ever spoken, Gregory. No truer words ever spoken. I like you. You're not like the other people. Here. In the world.

Joe #2 enters.

Joe #2: Okay. Finally. I am going to have the sherz... the shearz... the.... Fuck, what do you call it?

Waiter: What the fuck do you call it?

Joe #2: I don't know. I can see it. It's like the second thing listed in the entrees. What am I thinking? You know the menu.

Waiter:	I can't. He doesn't like people reading to him.
Joe #1:	He's right. I don't.
Joe #2:	All right, whatever. Did you get that pen and paper?
Waiter:	You just got back right now.
Joe #2:	This would be so much easier if you just had menus like other places do.
Joe #1:	He's not wrong about that.
Waiter:	But we're paperless.
Joe #1:	They're paperless. What're you gonna do?
Joe #2:	Or maybe if you had the menu posted in various spots throughout the place. Printed so big that people could see it from wherever they were sitting. I might not be in this jam right now.
Waiter:	That's not a bad idea.
Joe #1:	It's not. I could get on board with this.
Joe #2:	Here's what I'm thinking. Right there. Take that plant box out. You put a menu hang right there. All the people in those two sections could read it easily, and likely a lot of those folks by the window could refer to it in a pinch as well. But their primary view would be right there. Next to the door to the kitchen. Take down all those corny black and white photos and put a menu up there that two-thirds of your tables can see. And then, for the people in the front, it's easy. Right above the restroom signs.
Joe #1:	I don't know about that.
Joe #2:	Why?
Joe #1:	Right there by the shitter? Doesn't seem right.
Waiter:	Not only that. Say some guy has a bad meal. Or even a good meal, and it has nothing to do with our food, but

he got salmonella from the omelet he had for breakfast, and he's come down with a sudden case of the shits. He's looking for the men's room and while at it, he has to be reminded of everything he could have possibly eaten in this establishment. He takes that with him into the can. And then, he defiles the john. I don't want to be blue, but, I mean, he compromises the integrity of the room. You know what the fuck I'm talking about. And now, for the rest of his life he's got those two thoughts juxtaposed in his scrambled-up, mush brain. That's bad for business.

Joe #2:   That is thinking ahead. Do you play chess?

Waiter: No.

Joe #1:   So, we scrap the bathroom menu. And just leave the one at the front for those people. I mean those are the cheap seats and all. Right by the shitter. Fuck 'em.

Waiter: I like it.

Joe #2:   Great. What do we have to do to make this happen?

Joe #1:   You know some people, Greg?

Waiter: I think I might.

Joe #1:   You don't mind I called you Greg, do you?

Joe #2:   He does that to everybody.

Waiter: I don't mind.

Joe #1:   I don't want to shorten up on you if you don't want to be shortened up on. I knew this woman, called herself Kimberly. We went to the same gym for a long time. We knew each other well. I guess you could say we were friends. One day I called her Kim, she slapped the shit out of me...

Waiter: It's okay. My friends call me Greg. I only use Gregory on my bank account and here. I thought it sounds a little more sophisticated.

Joe #1:   It doesn't.

Waiter: No?

Joe #2:   Makes you sound like an asshole.

Waiter: That's not nice.

Joe #2:   It's not. I know. I'm just saying.

Waiter: You guys ready to order?

Joe #1:   Yes.

Joe #2:   Let me go look.

Waiter: Okay.

Joe #2:   Better Yet. How about this, Gregory. I mean Greg.

Waiter: You're the one that said it made me sound like an asshole.

Joe #2:   It does.

Waiter: Then why did you say it again? You think I'm an asshole?

Joe #2:   You know I think the world of you, Gregory. Greg.
            God Damnit!

Waiter: I'm just fucking with you.

Joe #1:   I like this fucking guy.

Joe #2:   I love this fucking guy.

Waiter: So, what's your plan?

Joe #2:   I'm going to go check the menu. Joe here, will keep an
            eye on the scotch. And you go grab me a pen and paper.

Joe #1:   But why do you need the pen and paper, if you're going
            to go look at the menu for a second time? Just remember
            what you want this time.

Joe #2:   I intend to. The pen and paper is for... in case... the future.

Joe #1:   The future?

Joe #2:   It's pre-emptive. You know. In case the shit goes down.

Waiter: What shit?

Joe #1:   Yeah, what shit?

Waiter: No. You know what. I don't give a fuck. I'll do it. If the shit goes down, I got your back. Joe, you check the menu. Joe, you watch the scotch. I got the supplies.

Joe #1:   You sure you weren't in the military?

Waiter: I'm pretty sure I wasn't.

Joe #2:   Wait. Which Joe does what?

Waiter: Well he...

Joe #2:   I'm just fucking with you.

Waiter: I like you fucking guys.

Waiter exits. Joe #2 Exits. After a long pause -

Joe #1:   *(Singing to himself)* 'It's not the heat / it's the stupidity / it's not the drugs / that did this to me.' *(Whistles).*

Joe #2 enters.

Joe #1:   You got it this time?

Joe #2:   I do. I think I do. I'm pretty sure I do. I might.

Joe #1:   Don't fuck it up.

Joe #2:   What are you getting?

Joe #1:   What the fuck you care what I'm getting?

Joe #2:   Just asking.

Joe #1:   Mind your business.

Joe #2:   You didn't get nothing with capers, did you?

Joe #1:   Why?

Joe #2:   You shouldn't eat capers.

Joe #1:   Why not?

Joe #2:   Nobody knows what they are.

> *Waiter returns. He puts the pen and paper on the table and, oddly, they all get up and hug.*

Waiter: We get it all sorted out there, Joe?

Joe #1:   Who?

Waiter: You're fucking with me.

Joe #2:   I like you, Gregory. You're not like the other people. Here. In the world.

Waiter: So, what will it be?

Joe #2:   Damnit!

Joe #1:   What?

Joe #2:   I forgot.

Joe #1:   You dumb shit.

Joe #2:   I had it. And then. Gregory. He distracted me.

Waiter: What the fuck did I do?

Joe #1:   Don't blame him.

Joe #2:   I got to thinking. See. You don't get to think whatever you want. You were right. I wanted to be thinking about food. Food, motherfuckers. Food. But instead, I was thinking about...

Waiter: What were you thinking about?

Joe #1:   Yeah, Joe. What were you thinking about?

Joe #2:   Just... .... Nothing.

Joe #2 sheepishly takes the pen and paper and exits.

Waiter: Oh, so I talked to the manger.

Joe #1:   What about?

Waiter: You're idea. The menus.

Joe #1:   What did he say?

Waiter: He was into it. You want to meet him?

Joe #1:   Now?

Waiter: He's right over there.

Joe #1:   Yeah. Yeah. Yeah. Sure. Let's uh... Let me collect my thoughts, here. Where did we say we were going to put them? I don't know. Maybe we should wait for Joe. He has some thoughts on this.

Waiter: I can tell him to stop by the table.

Joe #1:   You got to kick him part of the tip for that?

Waiter: What?

Joe #1:   You know. If he's got to come over here to your table. If he's got to do your job, what does he need you for?

Waiter: I see.

Joe #1:   I'm going to tell you two things, Greg. Because I like you. You're not like other people. Here. In the world.
One, the customer is always wrong.
And two, the boss is always an asshole.

Waiter: He is kind of a dick.

Joe #1:   Maybe I should have a few words with him.

Waiter: Maybe you should.

Joe #1:   Be right back. Watch the scotch.

Waiter: Got it.

> *Joe #1 exits. Waiter takes another pull off the scotch. Joe #2 returns.*

Waiter: So? –

Joe #2:   Shhh. Don't distract me. *(Long pause)* I can't tell what I wrote because I wrote it in waiters' shorthand. Hell, I've never been a waiter. I don't even know if waiters' shorthand is even an actual thing. All I know is I see the girl at the breakfast diner always scribbling down initials when someone orders something. So, I figured it was a thing. Is it a thing, Gregory?

Waiter: It can be.

Joe #2:   I thought I told you to be quiet. *(Long Pause)* That's my problem I always think everything is always a thing. And what the fuck do I know? I know this. Life ate me up. I could never do what it was that I wanted to do. Because I got caught up thinking everything is a thing. But no thing is a thing. I know that now. And I'm hungry.

> *Joe #1 Enters, pats waiter on the back.*

Joe #1:   You're good.

Waiter: Yeah?

Joe #1:   Extra dollar an hour too.

Waiter: No shit?

Joe #1:   Next pay period. Not this one.

> *Joe #1 pours three scotches.*

Waiter: Figure it all out?

Joe #1:   I did not.

Joe #2:   Me neither.

Waiter: And yet here I stand.

They toast in silence.
They drink.

—The End—

JULIA WILLIAMS and VICKI WALDEN as Elm and Tip in *One Boppa*

One Boppa, in two acts*

Premiered **November 2016**

Prop Thtr / Chicago, IL

written by **BEAU O'REILLY**

directed by **Matt Rieger**

performed by:

Meredith Lyons
Matt Rieger
Vicki Walden
Julia Williams
Ryan Hogan Wright

THE

PLAYS

* see endnote, p. 285

SETTING

The play takes place in Chicago, sometime after the millennium. The first act takes place 4 years after the second act.

CAST of CHARACTERS:

TIP, 30 to 45 years old
Eccentric woman in her dress and speaking, any size.

ELM, her sister, 30 to 45 years old
Tense, with a need to have both feet in the real world.
Pedantic, stern, attractive, any size.

ANDI, 28 to 38 years old, probably the youngest
Soft in manner, prone to laughter and weeping.

SERGEANT TENDERBERRY, a cop
Very excited and pleased by small things.
Could be any adult age, male.

FRED, the other cop
Very calm and makes a point to be decent.

STAGE

The set can and should be simple: an apartment without much in Act One; a restaurant, without much in Act Two. Both rooms need a door and a window. They can be representational or realistic.

Scene One:

*Tip comes out on stage, swings a log and throws it towards a
window; sound of breaking glass.*

Scene Two:

Elm, Andi and Tip at a house where Tip is plant sitting.

Elm: What? What do you think anarchy is, Tip? Do you even—

Tip: "An agreed upon non-hierarchical system derived from
          a conscious worldview."

Andi: Maggie Crain called me.

Tip: "These are my dogs, my treasures...unfortunately, but
          treasures that urinate. Mine is the busy life and I will never
          walk them, my treasures, you will walk them, you are not
          my treasures—treasured dog walker...that is what I pay
          you for a position of trust that Maggie creates."
          That Maggie Crain?

Elm: We only know one Maggie Crain, Tip, come on.

Andi: She said a funny thing happened a month after
          she left you with the dogs, Tip.

Elm: The picture window fell out, and the dogs
          were just sitting there?

Tip: In the dog room, on the dog sofa?

Andi: I think so...and the dogs, Myrta and Peter...

Tip: Merdefoot and Pissoir. Bark. Bark.

Andi: Started barking, both of them...and she was looking out the windows to see what they were barking at.

Tip: Squirrels! Squirrels gone manic all over that backyard.

Andi: And the glass in the picture window trembled.

Tip: "Trembled." Is that how she said it? "Trembled?"

Andi: Yes. "Trembled." And then fell, all in one piece, it fell out and shattered on the lawn.

Tip: These dogs have very hi-pitched barks. I always wear earplugs—walking the dog in a bag of silence.

Andi: She asked me if I had heard anything about the window. Had my sister said anything had happened to the window...

Elm: You didn't tell Andi, Tip.

Tip: I didn't think she would want to know, Elm.

Elm: Of course Andi would want to know...it was her friend, Maggie Crain, giving you work.

Tip: Sometimes not knowing is better.

Andi: I wanted to know. Of course I wanted to know...I still do, Tip, what really happened?

Tip: The window got broken.

Elm: Tip broke it with a log.

Tip: Elm told me to—

Elm: I told you to get in the house because I had to go to work and you needed me to hold the dogs because you're such a fool, for you that meant break a window...

Tip: ...it was the dog, that Pissoir.

Andi: Peter...broke the window—

Tip: It was his fault...that dog is terrible about basic dog stuff. He jumps up—hits your breasts when you're trying to put the leash on, and you know how they shit and you're supposed to plastic bag it...Pissoir will shit on the run with his ass at an angle—the whole length of the sidewalk and you have to bend over and bend over and bend over and bend over while plastic bagging with one, with both tugging at the leash in the other hand.

Andi: Tip, how did Peter break the window?

Tip: I was in the dog room—you know how it opens on the backyard...

Andi: The patio.

Tip: The back yard. Usually I really walk the dogs, I'd rather walk plus I am getting paid, I try to be ethical...though it's just turd patrol. Boppa-

Andi: That's right—Boppa met the Shriek...

Tip: And he fled. Boppa ran from the Shriek.

Andi: Boppa ran from the group. The group. You're very lucky
         to have the group.

Tip: Ten years and don't I know it?

Andi: What are you guys reading now?

Tip: The New Bible.

Elm: The Bible?...you don't even believe in God. And Boppa.
         The only god Boppa believes in is himself, himself smiling
         in the mirror, like he just ate the last piece of chocolate and
         he thinks no one saw him do it, that he got away with it.

Andi: Elm, stop that. Boppa is nice.

Elm: Is he?

Andi: Compared to most men, yes. He is sweet, he is gentle,
         he's nice, he's just gone a lot.

Elm: Gone? Is that where he is ? I knew he must be somewhere.
         Somewhere out of the 'I am responsible' zone.

Andi: Boppa doesn't punch. He doesn't snarl at the women in
         his life. He listens to us talk; he likes to know how women
         do things. He likes us. Most men—

Elm: We are not going to compare poison to poison
         now are we? Andi? Arsenic to rat poison?
         Because poison is still poison.

Andi: Boppa is not a rat. You don't think he is a rat, do you Elm?

Elm: Well, a mouse. Rats are at least aggressive.

Tip: I like mice. Mice are nice; mice, mice, nice, nice. Mice are good, the way they move.

Elm: What? No one likes mice, their vermin, that's like liking vermin.

Tip: I like Boppa. Boppa is my favorite man.

Elm: That might be creepy, Tip.

Tip: Its not, though. The world has people in it, I see that, but some you like, you recognize. Tilly the Shriek says we are lucky to meet anyone that gets us at all. Tilly the Shriek says the problem with all these past lives of ours is that they were so complete that they wipe us out for this one, this one can feel like a copy of a copy, like a bad xerox. Its like swimming across the lake, Tilly says, we use everything we have to get across and then back in the water, girl, we have to use everything we have to get back again.

Elm: Jesus, Tip, what is going on. What is with all this religious murk? Are you really believing in god now?

Tip: In the new Bible—

Elm: No new bible, no new bible, God yes? God no?

Tip: I believe in storytelling. The book of Job...all those hideous things; man, God, the hardass drama...all that wonder... women made out of ribs. Serpents out of apples. Back when miracles happened, before they even had a name for them, stories pouring out of the head of an almighty being, that is rich, that is juicy.

Andi: Genesis.

Tip: The Book of Numbers.

Andi: Which nobody understands, except this specific room of rabbi-mathematicians who are so smart that all they do is raise eyebrows and wrinkle foreheads and insist they know. Do you suppose, Tip, that Tilly the Shriek has ever been in that room?

Tip: She has. She has. Tilly the Shriek says it's like the Mensa All Stars in there, the brainpower is insane.

Andi: Glowing. I can see it glowing. If a person, a normal-like-us-person, sees all that brain power in the sky that person will never look at the sky the same way again. Will it be planets? Stars up there? Whichever it is, it is so fine,

Tip: Give me brains.

Andi: Big glowing Mensa brains.
         Now that is something to envy.

Elm: Stop it, please. Both of you. Tell me about the dog.

Tip: I was late for the group. I called Tilly the Shriek and I said don't let Boppa leave when he gets there, make him stay, he's bringing the Gnostic Gospels, which was a lie, cause Boppa never read the Gnostic Gospels.

Elm: He just wants all the cookies and the cake.

Andi: He just wants to see how long he can stand sitting next Tilly the Shriek.

Tip: Boppa says its good for his patience, a test like that. And he likes the rest of the group: Matthew Mark Luke and John, those are great names for bible study, Boppa thinks, are they really these boys names with their long beards that look like they just stepped off the Halls cough drop box...Boppa wants to know if that is their real names and I could have told him three David's and a Billy but Tillie the Shriek, shrieked 'no no a man's name is like his intimate organs', it is his business...Tilly the Shriek. Tilly the Shriek, just keep saying it, her name carries so much psychic weight.

Andi: That's what Boppa says.

Tip: That's what Boppa knows. Tilly the Shriek's mother named her that; did I tell you, on the day Tilly was born?

Andi: No! Tillys mother is holding the baby say, and the baby is crying, wailing to beat the band.

Tip: Shrieking. That baby was shrieking, baby Tilly is shrieking.

Andi: At her first sense of the world, how massive it all is.

Tip: Massive smell. Massive light.
Massive touch, massive touch.

Andi: Cooing. Cooing, someone's cooing ba-a-by. Ba-a-by.

Tip: I would shriek. Wouldn't you?

Andi: I would shriek. I would.

Both start shrieking.

Elm: Stop that, both of you. You are waking the dead.

Andi: *(Scared.)* Really?...my...mom?

Elm: It is all right Andi. The dead don't wake from noise.
          They are dead.

Andi: *(Scared.)* Why would you say that then?

Elm: It's a figure of speech. It means your to—

Andi: It's a horrible figure of speech. Wake the dead.
          Can you imagine?

Elm: No, I cannot, but I am sure you can.

Andi: I can, I really can.

Tip: I can too.

Elm: God I hate it when both of you are weird at the same time,
          I really do. I feel more alone than usual, like the therapist
          just told me that my depression support group really all
          have brain tumors, which happened, by the way. A whole
          room full of people feeling terrible, offering me support
          and they all find out they have brain tumors; all except
          me, I just feel terrible because I feel terrible. You guys just
          underline that, you say feeling terrible, everything seems
          weird, how about this, this is weird and this, this is weird.

Andi: Elma. We don't do it on purpose.

Elm: Tip does. The world isn't bad enough without having to
          think about—

Tip: Homunculus.

Elm: Don't.

Tip: I am just saying, in the 1600's people believed that every drop of sperm was a little human creature waiting to come here.

Andi: Can you imagine how crowded it must feel in every drop of sperm, everybody elbowing for a place in line, save me some of that bread, that cake, that lotto ticket.

Tip: When you think about it modern us people have it easy, we understand biology—

Elm: Why think about any of this? Why tell anyone you are thinking about this—

Tip: I was thinking what you said about the dead, I was trying to balance all the dead coming out of a saying, a word, how words can catch a hold—

Elm: Stop it. Stop it, whatever your reasons. Your reasons are deliberately annoying and I won't have it.

Tip: Elma won't have it; Elma won't have it, listen to you, puking up at the crazy sister, telling her how to behave. How to talk. Really Elm? You don't want me talking. What would you have me do, big sister, normal woman? Electrical charges to the head? Horse pills?
           Get me one of those dogs, those dogs that take care of the mentally marginal? What, Elma, what?

Elm: I am not saying that, Tip.

Tip: Then what are you saying.

Elm: Tillys mother wouldn't do that.

Tip: What?

Elm: Call her Shriek. Mothers don't hear a baby crying
           and think Shriek Shriek, what is that terrible sound?
           They think—

Tip: How do you know this?

Elm: Everybody knows that. Women are...we like babies.

Tip: Do you know Tilly's mother?

Elm: I know women. Where was the father?

Tip: I don't know anything about the father.
           Do you know him?

Elm: I know fathers.

Tip: But not the father of my friend Tilly the Shriek.
           You don't even know Tilly, do you Elm?

Elm: You know I don't.

Tip: Oh, I know you don't. You don't know any of my friends.
           Do you Elm?

Elm: I do, I do. The guy who talks to the squirrels.
           In the made up language.

Tip: It's not made up, it's Chinese.
           My friend is speaking Chinese.

Elm: It sounded made up. He was mumbling and there were
           all these squirrels all around him, it was weird.

Tip: They were squirrels. He was feeding squirrels.
         What would you do, kick them?

Elm: I would, and do not tell me that that would not be right.
         Squirrels are aggressive.

Tip: And I am the weird one?

Elm: Let's get back to the dogs. Andi has been waiting to hear
         about the dogs, what happened—

Andi: I have? I thought I was happy thinking about Tilly the
         Shriek and the Shrieks mother...

Tip: An amazon with a library card and a PhD in forensics,
         a shelf full of Martin Buber—

Andi: Is she good looking? She is good looking. Stunning!

Tip: 6 foot, hair like Rapunzel.

Elm: Please go back to the dogs, I am begging you. My brain
         is collapsing inward. Mercy, Elm. I will remember your
         friends better, I will meet them and try to care about
         them. Just tell us what happened with the fucking dogs
         so we can go home alone and mourn the littered hamster
         cage of life—

Tip   Take it easy here Elm. This going on luridly is not your
         thing. You are to stay solid.

Andi: Boppa always said you are like the last wall of Jericho,
         obstinately standing after the walls come a tumbling
         down—

Elm: Fuck Boppa. Dog story completion or I walk.

Tip: It's not that good a story.

Elm: Oh don't I know it. Tell it .

Tip: I took them out back, the dogs, and we threw a ball
          around. Merdefoot wasn't interested, she stopped
          looking at where the ball was headed...you know how
          they watch with their heads, the whole head staring, she
          wasn't doing that. Pissoir would run around. But that
          is what he always did, 'woof, something is happening,
          woof, run around.' It was a tennis ball. I would throw it so
          it would bounce off the brick of the garage, off the tree...
          Pissoir would lose it after the first bounce, he would run
          yapping and jumping as if the ball was in the air right over
          his head. I'd have to go get it and throw it again.

Elm: Why didn't you just throw it straight?

Tip: What?

Elm: Throw it straight in the grass, so the dog could see it and
          go get it.

Tip: That seemed too easy.

Elm: But you say the dog never got the ball and you had to
          go get it and throw it again...that's harder. It's harder on
          you; it's harder on the dog.

Tip: I thought the dog should learn something, though.

Elm: You didn't even like the dog. What do you care?

Tip: Theoretically, the dog should learn and if I'm the dog's
          caretaker—

Elm: Theoretically, the dog should learn? Listen to yourself... how do you even live, clutter brain?

Andi: Elm, could you please stop being mean to Tip? This is hard on all of us.

Elm: Is it? Why? Because it's stupid thinking from the bottom of a big clutter brain.

Andi: Stop it, Elm.

Elm: She's impossible. Listen to her, big big clutter brain.

Andi: Too mean.

Tip: Maybe I really could just kill you with my brain. Emit such poison—

Andi: Please Tip. Tell the story, tell the story. All of this is making me sad.

Tip: All right. My bag was in the dog room. That's important. The keys were in the inside lock, the door was open.

Elm: The door swings out, into the yard. That's important—that's a crucial detail.

Tip: It is...I threw the ball; it bounced up onto the roof of the garage and Pissoir leapt all over the yard, hoping to catch the ball. He reached the open door, leapt up with both front paws extended. The door slammed shut...

Elm: Keys inside, door locked, dog walker and dog outside...

Tip: That's right. Plus, I had to get to the group...that day we're to discuss the Sermon on the Mount...

Andi: Blessed are the meek for they shall inherit.

Tip: Blessed are the clear of heart...

Elm: Stop that, please...both of you.

Tip: Plus, it was hot and I had been moving around, I felt weak and dizzy.

Andi: Really? Just from moving around? Are you all right, Tip? I mean, every day.

Elm: She doesn't eat protein. Do you drink water? Had you drunk anything that day?

Tip: O, o, water. Look at that, water in a glass. Wow. Water below the toilet seat. Wow, water—

Elm: Water is life, you idiot. I drink a lot of water. Look at my skin, perfect; now look at your own.

Andi: What did you do?

Tip: The gate was locked, but I figured I could climb over the garage...of course the dogs were barking and I thought, "Shut up, shut up, the neighbors..." Maggie Crain lives in a nice neighborhood. And people climbing over the garage...there was a laundry mat on the corner.

Elm: She called me.

Tip: I tried Boppa first. He didn't answer.

Elm: Of course not. Does he ever answer?
        "I want you girls to feel like you can call me
        whenever you need to. I'll never answer but..."

Andi: Do you call in the morning, early?
        That's when he answers.

Elm: This was the morning. Early. Wasn't it Tip?

Tip: He was in his yard, flirting with the gardener.

Elm: Boppa's building has a gardener?
        They don't even cut the grass.

Tip: That woman from next-door...Ronnie.

Elm: A gardener? I thought she was a substitute teacher.

Tip: She gave him that amaryllis in a pot once.
        That's gardening.

Elm: That is not gardening...that's fooling around with things.

Andi: You called Elm.

Tip: I did.

Elm: She did. I came and I helped her.

Tip: Very reluctantly. I practically begged.

Elm: I was doing something and you didn't beg,
        you demanded. "You have to help me, Elm,
        HELP ME right now," and I did.

Tip: You did. You were very sour about it, though.

Elm: Sour? I interrupted my day, my only day off out of like twelve days straight of running the Dreamfast festival, 12 days of answering every stupid question from every stupid performance artist on this fucking planet, and I have to help you with your stupid situation.

Tip: People are supposed to feel like they can ask their sister to help with their stupid situations, Elm.

Andi: This is true, Elm.

Elm: Well, ok sure...I think like that.
But what if that sister is an idiot?
With Tip it is constant. Stupid crisis after stupid crisis.

Tip: I think if you stop using "stupid" and "idiot" when you're talking about me I won't have to fall asleep hating you tonight Elm...I was not being stupid. It was the dog.

Elm: Dogs don't make stupid situations. People—

Andi: All right! All right!
What did you do when you got there Elm?

Elm: Climbed over the garage with my sister to hold the dogs while she tried to open the door...

Tip: The dogs now were very confused and barking and whining and leaping...

Elm: They'd been left alone in the yard. Maggie Crain's dogs are never alone, of course, they're—

Andi: Strange women climbing over the garage and—

Tip: They're just badly trained, Maggie's dogs, always right on the verge of breaking out of control...plus Elm was slow and complaining and...I couldn't concentrate and get the door open...Elm said, "Break the window..."

Elm: I said, "Try the window." "TRY the window."

Tip: There was a log there, old firewood...
it was all chewed on by the dogs and prehistoric looking like an old bone...it looked like something you could swing and crack away with.

Elm: She swings this huge log...

Tip: Like a bone, like swinging a troll bone...

Elm: And she smacks the window with the troll bone.
And I yell, "Tip, don't!"

Tip: You did but by then I wanted it. I felt great,
to get to attack Maggie Crain's big picture window.

Elm: You did.

Tip: Crack, crack that old bone thing against
that smooth glass. Wow.

Elm: She had to hit it like six times—the whack cracks bouncing all over the neighborhood, the dogs in this frenzy and I'm listening for the police, someone's called them by now...

Tip: And then the window breaks. It like, implodes,
the glass so thick and heavy, it doesn't shatter
and fly in all directions.

Elm: It falls in these huge chunks like scales.

Tip: Right. Dinosaur scales dropping slowly, reluctant to move through space. Now there's a big hole.

Elm: But you keep swinging the troll bone.

Tip: I liked it...breaking things...that...

Elm: "Tip, stop it. It's done. That's enough.
          The cops will come."

Tip: What?

Elm: "Just go in the house now, get the keys."

Tip: And I did...I opened the door, the dogs running in,
          desperate to get in, like outside was so awful for a dog.

Elm: Of course it wasn't over. The window was open,
          the house was open, and Maggie Crain was
          coming home on Sunday.

Tip: It was Friday and I had to go to the group.

Elm: I had to do my own...stuff...This wind has started to blow
          in off the lake and I thought 'disaster.' No cops, though.

Tip: No one looks out the back window in Lincoln Park on a holiday. If something is breaking it's breaking far away where no one has to hear it. The dogs sat in the house all day...they didn't know the window was open. It was hot and they panted on the couch while the window was open–

Elm: While Tip and Tilly and Matthew-Mark-Luke and John talked about what Jesus in the New Testament had to say about life, a Jesus that not one of them believed in, Maggie Crain's house was wide open and anybody could have walked away with it. That's our sister Tip.

Tip: I worried about it all day, Andi. I didn't' even enjoy the discussion that night and Tilly does.

Andi: What?

Tip: Believe in Jesus or at least, what he says about things. Love, forgiveness...

Elm: Doesn't the world make you want to fall apart? The way everyone runs around slamming off of each—

Tip: I love Tilly the Shriek, we're friends. And that is a surprise; the Shriek is a difficult person.

Andi: Well, that's good.

Tip: Tilly the Shriek wants love and forgiveness for everyone everywhere. Doesn't that help? People? Us?

Andi: It does, actually.

Tip: I got back to Maggie Crain's and I was relieved that no one had broken in, at least I didn't think they had...the dogs were weird, but they were in the dog room and they are always weird. They are terrible pets, those dogs.

Elm: Well, if you'd stop terrorizing them, breaking things around them.

Andi: What did you do? How did you fix it?

Tip: I called Boppa. He said call the window replacement people, which was a remarkably reasonable suggestion–

Elm: For Boppa. For most people it would have been, "Just go to the gas station, you're out of gas get gas, you break a window go to the hardware store, but our family..."

Tip: Is it self-loathing that leads you to hate our family or...

Elm: I don't hate our family, I—

Andi: You replaced the window. How much did it cost?

Tip: Maggie had paid me for the three days they'd be gone...
          120 dollars, replacing the window cost $280.00. Boppa
          called me. He must have heard.

Elm: I told him...

Tip: You....?

Elm: Yes, I did. I wasn't just going to leave you to figure this
          out. What did you think? That it just occurred to Boppa to
          help you?

Tip: Yes, that is what I thought.

Andi: I have to say, that it often "occurs" to Boppa to help me.

Elm: That's you, that's you.

Tip: I worried about it all day, I didn't even enjoy the
          discussion that night. Doesn't the world make you want
          to fall apart? That's what I kept thinking, it feels like dogs,
          it feels like sisters. Which should be nice or familiar but
          what it feels for real, is like I can't, I can't, which is bad
          enough and then it spins into you can't, you mustn't
          ever, you never should do that, all is forbidden. I mean
          normal things, comfort, natural responsibility, and it's
          not like things are shutting down mentally which is what
          everyone is always saying it is, it is more like opening up
          a brain but in a huge way, a huge way, a waterfall in a
          tunnel on the straining ass back of Atlas, who is more
          giant than giant or—

Elm: What are you talking about? You're not talking about anything you know that, right..

Andi: I have to say that it makes sense to me especially the part about Atlases' ass crack.

Tip: I didn't say that...did I say that?

Andi: I am pretty sure I heard ass crack and I know I didn't say it ...I get very nervous when I hear ass crack usually,
I think what does he want erotically,
do I even know how to do that?

Elm: This is not good, the two of you making sense out of erotic nonsense. Let's come back down on the ground, please. The dogs.

Tip: Like I say I got back to Maggie Crain's...the dogs were weird, but they were in the dog room and they are always weird. Licking...Why do pets lick without being invited? They are terrible pets, those dogs.

Elm: It's you, terrorizing them, stop breaking things around them. Leaving open wide spaces full of backyards and wind, and how did you fix it? You make me fix it, I called Boppa and I told him that if he didn't help you, I would but I didn't think it was fair because Tip has a group and I don't have a group.

Tip: Boppa called me. He said I can give you $100...O.K., $180, and I have seen these window makers. A clan of them floating down Laurence Ave, with these long storefront windows, like a half a block long. These windows were on a dolly, this impossibly long dolly so everything floated and glistened, and the workers were all glowy. Skinny shiny gypsies with gypsy beads and a sign that said, "We'll fix it, and here's the number."

Elm: God. You and Boppa can't even call a normal—

Tip: I called and they came. It was Sunday morning, so,
          early—and they did float. Boppa was right about that.
          And their beards were all blowy and perfumed, I think,
          everybody smelled like flowers. They didn't speak up,
          very soft Spanish voices like leaves, murmuring, and I
          thought Cuban. But Boppa said Tearero Del Fugue.

Elm: But he doesn't know where that is, and he has the
          intuition of a housefly, so that has got to be wrong.

Tip: Plus, they made me think about Cuba, so I'm thinking,
          "Cuba," and this was weird—the dogs bark at everything
          and they didn't, once the flower Cubans were in. One of
          them, the tallest, he was wearing all these vests with
          tools in the pockets...so maybe he was the boss; he
          knelt down and sang to Pissoir and Merdefoot and they
          shuffled up to him. And from then on those dogs were
          quiet, if you had seen them you would have said what
          well behaved dogs are these...I was watching this and
          the other two flower glass men moved past me on cat
          feet—I mean I didn't hear them go by. And it was so early
          and Sunday, we should all be thinking about stained
          glass and mumbling the Hail Mary...I couldn't talk to
          them about the window. We couldn't understand each
          other at all, they had seen broken windows before, they
          knew what to do. The dogs stayed quiet, the tall vest guy
          crooning to them in this tiny little voice. The other two
          rolled the window in and lifted it into place...you could
          tell that they were strong, lifting the window with these
          rippling backs and arms, and I'm sitting watching them,
          very peaceful, like I'm on mushrooms or a ten day fast
          or something. And they—the flower glass guys—are
          posing in the rising sun and it was rising, I mean really
          rising, glorious, and then they were done and gone. The
          room felt empty, like all the aura that had ever stumbled

or accidently floated into Maggie's place had just floated out, with these flower Cubans. The dogs stayed quiet for hours, and then they slept...their tails flipping and paws running after a dream squirrel. I packed up, left before Maggie Crain got home. I don't think I could see her without telling her the story. And now I didn't have any work and I owe Boppa $100, well 180, so the whole thing was a disaster except for the flower glass people, who were like angels, which I had never seen before. And I think I always wanted to. Angels...

Andi: I used to see them all the time, when I was a kid. On a tree—oh look at that, and angel, on a cloud, my fluffy angel. The sky was all these fluttery blob shapes...but now it's like sludge. Smudging everything—coal dust between your eyes and heaven...it's very sad to lose the light like that...

Boppa told me once, when I was a little kid and everybody felt crazy, that he, Boppa, sees the angels.

Elm: Oh, I'm sure he does. But is that a good thing?

Tip: Boppa sees everything. You can see it in him—his eyes go all global. That must be something for him.

Elm: Nearsighted. And cataracts that glimmer, they are so thick. The man can't see a breath in front of him and he remains too vain to wear glasses.

Andi: You think so Elma? I don't think that is it. Boppa has magical eyes. Your eyes are like his, Elma. Magical eyes.

Elma: I look nothing like Boppa.

           Door swings open.

Tender: Oops! Did you see that Fred? That door flew open, I barely touched it no pressure at all, no physical aggression, which is good, because I don't like physical aggression. That door flew open, what hinge work. What a balance of materials went into the building of this door Fred!

            I am going to do that again, what do you think Fred?

Fred: Please do so, Mr. Tenderberry.

Tender: *(Goes out and opens door again.)* Oops!

Fred: Wonderful.

Tender: It is, isn't it? You didn't build this door misses?

Fred: Decorum, Mr. Tenderberry

Tender: Right you are Fred. I am sorry, misses, no intention of being rude, good morning to you and yours. It is just what a, wow—that hinge work. You didn't build it, did you? How long have you lived here?

Tip: *(Guessing.)* 3 weeks?

Tender: 3 weeks. It would be next to impossible to build something that perfect in three weeks. The hinge work alone. Would it Fred, be possible...?

Fred: Well the hinge work alone.

Tender: Exactly. The hinge work alone.

Elma: LOOK! GET THE FUCK OUT!

Tender: I am sorry, misses? What?

Andi: What she means, sirs...men people...this is a private residence.

Tip: We live here and Andi has a pistol!

Elma: Don't say that.

Tender: Do you have a pistol, misses?

Andi: No, my sister just gets excited...about everything.

Tender: Do you live here, misses?
          You the one that owns this marvelous door?

Andi: I don't, no. I don't own anything. Ever.

          They all look at her awkward.

          Its not a belief system. I just...don't...
          I'm a failure, I guess.

Elma: No you are not and that is remarkable, considering your parentage. LOOK! You two boys, get the fuck out, still.

Fred: Well we are police officers, maam. If that helps.

          Awkward pause.

Tender: I don't think that does help, Fred.
          Yes, we are cops, misses.

Elma: God, this is not good.

Fred: Its not all we do.

Tender: Curry. Fred makes a nice curry.

Fred: Table tennis.

Tender: We are both pretty good at that. Fred has a steady serve.

Fred: Mr. Tenderberry has got a slashing left hand.

Tender: Book club, every Sunday.

Fred: Mr. Tenderberry attends it; I get to hear all about it.

Tender: Every Monday morning in the squad car.

Fred: A full report. Very satisfying, it feels like I read the whole
            book myself.

Tender: We are on Alcott now, Louisa May.

Fred: Mr. Tenderberry is not sure why.

Tender: No one is sure why, I mean the whole book club.

Fred: Lets see, what else? We both date women.
            Infrequently, because of the job.

Tender: But it is always satisfying, mutually.
            To every one in the date, I mean.

Fred: And the marathon. We are considering that this year.

Tender: Running in it.

Fred: That's right, running. Not just security or something.
            We are people, is the point.

Tender: I am sure there is more.

Fred: There always is. More. More. But people. We are people.

Awkward.

Andi: Would you like something, water, tea...water?

Tender: I thought you said you weren't living here, misses.
And didn't have a gun, hiding under the teapot,
in the cupboard, say?

Elma: She doesn't and it is not.

Andi: No. I just thought Water! Tea! Everybody has that;
everybody would want you to be welcoming with that.

Tender: I am addressing the whole room now.
(Getting out notebook.) Who lives here?

Tip: Justin and Martha Agerich and they are in Tulsa.

Tender: Are you squatting, misses? Does anyone still squat, Fred?

Fred: In Europe. Berlin. Amsterdam.

Tender: So, not squatting.

Tip: I am plant sitting.

Tender: Plant sitting.

Tip: Living here while watering the plants.

Tender: *(Looking.)* Where are the plants?

Tip: On the back porch. I moved them on the back porch, that way I don't have to water them.

Tender: But watering the plants is your purpose for living here, that is what you said. Isn't it Fred, what she said?

Fred: Indeed.

Andi: Rain! Rain! It is wonderful for plants. Open up, you leaves. The waters are dropping from the heavens, moving thru the clouds filled with the wonder of cloud essence, kissing off the tree tops, rubbing up on oak and acorn, bark and knot hole, before dropping straight down on the Justin and Martha Agerich houseplants that my sister in all her excellence has placed on the back porch.

Tender: Cloud essence! That really sounds like something, cloud essence; don't you think so, Fred?

Fred: I do, wonderful.

Andi: Would you like to see the cloud essence, sirs...men people. I could take you up on the roof. It is a high roof–

Elma: Andi! Stop talking to these policemen. You people, we haven't done anything, none of us have. My sisters might be weird, but they are fragile–

Tip: I am not fragile, Elma. And only weird depending on where I am. In some places I would make Abraham Lincoln look like an alchemist. Andi, are you fragile?

Andi: No no I am not that, I am emotional...about everything. I see beautiful things and I think Beautiful! Beautiful! So beautiful, sometimes that is overwhelming. I am overwhelmed by beauty, I guess.

Tender: I feel that way, too. Beauty, Beauty overwhelmed...
what about you Fred?

Fred: I don't feel that way, Mr. Tenderberry.
I remain even keeled when it comes to beauty.
But I do feel sympathy for yours and the...client's feelings.

Tender: Thank you, Fred.

Tip: I see mud on mud on mud.

Elma: Stop talking all of you. Cops. What is the problem?
Why are you here?

Tender: Right then. Down to it. Which one of you is Tip?

Tip: -I-

Elma: What did she do and why do you want to know?

Tender: There's been a complaint from a Maggie Crain.
Destruction of property. Vandalism. Broken glass.
Could be an arresting matter.

Fred: They take that seriously, we take that seriously.

Tip: -I-

Elma: I am Tip McGinty and my sisters have nothing to do
with anything I ever do.

Tip: -I-

Elma: Stop talking sister and allow me the dignity of
my own misfortune.

Phone rings.

Tender: *(To the phone.)* What's the story?

Andi: How about that tea, people?

Fred: I only drink the coffee, maam.

Andi: They don't have...we could go out...I will go out,
          Starbucks or...

Fred: Well that is kind of you, maam, but you're not
          responsible for my caffeine intake.

Elma: Jesus Andi. You don't have to be nice to him.
          He is here to arrest your sister.

Andi: I am sure he doesn't want to, though. Do you want to, sir?

Fred: Sometimes I wish I could just walk away.

Andi: Lets try, let's, lets go now. Theres a nice coffee shop
          somewhere, a wonderful coffee shop.
          We can walk together.

Elma: Andi.

Tender: All right then misses. Leslie McGinty is your dad.

Andi: Boppa?

Tip: No one ever calls him that, Leslie.

Elma: It's Boppa this and Boppa that.

Tender: Well Mr. McGinty is down at the station right now.
          He is cleaning this up, your father. Says he saw the whole

thing—four young men with beards, he says "Looked just like the Halls Brothers cough drops box"...only they were carrying big Bibles, walking thru Lincoln Park backyards, proselytizing, your dad thought it was weird but he recognized them as your friends, Tip McGinty. Mathew Mark Luke and John. One of them flew into a Holy Rage, Mr. McGinty says and threw his Bible right thru this big window, shattering the glass. We get a lot of that these days. Holy Rage in Lincoln Park. Something weird there, eh, Fred?

Fred: Money without substance as a way of living
           is how I see it.

Tender: That does make sense doesn't it Fred?
           Mr. McGinty says you didn't want your friends in trouble; Tip McGinty...Thought you could clean it up yourself? That about the size of it, misses?

Tip: -I-

Elma: That sounds like me, officer.

Tender: Our work is done here, Fred.

Fred: I hate to see us go, Mr. Tenderberry.

Tender: I know you do, Fred, but somebody has got to catch up to that Mathew Mark Luke and John. You wouldn't have any last names for the afore mentioned would you, misses?

Elma: Faith, hope, charity and...

Tip: ...earnestness?

Tender: Your guessing, that's a guess.

Tip: That's true, and not even a likely one.
Ethicality...is that more possible?

Elma: No and its not a word either, clutter brain...
if you're going to fabricate something make it—

Andi: *(Who has been staring at Fred.)* Can I give you my number,
Fred? You could call me.

Fred: Well that is some idea, maam. Please do.

Andi: Do you have a pencil or a phone?

Fred: *(Pointing at his ear.)* Just tell it to me here. I'll remember.

Fred: Thank you, maam.

Elma: Andi, are you all right ?

MEREDITH LYONS as Andi in *ONE BOPPA, in two acts* >>

– ACT TWO –

Scene Three:
On the street. Elma on the phone. Tip is on the street too.

Elma: You didn't do what you said you were gonna do, Steve, I'm pretty sure of that.

Steve: *(Off stage, on phone.)* But! But!

Elma: But?? But what? You did or you didn't.

Steve: I am doing it now. I'm really trying to do it right now.

Elma: No. No. And if this is what you people call good orderly direction, then your god needs to develop some grit. Lame—

Tip: Excuse me. Excuse me. Miss or Missus or whatever shouting mass of mouth you are. You are talking too loudly. If you have to shout into your phone and we are standing here to then WE ARE HEARING YOU SHOUT and you don't have to be brilliant to—

Elma: Steve! Steve! I have to go. Someone is being annoyed— No! *(Off phone.)* I'm sorry. Is there a problem? Wait. Tip?

Tip: Elma?

Tip & Elma: Was that you shouting?

Elma: What are you doing, shouting like that?
          I didn't even recognize you—

Tip: I didn't recognize you. I thought, Loud! Selfish person!
          On the phone! No way am I related to her.

Elma: So you yell like an insane person—

Tip: Well I objected. If I had known it was you
          I wouldn't have—

Elma: That doesn't help me. My sister is yelling at people in a
          public place.

Tip: You were being loud though. Come on, Elm.
          You know loud.

Elma: His phone doesn't work. His phone never works.
          So I have to shout just so he...hears me. I don't even—

Tip: Chris?

Elma: Steve, my boyfriend's name is Steve, Tip.

Tip: Wasn't there a Chris though?

Elma: Two years ago for like five minutes.

Tip: That long ago? Was that before "Snuffling Rupert"
          and the cab driver from Canada?

Elma: Wales. He was from Wales. I'd never date a Canadian.
          They're so lackluster. "Snuffling Rupert" *(both laughing)*.

Tip: "Snuffling Rupert the human puberty machine."

Elma: God, that's what Boppa called him: "Snuffling Rupert."
What was I thinking?

Tip: That teenagers really know how to love
middle aged people?

Elma: He was like 24, Tip.

Tip: I bet he remembered all that teenage stuff like it was
this morning though. Did he have a nice—

Elma: Don't be mean, Tip.

Tip: Was I being? I think I'm just trying to keep track.

Elma: Mean! Mean! Mean!

Tip: Let's see, my sister loves mullet heads on skateboards
who skate all night for a bong and a yogurt shake. No,
no, my sister loves weight-lifting accountants who fly
their own baby planes down to Cancun for the weekend.
No , no, my sister loves skinny little rat guys with a poker
habit and an amphetamine—

Elma: You like Steve.

Tip: Do I?

Elma: You do. You said you do.

Tip: I do, I do. He has all those books. Piles and piles.
He's a book collector.

Elma: What are you talking about?

Tip: You took us to his room. Me and Boppa. It was full of books. And I thought, this is all Rimbaud by the window ledge and William Carlos Williams in the spider plants. And who's that? Allen Ginsberg crawling into my lap? And I said to Boppa, Bop! This guy's got a lot of poetry. A poet fellow with Elma! Now that's a surprise. I wonder if she knew before the sparks started to fly. And Boppa said—

Elma: Steve doesn't read poetry and I don't wanna know what Boppa said.

Tip: No? Then why—

Elma: It was Borders. You met us at a Borders.

Tip: God that's good. I like Borders. You can read and wander around. Steve has a moustache.

Elma: Yes he does.

Tip: All the men you go out with have moustaches.

Elma: That's probably true. I like a nice moustache.

Tip: Is it the kiss? The way it brushes your lip?

Elma: Yes, the moustache kiss. I do like that.

Tip: What about in other places? The way it brushes your belly? The way it sweeps your thighs—

Elma: I really don't want to talk about how something sweeps my thighs, Tip.

Tip: No?

Elma: No. That's inappropriate. An inappropriate conversation.

Tip: Really? I thought it would be nice to think about.

Elma: Stop talking to me about this, please.

Tip: All right.

Elma: Clutterbrain.

Tip: Sure, but why is that a bad thing again?

Elma: Have you looked at the world, Tip?

Tip: Yes, yes I have.

> *Door opens. Mr. Munch sees them and slams it shut.*
> *[I don't think we have to see Mr. Munch.]*

Tip: Rude?

Elma: I don't think so. He doesn't like to open until Andi's here.

Tip: Andi takes care of the people.

Elma: She does.

Tip: Andi is coming? I could use a little taking care of—

Elma: She is. She's late.

Tip & Elma: She's always late.

Tip: It's ok though.

Elma: No it isn't. She knows we need to talk.
Is something wrong with Boppa?

Tip: Do you think so?

Elma: I'm sure I don't know.

Tip: Have you seen him? Boppa?

Elma: On the e-mail.

Tip: How did he look to you?

Elma: Like he's on the e-mail and being reproduced digitally.

Tip: What?

Elma: I can't tell what he—

Tip: He wants to go camping with all of us.

Elma: What? He can't even walk.

Tip: He can walk.

Elma: Not really, he shuffles.

Tip: That's walking. I'll go, I'm going.

Elma: Boppa can't hike.

Tip: He wants to go hiking now?

Elma: You have to hike if you want to camp.

Tip: You can drive. There's driving camping. Load up the red rusty Ford and park with that fleet of SUV's. Why not?

Elma: That sounds hideous Tip.

Tip: We can help him hike. I'm going to go.

Elma: I'm not helping him hike.

Tip: You like Boppa.

Elma: Sometimes.

Tip: You love him.

Elma: Not enough to hike with him stumbling all over the place I don't.

Tip: You're mad at Bop?

Elma: Only when I am. Tip, if you act weird and scream at people, no one will listen to you about anything.

Tip: What are we talking about now?

Elma: Your conduct earlier, shouting at me while I was on the phone. Do you do that all the time?

Tip: Not all the time. Sometimes I just walk on by and think, terrible human conduct. How can anything good come out of that?

Elma: People think you're crazy if you do that all the time.

Tip: Let's see. Do I care at all? No I do not. I was trying to get your attention. Sometimes I have to be loud.

Elma: You didn't know it was me. What if I had just turned around and punched you in the face?

Tip: I wouldn't like that but I knew you were a woman. Woman's figure, woman's voice.

Elma: So?

Tip: Women don't usually hit each other.

Elma: You count on that? You say, I'm gonna bug this woman because I know she won't hit—

Tip: It's not calculated like that. I'm not calculated.

Elma: I will tell you this. Sometimes I am so annoyed with you that I would like to hit you.

Tip: But, but, like to isn't doing it.

Elma: You're wearing a black eye patch.

Tip: It's green, actually. Blackish green. I think the green softens the fierce. It's still fierce, but soft fierce.

Elma: A bus driver punches you in the eye and scratches your cornea and you think this is how people live, Tip?

Tip: He punched me in the back of the head, actually. I scratched my eye on the broken bottle on the sidewalk when I flew off the bus after the punch.

Elma: That was a man punching you after you behaved badly. A man hitting a woman. You said—

Tip: Because I told him he was a jackass whose soul was damned to the fiery pits of Hades where a two-headed dog reamed him eternally after he snarled at Boppa for getting on the bus slowly. Boppa has a new hip.

Elma: Boppa probably spit on him or—

Tip: He didn't. The saliva just flies when Boppa talks. He gets excited. Come on, Elm, you would have objected.

Elma: You look weird with that eye patch.

Tip: (In a pirate voice.) Up your Davy Jones,
         you scum-sucking dogs!

Elma: You're my sister and I know why you are so weird.
         I have compassion for how fucked up and crazy you are,
         but if I didn't—

Tip: You hit me, that one time in the attic
         when I ruined your blue blouse.

Elma: I never did that.

Tip: You did. You hit hard too. I mean hard. I think you knocked me out. I know my conscious brain left my body and when I came back I thought Man, my sister can really hit. How can she? She's like a pile of twigs.

Elma: Tip that wasn't me.

Tip: What? It was too. You loved that blue blouse and I was like 12 and spilling everything. You said it was grape juice but it wasn't. It was purple wax from Wendy's purple wax candle. But it was purple, which was bad enough because I always have a terrible time with purple.

Elma: Tip, it wasn't me. I didn't even meet you until you were 15. Clutterbrain.

Tip: No it was. My sister hit—

Elma: It wasn't me. It must have been Andi.

> *Mr. Munch opens the door.*
> *Glares out and slams the door.*
> *[I don't think we have to see Mr. Munch.]*

Tip: Andi's really late.

Elma: You think?

Tip: You think she's too late for Mr. Munch?

Elma: Andi's hard to fire. Was it Andi?

Tip: Andi? She would never hit me.
Now she's like a sucking-on-a-soft-straw-summer girl but when she was a little kid—

Elma: *(Annoyed.)* Cake, I know.

Tip: Right. She was cake.
Plus she didn't live with us until I was 17.

Andi: *(Entering.)* 14, you were 14. And I never lived there, Tip, I just stayed over!

Tip: That was great though. We put up that tent under Wendy's piano—

Andi: That WAS great! Hi you guys! I'm late, I'm late! Woof woof couldn't find his shoes. And he wants to walk, he's insistent about it and Charlie thought it was a school day but it's not a school day. Charlie gets upset without school. Elma, you look so beautiful, look at you!

Elma: *(Pleased.)* You think so? I have been working on my skin.

Andi: You're glowing. Isn't she glowing, Tip? Skin like a sunrise.

Tip: I thought that was a glower, actually, not a glow.

Andi: A glower? NO, Elma's gorgeous!

Tip: And, did you hit me over that blue blouse?

Andi: When you were 12? I hadn't met you yet.
No that was Wendy. Tip. I have to go in.

Elma: Your boss came out twice.

Andi: Really? Mr. Munch can't open without—

Tip: My mother knocked me out over a blouse? I hate to think that, she was a very nice woman.

Andi: That was the year she was mad, though. You told me.

Tip: I told you that?

Elma: Are you keeping track of this at all, Tip?
You didn't know us until we were teenagers.

Tip: Kids shouldn't get knocked out by their mothers, though. That's probably traumatic. Is it, And?

Andi: I'm sure that's true but could we talk about it inside?

Tip: It's really cold.

Andi: And I'm really late so in we go!

Elma: Will Boppa find us?

Tip, Elma, Andi: He'll find us.

> *They go in.*

Andi: Hello Mr. Munch. We can open now.

Elma: Is he mad?

Andi: No, Mr. Munch doesn't get mad like that.

Tip: No storming around? No smacking the wok with the frying pan? No spitting in the French fryer?

Andi: Mr. Munch hates the customers. The customers give him the willies, he says, and the longer I'm not here, the more he's gonna have to talk to the customers and the more Mr.Munch worries about how horrible that is going to be, the less he can concentrate on cooking. Mr. Munch likes to cook, that's his job really. And Mr. Munch likes to cook on time, which means things go in...and then they come out. 10 o'clock, pot roast with the oven-brown potatoes goes in. 10:30, the three berry pie goes in. 11 o'clock, the kimchee and spiced-beef special goes in. 11:15, the split pea soup which Mr. Munch cooked yesterday goes in, now the rice in a pot, now the corn, now the succotash. 11:30. Out come the pies. 11:45, out comes—

Elma: I think I get it, Andi.

Tip: I think I'd like to eat it, Andi.

Andi: *[Through the door, I don't think we see Mr. Munch.]*
Mr. Munch, could you please come out of the mop closet
so I can use the mop? Mmm! Mmm! It smells so good, I
don't think anything is over done, just baking away. I am
fine, Mr. Munch, you are kind to ask. Charlie was eating
your rice pudding from yesterday. He didn't want to
stop so I waited with him. That boy loves your food Mr.
Munch, you know he does...They are great customers!
They are patient and we are lucky to have them! *(to the
sisters)* He doesn't know you're my sisters, he thinks you
love his food, wink-wink. Tip?

Tip: Oh that succotash! I've been craving it all week!
Succotash!

Andi: Elma?

Elma: What?

Andi: Elm!

Elma: Do you think he'll write that three berry pie recipe down
for me waitress? I envy his crust so!

Andi: I don't think he will, no. That's a secret recipe, that crust.
But you can come here every day and have some fresh
pie! *(Whispering.)* Thanks, Mr. Munch is moving towards
the stove. Do you guys want the kimchee beef special?
Mr. Munch likes to serve it fresh and hot.

Elma: Vegetarian.

Tip: Garlic bread. And rice pudding. Rice pudding.

Elma: Tip, when was the last time you ate?

Tip: I don't like to eat in the morning.

Elma: Yesterday? You ate yesterday?

Tip: Muffins, lemon wedges.

Elma: It's up to you if you insist on being poor, but—

Tip: "Oh, those impossible poor! Insisting on starving while the rest of us have to do the right thing and never miss a meal!"

Elma: When you do eat you should at least eat protein.

Tip: I like lemon wedges. Where are we sitting?

Andi: Sit by the door so Boppa will see you.

Tip: I don't want the booth.

Elma: Sit at the table.

Tip: The table is in the corner.

Elma: Where we can see out and Boppa can see in.

Tip: He'll find us. Don't you think Boppa will find us?

Elma: I do, but Andi asked—

Tip: I can't sit there. Boppa will find us, there's no one else here. I'm moving.

Andi: The place fills up at lunch time.

Tip: It's noon-thirty.

Andi: They'll be coming in hungry. Here's the succotash.

Tip: Succotash? Yuck.

Andi: Here's the split pea soup. But Elm, there's ham—

Elma: I can't eat that.

Tip: I'll eat that.

Elma: We should split something. A green salad with
          oil and vinegar. Can you ask Mr. Munch to
          add bean sprouts and tofu?

Tip: I'll have the garlic bread and lemon wedges.

Elma: We're not sharing that. Green Tea.

Tip: Sarsaparilla.

Elma: They don't have sarsaparilla.

Andi: Here's your Sarsaparilla, Tip.

Elma: Do you have any money, Tip?

Tip: No. I don't. And I don't have a job or a husband or a future
          but it's so nice of you to ask, Elma.

Andi: I have money. Here's some bleu cheese.

Elma: You don't, though. Charlie and Woof—

Andi: Are happy children. Here's the salad, Elm. And the oven-
          roasted potatoes and the pot roast.

Elma: You can't pay for this. Tip, Andi can't pay for all of this.

Andi: Do you think the lunch rush is coming?

They all stare at the empty room.

Elma: It's very empty, And.

Tip: There's an echo.

Andi: Well I can sit until it fills up! That's nice! Mr. Munch, they ARE good customers! Very good tippers! *(Whispering.)* He thinks you're very good tippers and that's why I need to sit and talk with you, wink wink.

Elma: We're not, though.
          Last time I don't think we even left anything—

Tip: I don't have any money. I couldn't even take the bus. Plus I hate the bus driver—

Andi: *(Slipping Tip a ten.)* Here, just leave this on the table.

Tip: Ten dollars? That is quite a tip.

Elma: Andi's worth it, Tip. Come on.

Andi: Mr. Munch will be impressed. A tip like that, it'll give him hope. Mr. Munch doesn't want to think this is a crummy little diner where no one likes to come.

Elma: Andi, I feel bad. I would tip, except Tip never has any money and Boppa forgets to pay.

Andi: That's ok, Elm, who cares? You don't think it's awful here, do you? The food's good.

Elma: It's great, if you like fat on sugar.

Andi: That succotash is healthy.

Tip: Did we ever get the lemon wedges?

Andi: I'll get some more.

Tip: This room is purple. The walls are purple.

Andi: There's a lot of red in it, though.
          It's violet, actually, Tip, violet.

Tip: Why would Boppa have us meet him in a purple room?
          There must be something wrong.

Elma: I'm sure he didn't think about it, Tip.
          This is just where Andi works.

Andi: Tip, do you have your sunglasses?

Tip: What? *(Beginning to panic.)* I'm going to, I'm going to.

Andi: No, you don't need to do that, wear mine.

Tip: Really panicking. I have to get out of—

Andi: Mine are yellow, Tip.

Elma: Put them on, Tip. God, I'll do it. *(She does.)*

Tip: Yellow.

Andi: That's right, yellow.

Tip: Yellow is a love color. Everything so yellow.

Andi: That's right, yellow everything.

Elma: You're getting weirder, Tip. I have to say that. Weirder.

Andi: She's fine, Elm. Don't be mean to her.

ELMA's phone rings. It is Steve.

Steve: Elma, can we talk now?

Elma: I'm sorry Steve, did you need something?

Steve: You didn't call me back.

Elma: I am with my sisters now.

Steve: I'm sure they won't mind. Hey you guys, do you—

Elma: They can't hear you, Steve.

Tip: Yes we can.

Steve: I think there's a lot more to say.

Elma: I'm sure you do, Steve. But the thing that you seem to always forget is that you say things, make things that you pretend to be promises and you don't keep them.

Steve: I cleaned the house!

Elma: That conversation was in May, though and this is February.

Steve: But the house is clean.

Elma: Bye, Steve. *(Hangs up.)*

Andi: Are you all right, Elma?

Elma: I am.

          Pause.

Andi: Is everything as sad as it seems to be?

          Pause.

Tip: Men and women are, as far as I can tell. Maybe I shouldn't
          say that. Is anyone in love?

Andi: NO, you're right, Tip. They are sad together and—

Tip: Apart. And children are just a set-up
          for more men and women.

Andi: That's awful. Isn't that awful, Tip?

Tip: Which just leaves the pets—animals in name only.
          Their savage natural selves blunted by overeating
          and Nembutal.

Andi: *(Really sad, ready to cry.)* Oh god.

Tip: And the old people, thank god they're headed toward
          neuter.

Andi: *(Crying.)* I can't live like this.

Elma: All right, all right, Tip, stop it.

Tip: What?

Elma: You know. And is sensitive, even if we're not.

Tip: I'm sensitive, god!

Elma: I'm not, thank god. *(Pause.)*

Andi: Charlie sent you guys messages.

Tip: Oh good!

Elma: I was wondering.

Andi: We wrote them down together. Charlie thought it was very important that we write it down together.

Elma: Smart boy.

Tip: Read it, read it!

Andi: "Tell Elma that Charlie says I haaaave you, Elma, I really haaaave you."

Elma: I haaaave you too, Charlie. I really haaaave you. I do.

Tip: And? And? Let's hear mine right now!

Andi: "You are the best one of all the, of all the, of all the bad people. Tip."

Tip: Yes. I finally have someone who recognizes me for the person I am.

Elma: It's not surprising that you have such great children, Andi. You're...but that Charlie finds Tip entertaining.

Tip: Now what did Woof Woof say?

Andi: "Aaaahgaaaa"

Elma: Good use of the vowels.

Tip: Oh suffering humanity, hear the howl of human anguish without filter.

Andi: I'm surprised Boppa is still coming. He has such a cold. *(Does Boppa's voice.)* A real hanky-shredder.

Elma: Boppa has a cold?

Andi: Bronchitis, actually. *(Doing Boppa's voice.)* "Coughs that are so deep in the lungs that my whole trunk flies up and down, the muscles all beating up on each other. Man, the body." He didn't look good.

Tip: All wincey, right? He's often wincey and achy at this time of...Boppa should live in the desert.

Andi: Right, or on a cliff. Like a dry cliff. A Navajo cliff.

Elma: Wait now. How do you know he's sick?

Andi: He looks sick. Green.

Tip: More white.

Andi: White and green. Fish faced, like, gills.

Tip: Yeah. With Boppa you can always tell.
          There's two Boppas.

Andi: Boppa sick.

Tip: And Boppa well.

Elma: Wait, you both saw Boppa? Yesterday?

Tip: The day before for me. Boppa was sweet.
He made chocolate cake.

Andi: Oh Boppa's always sweet to me. I can't eat the sweets though. He just pours on the sugar.

Tip: I like cake.

Andi: *(Looking at the door.)* Hello! Please do use the bathroom before reading the menu! I don't think he's going to stay, Mr. Munch. Mr. Green Overcoat only ever wants the curry...Wink-wink...Thank you for stopping by, sir!
Red curry on Tuesday!

Elma: Does he ever buy anything?

Andi: Coffee. When I give him a dollar...It is encouraging, Mr. Munch, activity equals achievement.

Elma: I haven't seen him for months.

Tip: Did you call him? You should call him, Elm.

Elma: He should call me.

Tip: He doesn't think like that.

Elma: He should, he's the parent.

Andi: He's 65.

Elma: Which means what? He's not responsible?

Andi: He has his ways.

Tip: Which means you could be nicer to Boppa. At least adult. Ask about his life.

Elma: His life? What? His dates? How did it go with the waitress from the coffee shop, Pop? Did you surf the net together whilst stroking each other's thighs carefully so as not to strain a muscle and have to go to the acupuncturist? How am I supposed to ask my father about his dates?

Andi: The waitress.

Tip: 38!

Andi: She looks young, though.

Tip: Baby face.

Elma: Of course our father dates inappropriately.

Andi: I think she loved him.

Tip: Well she liked him.

Elma: You have to admit, inappropriately.

Andi: I don't know that. Boppa is private. He's discreet.

Tip: *(Doing Boppa voice.)* "Great truths are told in bed."

Elma: Yuck! What is private about that?
          And why do you even know he says that?

Andi: I think he's just unlucky in love. He's very interested in women. And he's careful, he's not aggressive.

Tip: Well there was that time with his landlord's cousin.
          Tender Terry in the laundry room.
          They'd just met at like 11 and—

Andi: He'd just had that hip operation.

Elma: Replacement. It was a hip replacement.

Andi: Well the hip, he couldn't move around much and—

Elma: So they did it on the dryer on a pile of sheets, in a public place, in the middle of the afternoon.

Tip: Tender Terry said it was good there, warm. And the dryer moved around. *(Shows with her hands.)* And the laundry room was in their building. It's not exactly public.

Elma: Why did Tender Terry tell you anything about this, Tip?

Tip: Boppa was worried about her, I think, after. And he told me about it and I made a point to meet her.

Elma: Why was he worried?

Andi: Hadn't he just got his ashes hauled?
           That's when I'm the least worried.

Elma: His ashes hauled? Who says that?

Elma, Tip, Andi: Boppa.

Elma: More yuck, why was he worried?

Tip: He thought maybe it all happened too fast and Tender Terry was not all right, sexually.

Elma: So he fucked her and then worried...
           Why didn't he just walk away?

Andi: That would be rude, don't you think? If she was needy?

Tip: That's what Boppa thought. Someone offers themselves to you, *(Doing Boppa voice.)* "There's a fire in the engine room, you gotta throw on the coals."

Elma: I hate that, I hate it. Our father—

Andi: It is uncomfortable, Elm, to know stuff about your parent, but I don't know what else Boppa should have done.

Tip: Plus he was moving very slowly, so there was a lot of eye contact, and you know how we are about eye contact. We can't resist it.

Elma: We're gonna stop talking about this now.

Andi: Yeah, Tender Terry. Was she all right, psychologically?

Elma: *(She means it.)* Stop it. Stop it, stop it.

Andi: It's better to talk about things, Elma.
If you push everything back in—

Tip: You just back up bile—

Andi: And you know how we are with bile. There's nothing worse than a world of pus. Is the world just pus, Tip?

Tip: Did Woof Woof find his shoes, And?

Andi: Oh, no. He didn't, but he's still a baby. He found some bowls and he put his feet in the bowls. And I think he thought, Clomp clomp. Woof woof.

Elma: You keep bowls on the floor.

Andi: Well Charlie likes bowls. They're cool and nice shapes. And everything Charlie likes—

Tip, Elm, Andi: Woof Woof.

Andi: Right, like that. Boy babies are really great.
They're fearless. They'll play with everything.
Were we talking about Boppa?

Tip: Always.

Andi: *(Looking at the door.)* Hello! No I don't think we need the incense or the flowers today! You'd like some water? Help yourself! The bathroom is always open! No, Mr. Munch, I don't think they are going to stay, they're only interested in the...wink-wink...sauerbraten and the sauerkraut and you know that's only on Mondays.
But there certainly were a lot of them, weren't there? And I'm sure they'll come back.

Tip: Who were those people, Andi? That was a lot of purple.

Andi: No, no. I think it was orange. The rajanishas.

Tip: Come on, that wasn't orange, that was purple.

Andi: No, no. It's the yellow sunglasses and neon lights.
It makes orange look funny.

Tip: Purple isn't funny, it's disturbing.

Andi: Maggie Crain was Boppa's age.

Tip: Maggie Crane. Her yard was full of lilacs.
Lilacs groaning with purple. I hated going there.

Elma: Well she was 50.

Andi: That feels the same.

Elma: But it's not. It's not at all. I hope when I'm fifty, people don't say, oh she's about 65.

Andi: Maggie Crane had all those things.

Tip: Houses, cars, Republican leanings.

Andi: I thought this would be nice for Boppa. She can take him to the health club. And Boppa can swim in a nice pool instead of walking in a puddle.

Elma: He screwed it up though, didn't he? Tore the sail on the sail boat or scratched the Ferrari?

Andi: Boppa said it was very hard to stay at Maggie's house. The wealthy things, all that lovely wood, and brilliant electronics made him want to break things up, load the e-mail with spam, and sleep in the yard. *(Doing Boppa.)* "Me, I was born in a pool hall, you can't live a lie, Andi, even if that lie has got you fat and sassy and living in the lap of luxury."

Tip: Maggie does have quite a lap.

Andi: Maggie Crain told me that she liked Boppa but that dating Boppa was like dancing with an anarchist.

Elma: Which is called bad. Bad dancing.

Tip: Boppa's not, though, an anarchist.
          He's more, do whatever you want.

Elma: What? What do you think anarchy is, Tip? Do you even—

Tip: An agreed-upon non-hierarchical system arrived at from a conscious world view.

Elma: Well it's not, it's chaos, it's crap. Boppa hates me.

Andi: Boppa doesn't hate you.

Tip: Boppa doesn't hate.

Elma: Oh he does. He does. When I was 15, he said, I'm not sure
          I know who you are. Who says that to a young teenager?

Tip: Everybody? Or they should.

Andi: I wasn't there, Elma, but maybe he was being honest—

Elma: That is a terrible time to be honest with a child...When he
          came to visit, when he stayed in that hotel for a week,
          all we did was walk around the malls from one
          bookstore to another.

Andi: Boppa likes to walk. We always walked,
          only it was the park. Boppa had a dog.

Tip: Wilbur. Wilbur Romping Bottoms.

Andi: You knew Wilbur?

Tip: This was before we met. Boppa said Wilbur was his
          neighbor's, Mrs. Murky's.

Andi: That was me, Mrs. Murky. Boppa called me Mrs. Murky.
          Wilbur Romping Bottoms was my dog.

Elma: Everything about this man is terrible.

Andi: No, no. He was nice to be with when I was a kid.
          We would read. Boppa would see a fly and say,
          Look, Missus, the angels are—

Elma: No no no!

Tip: What is wrong with you, Elma?

Elma: This is MY time to remember. I was remembering my father, and it wasn't all nice. Flies that are angels and princesses.

Andi: Well there weren't any princesses, there were more like vaudevillian-trained bats.

Elma: My turn.

Andi: All right, all right, Elm. Where are you, walking the malls.

Tip: Walking the malls, bookstore to bookstore.

Andi: All day. That doesn't sound awful.

Elma: Well it was awful.

Tip: Did you talk, you and Boppa?

Elma: Boppa did. All day. About Shakespeare's sonnets, why they're the most romantic. And palindromes, the ultimate evidence of the great god on a roll. And how to win a spelling bee, even when you can't spell. And fly fishing from a boat with your grandparents when you'd rather be playing four square.

Tip: Those are the things Boppa talks about.

Elma: They are awful. Clutterbrain. Of course, I'd never talked to him before. I would've remembered—

Tip: How do you win a spelling bee
        without being able to spell?

Elma: Develop a tick like a dancing leg, that distracts them, the judges, and then mumble the word so fast that they think they've heard all the letters.

Andi: You remember all that? You must have liked—

Elma: No no no. I was horrified. He didn't talk about any of the things that I expected from a parent. How-were-my-classes-who-was-my-favorite-teacher-did-i-want-to-go-to-college? He didn't ask me any of that. He didn't ask me any questions.

Andi: He let you talk? Did you talk?

Elma: Every once in a while he would pause, look at me with this big smile. Staring, but weird, like I was a fish in an aquarium that he had never seen before and then he would nod. And nod again. Like he was waiting for something to happen.

Tip: He was waiting for you to say something about your teachers, your classes or whatever.

Andi: He probably didn't know that he was expected to ask questions. Boppa and his people they just talk.
They're talkers.

Elma: I didn't know what to say. I'd just met him once before, with my mother, at a bus station coffee shop. I didn't even know why we were going there. My mother said, 'We have decided, Lester and I, that you should know your father." Who is this "we" mom? We? We? We had always been me and mom. Mom and me. And now there's this Lester. We never called him Boppa, that's your side of the family. His name is Lester. Boppa is a baby name—

Andi: Tip called him that. Boppa,

Tip: I was a baby. I had a trouble with all those P's.
P's were hell on my childlike embouMunchre.

Elma: I'm not talking about your childhood, Tip; we are talking
about mine.

Tip: For how long, though?

Elma: Until I'm done.

Andi: I think she needs to get it out, Tip.

Tip: OK, but if this is for all day.

Elma: Until I'm done.

Tip: All day then.

Andi: Tip, please, just listen to her.

Tip: All right. You're miserable in the bookstore
and Boppa says—

Elma: At night we would meet for chop suey and go
to the movies and—

Andi: You don't like chop suey, Elm?

Elma: It's all right, chop suey, it's fine.
It's just that it was every night.

Andi: I really like chop suey.

Elma: I know you do, Andi. That's fine for you, but I'm not you.

Andi: Boppa probably thought you like it because I like it.

Elma: He probably did and that's—...well. We go to the movies. It was a revival all blacks and whites which was weird because everyone looked poor and drained. The theatre was all musty and old-smelling. There was a drip in the first row, you could see it on the screen. Every five minutes the shadow of this drip would fall across the screen. The projector light was catching the drip and magnifying it. And one night I saw a rat, delirious, staggering up and down the aisle. Drunk on goobers and hording old popcorn. And I said, God, that's a rat. And Lester said—

Andi: (Doing Boppa voice.) "Oh no, that's a Chihuahua. Someone snuck in a Chihuahua in their pocket and now he's enjoying the movie." Boppa still says that whenever we see a rat at the movies. Charlie thinks the movies are Chihuahua ranches.

Elma: God he has a routine about rats—

Andi: What were the movies?

Elma: Preston Sturges, "Miracle at Morgan's Creek" and—

          Tip and Andi break into "Them There Eyes,"
          singing it in bass.

Andi: Boppa loves that movie.

Elma: That wasn't the song.

Tip: Yes it is. That's what Betty Hutton sings
           in the record shop.

           Andi and Tip sing it again.

Elma: That wasn't it. It was "Boom, boom. Boom, boom.
           Tolled the bell in the bay..." a song no one's ever heard of.
           Some obscure, awful—

Tip: I thought it was "Them There Eyes."

Elma: Have you guys even seen the movie?
           That song is nothing like—

Andi: Boppa would do the song.

Tip: Boppa would put on his Preston Sturges hat, his Preston
           Sturges pants, his Preston Sturges vest, and we would all
           dance around singing.

Andi: Yeah!

Elma: So you guys were together a lot?

Tip: After I turned 14, Boppa and Wendy told me I had a sister.

Andi: That was my mama...She didn't want me to have to think
           about how Boppa had left us and had another family...
           My mama is convinced that children are so sensitive
           that they'll fall over and never get back up if everyone's
           not smiling and cooing all the time. She does that with
           Charlie and Woof Woof, and she'll run whistling out of the
           room if she needs to cry, so the kids don't have to see
           a sad grandmother. And I say, Mom, that's nice, but the
           children aren't flowers. They can see you sad. And I hope
           it's true. I mean—

Tip: Boppa kept seeing you though. All the time.

Andi: He never did leave completely. But I think he liked it better when we could all hang out together.

Elma: That was easier for him, but Wendy and your mom were probably miserable. And he lied about that song. It wasn't "Them There Eyes."

Andi: Lied? He misremembered. That's...why would he lie?

Tip: Wendy said she was ok about your mom, And. And that they were never really together.

Elma: No no no. They were definitely—

Andi: But not really—

Elma: Fucking, making babies. That's real.

Tip: "Men," Wendy would say, "Men." And she'd grin and shake her head like, it's snowing, what're you gonna do?

Elma: You don't think that about men.

Tip: What? That they're (Shaking her head.) "Men."

Elma: That they're just wild forces of nature like that and we're not supposed to–

Tip: That's not what she thought. Wendy wasn't simplistic... She was easy about the world.

Elma: Passive, willing to be walked over.

Tip: Dead now, so you don't get to have an opinion.

Elma: Well I do have an opinion.
          You don't tell me how to see the world, Tip.

Tip: My mother—mine. No opinion, Elm.

Andi: She was a great woman, your mother.

Tip: Thanks, but. She wasn't. She was fucked up about men I
          guess. But she was my mother, mine, and I get to think
          about how I got my man things from—

Elma: Tip, you don't have any man things.
          Do you even know any men?

Tip: Boppa, Charlie and Woof Woof. They're men.
          They're boys, and they're in my life.

Andi: Oh they are, Tip, they are.

Elma: Men who are not your blood. Charlie and Woof Woof are
          children. Children are not men. *(Phone rings.)* I'm done
          with you, completely done with you. Is this Steve?

Steve: I wish you wouldn't say things like that Elma, God.
          I'm not garbage in your life I—

Elma: But I don't care, Steve, I don't care, because you, you're
          a terrible person who doesn't care about...guess who?
          Other people!

Andi: Elma are you all right?

Elma: *(Almost crying.)* No, Andi, I am not.

Andi: Oh Elma...I'm sorry...should we go to the lake?

Elma:	They just kick the life out of you and they make it impossible to stay calm or organized—And then they act like you are the heartless one.
Andi:	Have you tried just staying away? Girls? Plants? I've been enjoying meditation.
Elma:	I have a vagina, Andi.
Andi:	Well yes you do.
Tip:	And a very nice one, from what I've heard.
Elma:	A vagina doesn't "get it" from meditation.
Andi:	Well actually—
Elma:	I don't think I like girls.
Tip:	That's true, you don't.
Elma:	Who told you that? About the nice vagina?
Tip:	Oh I don't remember, I'm sure they all say that.
Elma:	But not to you.
Andi:	Rupert. "Snuffling Rupert."
Tip:	"The human puberty machine."
Elma:	Fuck! I bet he did. He told you too And?
Andi:	He did. He talked about you guys a lot. How you guys were together in bed. Your skin, which felt better than running shorts, your smell, which is like sweetened lake water, the little sounds—

Elma: Wait. When did he tell you all this?

Andi: I think right after you guys would be together.
That was usually in the mornings, wasn't it?

Elma: I had to go to work, and he had first period...

Andi: I think first period was skateboarding in the park, actually.
I'd be walking Charlie in the park and he'd come skating
up all rosy and flushed, like he had to talk about it.
I thought he had some kind of sexual Turret's.
He'd shout, "Skin! Pussy! Lake! Twat! Cock! Silk!"
But I don't think it was that. I think he was just excited.

Tip: How old was this boy?

Elma: 24! 24! He told me. Why was he so excited, And?

Andi: You're very beautiful, Elma, who wouldn't be.

Elma: *(Pleased.)* Really? Why did he tell you this?

Tip: People trust Andi.

Andi: They do. You could be done with men, Elm. I think I am.
They're lovely, but they do always carry the imperfection
of existence like a jug of moonshine.

Tip: I don't think that's cool.

Elma: What?

Tip: I don't think it's healthy, Elm.
To get away from mud. Air. Mud Air.

Elma: You don't think it's healthy?
        You don't know anything about men, Tip.

Tip: They put their pants on one leg at a time—

Elma: Nothing. You know nothing about them.
        When was the last time you even talked to—

Tip: I talked to Boppa yesterday.

Elma: Boppa doesn't count.
        You count your fucked-up father figure of a father.

Tip: Boppa's not my father figure. Boppa is my father.
        A father can't be a father figure.

Elma: If he's absent he can.

Andi: Boppa is not absent. C'mon Elma!

Elma: That's you, that's you!

Andi: Us! It's us. Me and Charlie and Woof Woof.
        Boppa baby-sits so that I can work.

Elma: Well who's babysitting now, since Boppa's coming here?

Andi: Tommy and don't—

Elma: Tommy? I thought you weren't speaking to Tommy.
        When was the last time you even mentioned—

Andi: We weren't. But that was too sad, so now we are.
        And Charlie loves to see Tommy.

Tip: Who is Woof Woof's father, Andi?

Andi: What? Don't ask me that, Tip.

Elma: Well it's not Tommy, that's for sure. That guy's such a wuss puddle it's amazing that he fathered once, let alone—

Andi: Tommy was lovely, is lovely. We made love in the rain, which I liked, in a gazebo, when we made love, which was only twice but—

Tip: But who's the other guy? The Woof Woof progenitor? That Jamaican dancer?

Andi: Tip, I don't want you to talk about this.

Elma: Have you looked at Woof Woof, Tip?
          It's obvious that his father's not Jamaican.

Tip: There's something in the eyes, though. Far eastern.

Elma: You think? Andi has that look. It's hers.

Tip: Really? *(They both stare at Andi.)*
          I think she looks just like us.

Andi: Why are my sisters speculating about my most private stuff, when I've asked them not to? My sisters whom I love, and who love me? Woof Woof is an angel.

Tip: Yes, he is.

Andi: Elm.

Elma: If I didn't hate the angel thing, then I'd say yes he's an angel, but I hate—

Andi: I used to see them all the time. When I was tiny-little, Boppa says. And I remember, when I was a kid, Oh, a white oak tree! Look at that, angel! Or, Oh! My cloud, my fluffy angel! The sky was all these fluttering blue shapes. But now it's like sludge, smudging everything. Coal dust between your eyes and heaven. It's very sad to lose the light like that.

Tip: Woof Woof sees the angels.

Andi: Woof Woof sees everything, you can see it in him.
His eyes go all global.

Elma: That must be something for him.

Andi: Oh I'm sure it is.

Elma: Tip—dating, men—when was the last time?

Tip: I don't think that matters though. I would like to be with men. Go for a walk. Twilight fishing maybe. The sun goes down, and everything goes warm and cricket quiet. The day heat, bouncing off the water for hours. Playing with the night chill. But the man still shivers, only it's not the cold, and he knows that. He forgot to leave when the others did, he just forgot. Because I'm right there and the wind is mixing with my voice and those sounds are the only ones he's hearing, because I'm making sense and I'm painting pictures in his picture brain, and he can't remember any reason to go. And maybe then the sun comes up, cuz time got funny as it disappeared almost, with us snuggling up, and him making my body roll. I mean all the muscles roll. This is what I'd like to do. Is any of that too weird? Not that I would care if it was it's just that if it was too weird, I would have to change my expectations, which I suppose I could do, but I don't want to.

Andi: It's not too weird...Tip, it's really lovely. Elm?
          Say the right thing, please!

Elma: It was lovely, but where does it come from, Tip?
          It's so romantic. You're not—

Andi: She is too! Look at her, she's a lover of men!

Elma: You DO look like that, a lover of—I'm sorry,
          I can't say that. Has it ever happened?

Tip: There was this scruffy fisherman by the lake once.
          He smoked this shag tobacco that smelled like an
          old German forest. You know. Hundred year
          old trees mulching.

Elma: That does sound—

Andi: Elm!

Elma: Did you guys fuck, Tip?

Tip: Not at all. We had eye contact thought, and
          you know how we are with eye contact.

Elma: How do you stay hopeful?

Tip: Oh I know what will happen. I'm a worthy person,
          I don't worry about that. Maybe tomorrow.

Andi: Or today. It could happen today. It's early yet.

Tip: That's true. And it's a long way back.

          The door swings open.

Tender:	My good nose, there is a touch of saffron laid over a healthy dose of hot pepper and garlic sauce on somebody's dinner plate. I was thinking only eggrolls, a modest amount, but this smell could turn a man around.
Tip:	Mr. Tendaberry?
Tender:	I am not sure I have had the pleasure...
Elm:	You have, five years ago...we are the McGinty sisters.
Tender:	Boppa's daughters! Of course you are...should have recognized you anywhere. Its the saffron under everything, it boggles the senses.
Tip:	You know Boppa now?
Tender:	Bird watching. I have taken it up...Boppa was ahead of me.
Elma:	Boppa bird watches now? I didn't know that, did you know that, Tip?
Tip:	He likes the whistles.

Tip whistles like a bird.

Andi:	Mr. Tenderberry, I am Andi.
Tender:	All right, will you take my order...I am thinking the 'Mr.Munch 2 chicken spicy' is what I smell.
Andi:	Have you seen Fred? I need to find Fred.

Tender: Fred? Fred is gone, misses...There was a snowstorm and a gunfight and a five alarm fire, all in the same night. Fred and I were in the thick of it. Fred saved my life misses but it cost him. Its quite a story if—

Andi: I need to see Fred, Mr.Tenderberry, I really have to.

Tender: The last I heard Fred was in a monastery far far away.

Andi: A monastery?...that seems so unlike him,
            the Fred I knew.

Tender: Or was it a chef school in the next county, just two towns away? It's been awhile, you see since I have heard from Fred, the odd postcard, and the group e-mail, even those have fallen off. Misses.

Tip: Woof Woof! Andi?

Elma: Fred the cop, Andi?

Andi: Shush! Not so loud, Elm. Mr. Munch might hear you.

Elma: What is that sound?

Andi: Mr. Munch. I'd forgotten about Mr. Munch. Mr. Munch! No, I know we haven't had a new customer for hours, but we have one now, he's very nice and he looks very hungry, he's a policeman and he wants the special, he will eat it. He will love it because it is very good and he will tell all his cop friends, we are not full today but we will be tomorrow. Oh Mr. Munch, please don't cry. Oh, Mr. Munch, not the mop closet! Mr. Munch! Wait, wait, hold on, I'm coming in. *(Slamming door.)*

            Phone Rings.

Elma: What? Boppa? You're not coming?

— The End —

HISTORICAL ENDNOTE:

One Boppa was originally written and performed as a one act, circa 2000; the second act was added 6 years later.

The original one act featured performances by Kathleen Powers, Teresa Weed, Kat McJimsey and was directed with Adam Rosenberg.

JULIA WILLIAMS, MEREDITH LYONS and VICKI WALDEN as Elm, Andi and Tip

ONE BOPPA, in two acts, 2015

JENNY MAGNUS in *Salvagers*

Salvagers

Premiered **February 2017**

Prop Thtr / Chicago, IL

written & performed by **JENNY MAGNUS**

THE
PLAYS

SETTING

The stage is set with a table and chair. Each character emerges from the performer's body visibly, nothing is hidden or magical. She puts the character on like one would put on an overcoat. Their stance, alignment, face, gestic body is all revealed to be a construction. The character transforms, then walks into the playing space in a way that is befitting their particular comfort with revelation, intimacy, communication. The monologues are played directly to the audience; these are stories, logics, realizations being told. There are moments of thinking within each monologue; the characters are meant to spend time actually thinking, making their way mentally through the lines of inquiry each one is setting up, and the actor should allow real time for these moments, not to rush them.

There is a pile of bricks on stage.* The actor enters, approaches the pile of bricks, takes one off and puts it neatly to the side. Throughout the course of the show, between each monologue, the actor moves a brick or two from the chaotic pile to a neat pile. She sings a fragment of a song at the beginning and end, holding a brick in her hands.

(sung)

You pick it up...

You put it down.

You pick it up...

You put it down.

You pick it up...

You put it down.

That's what you do.

The actor transforms into the first character.

* see endnote, p. 311

A middle aged man, possibly a former fighter,
kind of beat up, tough, a bantam rooster.
Very hesitant to share anything.

I guess I gotta talk about it...Uh, I don't think I can do this anymore.
I just feel....weak. Like my shtrenth has drained. I eat. I sleep.
But nuthin works right, like it used to do. As a kid, I felt weak.
That voice inside my brains would say, pssst, you're weak. You
know what, you can't do it. So I would come home after school,
defeated, get my chimps and dimp, and shut it down to watch the
3:30 movie. And then, that's when I saw Tarzan for the first time.
Elmo Lincoln, Johnny Weisemuller, Ron Ely. I loved those. That's
when I first started thinking about shtrenth. I'd see Tarzan be so
shtrong, swing on the vines, fighting the crocodile. I wanted to be
shtrong like that. I wanted to be creative-ly shtrong. And I don't
have the natural. All I ever had, really, was desire. I for sure wanted
it, to be shtrong. I wanted to be able to lift my weight. I could not
at first. But I worked on it. I dedicated my life to shtrenth. It all felt
upward. For a long time. Both upward, like, onward, sure, but also
like...forward...I learned it, how to be shtrong.

That's what feels different now. Now I know, I <u>feel</u>, it's all on the
downward. My best is behind me. I'll never be as shtrong again as I
was. What's worrying me is I lost my faith in shtrenth. <u>My</u> shtrenth.
I don't believe in it anymore. I used to take it for granted; once
I learned how, it was there. Always, underneath it all. I buried it
lots a times, compromised it, sure. But it would always come back

if I worked for it. Here's the thing: I went looking for it, recently. Recently, I was tryin' to do something heavy and I really couldn't do it. I tried workin towards it, how I always do. And it din't come back. I did everything I know. But I just can't...I can't anymore.

Now some of that's age, I know. There's a limit. I think about Jack LaLanne. I know that's what you're thinking. He pulled boats with his balls when he was 90. A real life Tarzan. He went way past logic, past physiology, past the odds. But then I think, you sir are no Jack LaLanne. Which I know. I never claimed that. But I think to myself I can be shtrong my way, to my potential. Right? Then I think, yeah, you reached your potential, like 15 years ago. That's all you got. All you get. Now it's just gonna be chimps and dimp and tv, you do the math. Then I think, why'm I sayin' this to myself? Why does it <u>seem</u> so true? It's that voice, in my head that sounds so right. But why? Then I think, at least don't lie to yourself. That is truly pathetic. That's worse than bein' weak. That is the way that madness lies. Then I think, *(pause)*. That's me telling that voice to shut the fuck up. I hate that fuckin voice. Part of the reason I know I'm weak is I can't beat that voice. That voice is the Jack LaLanne of voices.

So what I'm gonna do? I really think about giving up sometimes. Just giving up on shtrenth and be weak. But...I can't. I can't let go of my shtrenth. It's my...desire.

A young girl, on her phone constantly.
It's her best friend, the phone,
and though she is voluble,
she is also only somewhat self-aware.

Her speech is all upspeak,
many unanswerable questions.

Honestly, you guys, Hannah Anderson got kidnapped? And her mom and brother were murdered, and her house burned down? And her dog died too? All from this so-called family friend, who I am not even going to say the name of, because that just gives him the fame he wants... Wanted? And he had her kidnapped for like 6 days, travelling around, and camping, and seeing other people on horses in the wilderness but being too scared to say anything or ask for help? And she saw him shot full of 5 bullets right in front of her face? And, when she got rescued, and they told her about her mom and brother, she cried all night long? ALL NIGHT LONG?

And then she went on Ask.fm and answered questions about her ordeal? But not from the news reporters, she told them, well, really, she <u>asked</u> them to leave her alone? That this was private and her family needed privacy? Which is totally in her rights? Because she was processing, not reporting? She was directly telling us guys about her experience, and didn't need the news to take her experience and crunch it together and add anything? She was totally like a modern-day...uh, Edward Snowden!, you guys, just like him, she could directly talk to the people who needed to know, all her fans and her followers and her friends? And I read all this stuff, and read about how she felt and how she was scared all the time, and how the "family friend," her dad's best friend, got what he deserved in her opinion? She was super high key salty about it.

But then, I read about how maybe it wasn't even her doing the posting, that the chat she was on got taken down, and maybe it was totally like an identity theft, someone else posting in her name and making all this shit up. And actually, it made a kind of sense because I did think that someone who had just been kidnapped and had her mother and brother murdered and her dog murdered might be so traumatized that she wouldn't be able to post about that online and about her favorite color (pink), what she wanted to be when she grew up (a firefighter) and about Zac Efron, who is her bae? But then I thought, she is 16, and yeah, it makes sense that she would put her experiences out in the world like through this way? And she would think that losing her iphone, her ID, and her money was as horrible as the loss of her family? And her dog. For sure.

Then I saw a tumbler post about Ask.fm, and how it's this Latvian based site and kind of different than other social media sites because there is no way to report offensive comments, or increase privacy settings or find out who is behind anonymous bullying, and has supposedly led to a whole bunch of suicides and stuff? Yeah, in Ireland, but still...shady...And this website lets anybody see names, photographs and personal details of kids as young as 13, then anybody can post anything on the profile pages, stuff like sexual advances and threats of violence, bad bullying stuff?

And it made me think...WHY would Hannah Anderson pick a site like that to tell everyone about her ordeal, where like anybody can say anything, and is considered like a "stalkers paradise" by this security expert guy who told about it in a Daily Mail UK story? On Buzzfeed? And how if it wasn't even her, then we can't get too excited about it because its just trolling and fake...and...wait, you know what? She did even post a selfie when someone asked her for a picture? So...actually? I think it probably was literally her? And maybe she took the posts down the next day when she realized that there was something kinda weird to be writing about her favorite colors and whether she was sexually assaulted...like, in the same chat? And then I thought about, how would I know what the right thing to do is, if it were me, like, if I was a 16 year old, if my whole life had been violently altered and broken, and maybe posting online about it was just exactly the right thing to do because it made it seem real in a way, like, it isn't real until you tell about it? And this is how you tell about it now? And private means that it's hers to tell, as opposed to the hers that no one will ever hear about?

And you guys, I thought, who am I to judge Hannah Anderson, because she has to do whatever she thinks is the right thing to do in order to grieve? And all the stories coming out now about her postings and her taking down the postings and whether she should have posted any of that stuff in the first place is all really a judgment? On her, for sure? And aren't we all just vagueing around a judgment of the commodification of pain and the eros of suffering? Aren't we all licking it up like dogs ourselves and simultaneously scouring her language to read between the lines for clues to her damage, while indicting her unthinkable exhibitionism? Don't we all have to testify how everyone who read the initial posts, and all the stories about it after that, and searched key words and puts notifications on her name for their inbox secretly just wants to hear the juicy stuff, the gross details, even me, guys, I totally admit it? And it is so much better straight out of the horse's mouth than neatened up by a bunch of reporting and facts and background and stuff? And it being on line means you can ask the crazy personal stuff and not have to worry about spelling or punctuation, or feel the white hot scalding burn of shame for being turned on by it?

Anyways, it's been in my mind ever since I stumbled on it online when I was looking for back-to-school stuff and I wanted to get some of those super good Swedish socks. *(Thinks again)*. Because, yah, she has the same name as that Swedish company that sells pjs and Christmas sweaters, and like that?

A scientist, reading off a clipboard.
The list is at first baffling, unscientific,
but then increasingly clearly about the audience.

The mania of true passion.

Our love is the top of a balloon rising. Our love is the end of long day beer with feet on the table. Our love is the victory over fruit flies, ants, and silverfish. It is finishing a novel, a commission, a thesis. Our love is a starfish waving underwater, a slop sink coming unclogged, a perfect amount of ice cream. Our love is minky weather, rattan furniture that is actually comfortable, astral projection, coup contra coup. Our love is bendy straws, the end of a headache, rollos, and magic tricks that aren't stupid. Our love is a wide brimmed hat on a sunny day, fantasy novels you can't guess the ending of, the last piece of cake in the middle of the night, the best old-fashioned Italian place nobody young goes to.

Our love is a fog machine, Saturday afternoon. Our love is cold fizzy water, a blue scarf the color of the Mediterranean, fibs to protect feelings, snow days, the last note of Monster Mash, mechanical Turks of any kind, a trip to the seashore, a frying egg, and wooden chairs that don't squeak. Our love is a clean desk, the smell of hazelnut syrup, cotton sheets, and the funniest cat video. Our love is stinky cheese, wood grain, and flip flops. Our love is a new rug, the check engine light going off spontaneously, a new favorite record, windows facing a garden, Destry Rides Again, and suddenly "getting" quantum physics.

Our love is pancakes. It is eyelashes on a page. It is ceiling fans, and writing dates and mortgages being paid, and pratfalls and tushies. Our love is the first pill or drink, the diet kicking in, good sleep in hot weather, and saying the word "midwifery." Our love is Mondo's circle dress, introducing someone to Dr. Strangelove, the best strawberries of the last 10 years, trombone solos, ivies on the trellis, the package arriving, the cat from next door carrying her kittens in her mouth, down the sidewalk, one at a time, drum kits, giggling babies from Sweden, Klimt, pregnancy stories, corn silk, the quiet after demolition, walnut boats, rooster photos, cast parties, gold swings, biographies, highlighter pen smell, long hot dog sticks, piles of old magazines, dreams of thrift stores open only to you, fresh air when you're nauseated, kids on bikes, man pants, scratching an itchy butt hole, and the end of suffering. Our love is....our love IS! Our love IS! OUR LOVE IS!

Effete and english-y, a low-rent Quentin Crisp.
A wee bit drunky. Holding a cigarette for dear life,
but never taking a puff until the very end.

Slurring, but still veddy veddy proper.

I suppose I'd better say it. It really could be worse! That's what I tell myself. That's what I was told to think, when things seem extra dim. When it seems like I cannot stop doing all the...things...I am not supposed to be doing. When it seems like the whole world is going to...tilt...no, tip over into a pit. When it seems like there is no way to continue. But then I think, hey golly, it really could be worse!

The other day, I was sitting there, in my chair, by the window, MY chair, no one else sits in that chair, its broken into the shape of MY ass, with MY boogers and crumbs scattered into its tacky flowered cracks, and I had a feeling. A terrible terrible feeling. Oh, I've had 'em before, so I know what they're like, I recognize a terrible feeling, when it comes a'visiting me. And this one was indeed a visitor. The kind of visitor that one has a history with, the kind one hesitates to invite, because this visitor has outstayed its welcome in the past. So when I recognized this visitor, this petty, joykilling, vulgar, unimaginative visitor, I thought, oh god, not again. This feeling: so unutterably dull, so ghastly boring, it's just a shame it's got to show up and spoil the party. But here it is, and one may not ignore it, one must acknowledge the feeling, and welcome it in, however grudgingly. And this feeling was, predictably, that all is hopeless. That I, in fact , we all, have become the very thing I hate; strivers, aspirants, pilgrims, on haj, never progressing, never arriving. The Zeno's Paradox of effort. Forward movement is an illusion, you know the one I mean, the paradox of the tortoise and Achilles, that the distance can always be halved, and thus... dot dot dot. Well it's a paradox. It's a thought experiment, I don't think physical Achilles physically raced a physical tortoise. The point being that growth and change is an illusion. That I have not changed, the world cannot change, nothing changes.

Well, it was a dark moment. The darkness sichtbar, as they say auf deutsch. And as I sat there, staring out the window, running through the lists in my mind, of all the losses that have been sustained: the lost status, the lost money, the lost accomplishments, the lost eros, the excitement, the desire, the freedom, all the things I used to take for granted, along with all the losses in the world: the hope of progress, the possibility of development, the dream of justice (how embarrassing!); as I touched each thing in my mind, like my tongue will touch a rotten tooth, just to check, is it still there, has it miraculously healed, unexpectedly disappeared... (*wince*) oh no, no it has not, it is throbbing there, at the back, biding its miserable little rotten time until my attention even lightly sets on it again. As I sat there, contemplating the wreckage, (not too strong a word), this visiting feeling the results of our intention to ENJOY ourselves, for seemingly too long, and then finding ourselves living in the bubbling EEsops fable, is that how you say it, EEsops? Of the cricket and the ant, where one has played his fiddle all through the summer, while the industrious little ant has been working all along, and now that winter is coming, the fucking cricket is not prepared. Heard of it? The indignity. Bubbles bursting. To be in the wrong. To have bet foolishly, and lost.

Well here's the point: I had these thoughts, I felt these feelings, I sat and I sank. And then, a voice came into my mind, unbidden, fully formed, like Athena bursting out of Zeus's forehead, "YOU CANNOT SUCCEED IF YOU DON'T TRY..." That's it. A cliché. Well, thud. That is what years of the finest conversation and culture gave me in the moment of my deepest need. And what did I do? Of course I ignored it. That goes without saying. But then, it came again, like the little redrum finger voice, inexorable, unyielding, bullying. "GET UP" it said. "GET UP AND <u>DO</u> SOMETHING." I stopped, then, and had a think. *(Thinks.)* I thought, think for a moment, thinnnnk of what is even possible here. Think of how it really was, back then. Haven't we had these darkest hours before? Haven't the collapses been, well, part of it all, from the beginning? Haven't we been in a respiration of collapse and repair, collapse and repair, for all of our lives? It has always been a question only of <u>when</u> to start again. And once I realized that, I understood that in fact one thing had changed. What has changed is that I saw a pattern, I had lived long enough to see it as a pattern, and it would come again, the collapse, as would the repair... Well, yes, fine, it's not terribly profound. I recognize that too. But is it enough to hang one's hat on? To justify, "It really could be worse!"? Is it?

A young woman, outraged and baffled
by unwanted attention.

Holds a cell phone, but it's like a train wreck
she cannot stop looking at.

You know what? His dick just ain't that great. Oh my god, he keeps sending me shots and texts about his dick, his dick, his amazing dick, and oh my god, I have seen better dicks. It's like he thinks his dick is god's gift, and it ain't that big, it ain't that cute, it ain't that great. Oh my god, it's, it's, it's like he wants me to love his dick, to just, like, praise it, and like, raise it up above all other dicks, and I am like, look, your dick is fine, it's cool, but it ain't all that, you know? Where did you get this idea that your dick is, like, THE dick of all time? It ain't even THE dick of me, of my life, you know? And I think you should realize that you come off as kinda, like, weird, and like, pushy about your dick.

And then comes this last shot, the one that really hit the shit fan. Oh my god, there he is, showing off his dick, like how he does, and his kid is in the bed next to him, sleeping. Like, his kid, ok? His little kid is there, and there he is, with his stupid dick, and anybody, ANYBODY, would find that like, stupid and like, crazy, ok? Right?! Am I right about this? I mean, it's fine to have your dick around your little kid, especially a boy, but not like this. This ain't like, doot doo doo, we're taking a bath, we're changing clothes, we're the naked family, or whatever, no, this is like, DOOT! DOOT! DOOT! scary red light weirdout, texting his dick to some chick while his kid is asleep right there. I mean, am I right? This is like totally like being a dick ABOUT your dick, with a little pervy-ass ick shit added in.

And what it did to me, is like, what are YOU doing, getting texts from this dick-happy old dude, who ain't even that cute, you know? I mean, that's what my friends said, first off, like, he ain't that cute, he's old and kinda scuzzy and obvs a perv, so why is he sending YOU these dick shots? How much can YOU love dick to be getting all this dick attention and stuff? What are YOU putting out there to be such a dick magnet? And I'm like, I didn't ask him to show me his dick, I barely know the dude, he's some kinda dude from the news, we've never even fucked, oh my god, what can I say, he loves his dick! He just loves it.

It makes me wonder *(pauses, wonders.)* Did he always love his dick? Did he love it looking down on it as a kid? Did he love it from the first time he noticed it, or from the first time it got hard? Or did he only start to love it once he took a shot of it? Was seeing it on his phone the first time he really SAW it? And then, it was like, that's it, I've met my own true love? Only its, it's, like, just his dick? Or really, it's not his dick, it's just a SHOT of his dick. And how can you love that? How can the dude give up everything else in his life and be like, unable to leave it alone and get in fights, with other things, with his, like, career, his wife, his kid, I mean, his, like, dignity, right? It's like, he loves those shots more than anything else, and he aint leaving it alone until he's like, lost his will to live.

And, but, still, he keeps on sending me these shots of it, *(scrolling through phone)* it's like dick dick dick dick dick dick dick dick all day, that's all it is. I didn't ask to see his stupid dick. His stupid dick ain't that great.

A middle aged woman,
very anxious and saddish.

Her list is hard earned.
Making the best of it…

You imagine all the ways you can fail. You open the curtains and close the curtains. You rub your vagina and then smell it, not once, but lots of times. You become increasingly agonized over your own smells. You eat all the muffins. All of them. You "knock about the estate", as your father used to say, but you don't clean, as he did. You lean a little too far over the sink, putting all your weight on it, just praying that this is the time it breaks off. You watch movies back to back until you get the blinding headache. You steal the internet connection from your neighbors, because you figured out their password was "bernlust23", though you cannot understand how you figured that out. You try on all your bras, and because none of them fit, you step on one end and pull on the other ends. You create multiple first lines and last lines. You listen to a podcast of hoary pundits while taking several shits. You talk on the phone, and "reflect" back to your friends all the things they are doing wrong. You break out the crazy glue and fix all the chair legs that are woggling apart. You give up on crazy glue and use bungee cords to fix the woggling chair legs. You bandage the fingers that were glued by the crazy glue and pinched by the bungee cords. You fold your daughter's clothes and then unfold them because it's her job and she will never learn if you do it. You make lists of all the things some people like that you don't like. You watch dogwalkers out of the window and psychically dare them not to pick up their shit. You eat the things alone you would never eat together. You set up the drums, you move the drums, you re-set up the drums, you do not play the drums. You magic eraser the sinks and tubs, but tell yourself it's because it's fun to magic eraser and not that you are cleaning anything. You sit in several different chairs by multiple windows. You put everything under the table, except for the things that were already under the table. You sleep. You attempt your "work", which is sometimes actual work, and sometimes lists and lists of character defects and hopeless faults. You wait for someone to come home. You contemplate solitude while understanding that the place for solitude in your life has changed. You straighten but YOU DO NOT CLEAN. You put your foot down, finally.

A man of power, taking the stage,
all eyes on him. He oozes confidence,
everyone will listen, of that he is quite sure.

On occasion, he whips his head around because
something might be coming up from behind him.
Is there anything there?

Fuck you, Facts. I don't care what you say. I'm not listening to you, I am not going to say, Facts, you decide for me what happens, what has happen<u>ed</u>. No. I am not doing that. In fact, Facts, you can just shut up. Don't expect me to change what I'm doing because of you. I'm going to do what is right for me. I'm going to say what I think. I am not going to be dictated to by you, Facts. And who made you king, anyway? Who decided you were right? When someone says, this happened and then that happened, those are the "Facts," like on the news they say that, I say, no, it didn't. That didn't happen. Just because you say those are Facts doesn't make it true. I say, it's only you <u>saying</u> it's true. <u>I</u> say no, those are only words. That's "language."

You might well then say, what about observable reality? What about proven things, repeatable traceable concrete things that almost everyone else agrees on? I say, Almost everyone is not everyone. Then all of reality is subjective, you say? Yes, everyone should be able to decide whether they want to agree with Facts. And if they don't, if for any reason they think Facts are wrong, then they should say what <u>they</u> think. They should say their own truths, and maybe those are <u>their</u> Facts. But if everyone has their own Facts, what can we agree on, you might say. And yes, I would say, not much. Maybe that's just the way it is. You on your side with your Facts, and me over here with mine. And may the best Facts win?

And <u>can</u> we have multiple versions of Facts that can co-exist? Can we just have lots of different angles on things? I mean, why can't we? Why can't we each have our own takes and live with the complexity of that? The mixed-up confusing fucked up contradictory world of Facts that don't agree on basic things, like who was where first? And when was what decided by whom? And who is getting what? *(He thinks for a moment.)* Ok, yes, I can see some big problems with that. Sure, what if important crucial life altering things rest on directly contradictory facts? Which they absolutely would. Because those are exactly the kinds of things people lean on Facts for. They use Facts to help define and describe exactly those kinds of things, like boundaries, rights, punishments, ownership, history, and science. All that uses Facts.

And alright, sure, I understand why it does, why you need some-kind-of-something to put order in the world. I guess. I guess I see without that it can so easily turn into a mess. But look, it already is, it is a mess already, and alright, yes, my resistance to Facts is part of the mess, I understand that. But why should I be the one to give in? To give over to what may or may not be true? What if I really, REALLY do not believe in what Facts are saying? What if, at the very core of my being, that truth that Facts are holding up is simply not right to me; it rings totally false, makes me feel threatened? Am I actually supposed to gulp it down and like it? Am I supposed to go along with Facts that are wrong to me? I just cannot do it. I won't do it. And if I can't, I have to assume others can't or won't go along. Unless they are forced to. Go along. And if they are weak, or alone, or in the minority, they can be forced. They can be made to go along with Facts they don't believe in. Look, whole cultures are based on that. The strong force the weak to go along, and if they don't like it, they can just lump it. They can just...die, I guess. Then they're...fucked.

But I am not going to be one of those people. I am not going to be fucked. I am going to resist, to refuse to consent, to push back against Facts. Facts...I say, fuck you Facts. You don't own me.

A woman is rubbing lotion into her hands.
She is a healer, a person who spends all
day everyday with other people's pain.

But is she lonely, too?

I don't think I told you this. Did I tell you this? Stop me if I told you. A lady comes in for treatment the other day, a new patient, with back problems, couldn't bend over, likely a pulled muscle or even a herniated disc... We started off with real slow stretching, manipulation, some heat, and just evaluating her for range of motion, now did I tell you this? Ok, so then when we're talking, and I'm bending her legs up and down, making conversation, to distract her from the pain, you know how I do, I notice that her hands are all ripped up. They're covered in scars and cuts and scratches. I ask her how her hands got so bad, like what in the world happened? And she tells me this crazy story about her hands, and about how she hurt her back too.

She tells me she had just come from up by Detroit, where all those houses have "Demolished by Neglect" spray painted on them, and they're piles of bricks and rubble at this point. And she tells me, what she does is, is she climbs up on the piles and takes the bricks one at a time and makes a neater pile next to the house. What!? She says she's living in her car! Traveling around, she'll drive up to a house, park, and just stay there by the house until its done. And she does this all over the country, she goes looking for these houses and buildings that have fallen over, and she makes piles of bricks next to them. And her hands get all tore up because the bricks and stuff are sharp and jaggedy and broken. Her back is messed up from sleeping in her car, and climbing up and down, and carrying all the bricks. And to get the bricks, she's gotta deal with the, like, rebar I think you call it, plus the broken wood and stuff. So she's just taken it upon herself to climb on these big jumbles and collect up what's left and make these piles.

So, ok, that was one conversation out of the whole day, but I couldn't stop thinking about it. So in the middle of the night, I feathered Big Mike to wake him up. You can't shake him, or whatever because he'll jump up and grab for his gun, so you have to wake him up gentle, with your fingers on his face. I wake him up and I tell him about her, and I ask him, "...Hon, if you saw some lady climbed up on a collapsed house, what would you do?" Because I thought, neighbors would call the cops, and they could take it the wrong way, and carry her off to the hospital or something, like she was nuts for making these piles of bricks. But she's not stealing anything, or destroying anything, she's just making piles of bricks, so even landlords or the folks who own the buildings couldn't really press charges, right? Or so I was asking Big Mike, who wasn't too happy being asked about it in the middle of the night, and he did yell a little. Which then woke up Lil' Mike, and I had to get up and take care of him, so I never really got much of an answer.

Yeah...So then yesterday, when I was working on Mr. Demitrios' ankle, and he was grimacing and coming up off the table, and I had Sandy and Consuelo there doing squat breaks and using the rubber bands...I had just told this funny thing I was thinking about to Wendy, but she didn't get it, she was spraying off a table, and even her spray bottle was kind of snippy. Well, geez, I stopped talking to her, and I was watching Sandy and Consuelo work, to see they did it with the right form, and I was daydreaming about the job. I thought how the old, hurt bodies I'm trying to help heal were like those busted up houses. They used to be new and great looking, but now they are a big mess. And I'm the one showing up, climbing up on them and trying to salvage whatever I can off of them. That was a funny thought, and I told Wendy about it, but she didn't get it, so I let it go. She doesn't get a lot of my jokes, she want to hear what I'm thinking about, and she even thought my wanting to put up Halloween decorations and then to say how spooky it was, and was everybody scared, was sorta stupid. I just kept it to myself after that. I'm just tryna pass the time, talk to people...I don't know if we'll see that lady again. She moves around a lot, I guess.

A small song, sung to try to make sense,
because that is a way to salvage things.

I don't know what to think
I don't know how to feel
I kinda think my shit still stinks
Slipping on banana peels
And that is why I tear my skin
Interrogate the state we're in
Like shaman opening a frogs intestines
Looking for a clue

I'm feeling wide awake
I think I'm quite alert
I 'm wondering what stance to take
And if it's going to hurt
So that is why unzip my skin
Investigate what state we're in
Like fortune tellers digging through the tea leaves
Looking for a clue
To what the hell is going on right now?
I wish I knew....

Picking up the bricks, one at a time.

So you pick it up,
you put it down.
So you pick it up,
you put it down.
So you pick it up,
you put it down.
That's what you do.

Exit   *—The End —*

HISTORICAL ENDNOTE:

The *Trummerfrau* were German women, who, after WWII, were hired to salvage bricks one at a time off collapsed buildings. Trummerfrau means "rubble women."

H.B. WARD as The Great Galvani
in *The Art of Unbearable Sensations*

The Art of Unbearable Sensations

Premiered **February 2009**

**The Rhinoceros Theater Festival
at The Viaduct Theater / Chicago, IL**

written & directed by **SHAWN REDDY**

performed by:

**Guy Massey
Kathleen Powers
Diana Slickman
H.B. Ward**

SETTING

Evening, Late 19th Century

CAST of CHARACTERS:

LUDMILLA the Bearded Lady Emcee
An alluringly, scruffy mistress of ceremonies who is supposed to simply introduce the acts, but instead spends most of her time waxing about past loves, gender politics, and Parisian salon life.

THE GREAT GALVANI
A heart-broken tinkerer of dead frogs who proceeds to dissect everything from the famed Fiji Mermaid and Tom Thumb, to catastrophic loss and the need for distractions of bewildering beauty.

MADAME PETROVNA the Three-Armed Medium
A cranky, vindictive psychic with the ability to hold séances and speak to troubled spirits by candlelight, while also delving into her own demons and dark secrets of child abuse and abandonment.

DORIAN the Head Doctor Extraordinaire
A brilliant "doctor" who specializes in the now dismissed practices of phrenology. But he himself is troubled by migraines...migraines of murder.

STAGE

A traditional sideshow stage (no more than 12'x12'), complete with a raggedy backdrop and string lights. On the stage is a round table display covered in cloth, a chair next to it, and a crate off to the side. Directly in front of the stage is a dilapidated oriental rug (12'x6'). Off stage-right is a microphone on a stand.

SCENE ONE

LUDMILLA enters in the dark. A spotlight slowly fades in as she caresses a microphone and drips of sensuality. She is wearing an extravagant evening gown, ornate jewelry, and a long, scraggily, unkempt beard.

Ludmilla: *(Breathy and beatnik-like)* So uh, yeah...the other day? This, uh...creepy pint-sized little Frenchman, a puny painter in spectacles and a billycock bowler, fancy and all dolled up, literally, like a little doll, said he saw one of my tattered posters in a back alley while he was taking a piss. Said he was immediately mesmerized by me. My beauty. Said he had to see me in person, in private... after my show.

And so? He took me by the hand and began to kiss me on the inside of my elbow. Said he painted grand apocalyptic scenes of debauched decadence. The underbelly nightmare of Parisian nightlife. Of cringy cabaret corners and bed-bugged brothels in long brush strokes. And I said...

> *Beat.*

"Whoa. Take a breath, why don't you?"

> *Beat.*

He said... he was an aristocrat. That his family came from royal counts in the rich hill regions of Toulouse and Lautrec. And that his lineage dated back well over a thousand years to Richard the Lionheart. And so?

> *Beat.*

I curtsied.

Beat.

But he spoke with a rotten lisp and only came halfway up to my bustle. Thick and barrel-chested, and yet, he had tiny, little stick legs like a wooden child. Always tilting to the left. As if gravity was a form of blackmail.

Said, it was because he was a purebred. That his parents were royal cousins. And I said... "Oooh... inbreeding. Should I find a leash?"

Beat.

Sensing my disapproval, he said that his short stature was but a small price to pay. And I, in turn, asked him?

Beat.

If the pun was intended.

Beat.

As he leaned in on tippy-toes, whispering sweet and savory words covered in stale cognac and a life of regret, he said... I had that look. And then he offered me forty francs to pose for him as Jesus. And I said, "Jesus?" And he said, "Yes, Jesus." And I said, "Jesus!" again. And then he grabbed me. I said, "But Jesus was a man?" And then he immediately reached up and placed a stubby, sausage forefinger to my lips, "No," he said, "Jesus was universal. And you my dear, you've got that look." And I said?

Beat.

"Must... be the beard."

Beat, then sings in a melancholic tone.

The Art... of Unbearable Sensations.

Beat.

And with that ladies and gentlemen, I give you without ado, our very first act of the evening, The Great... Galvani.

The spotlight fades out.

LUDMILLA exits.

SCENE TWO

Wurlitzer Caliola Calliope's song, "Dardanella" plays as GALVANI enters in the dark and takes a seat on the stage. The music fades out. He begins crying, faint whimpers that turn into deep sobs. After a few moments a spotlight abruptly fades in catching him by surprise. He is wearing a mishmash of fine men's wear including a vest, top hat and cape. But everything is frayed, forgotten, and in patches. He has an unkempt mustache, is overweight, and glistens with sweat.

Galvani: *(In a mock-Italian accent)* You heard...nothing!

> *He pulls a dirty handkerchief from his breast pocket and blows his nose. Then he delicately folds it over and over again into a tiny sandwich and tries to put it back in his breast pocket without looking. Unsuccessful, he throws the handkerchief over his shoulder to the ground. He clears his throat.*

Before we can commence with this evening's amusements, twisted balloon animals and confetti specks, et al., I am contractually obligated to recite the following introductory advertisement by my employer. So please, for those of you who suffer from coprophobia, the...fear of feces, I urge you to kindly cover your ears at the present time.

*Rising from his chair and making his way down to
the carpet, he impersonating P.T. Barnum, as if possessed,
speaking in a bloated show barker's voice.*

Every man, woman and child...behold! For you have just paid your ticket to the highest of high class acts, and are now about to check the baggage of your own reality and embark on the most magnificent of journeys.

Oh yes! To a colossal magic-land where the beastly and grotesque bloom into bewildering beauty! Where lost and lecherous souls reign supreme on stage solely for your viewing pleasure and wonderful walking enigmas and human curiosities in cages can be poked with a stick for an additional price!

But! Before we can take that first step, I must implore you now, please...rub your eyeballs! And open up your minds to the possibility...of possibilities! For after all, it is a truth that has been well documented by numerous fortune cookie philosophers, that more persons, on a whole, are swindled, not by believing too much, but by believing nothing at all!

And oh the things I have for you to see! Oddities! Like William Henry Johnson, the mystifying man-monkey, missing link who speaks in a mesmerizing jungle language. Or the Nova Scotia giantess, Anna Swan, who eats raw meat and wears pillow casings for socks! There is the Woolley Horse, the Grand Aquaria with its marine monsters, the Ossified Living Statue, mechanical wonders and even the Thrice Thumbed Man!

Whispers loudly.

My gosh!

Beat.

And if this isn't already teetering on top of ostentation, then how about a monumental free street pageant lead by distinguished equestrians riding twenty decorated Middle Eastern trick stallions so skilled and cunning that you will actually think they have a conscious sense of themselves! "What are those creatures thinking?" you will gasp.

That's right folks! All this...and more! Much, much more! Including the Albino Iroquois Tribe, a learn-ed seal, the World's Worst Brass Band to Ever Play Under One Banner, Science Gone Wrong experiments, the Tattooed Greek Nobleman, cosmoramas, the Feral Starlet with No Undergarments, a unicorn goat, and even a Wax Statue Showcase of Noted Personages, comprising figures of celebrated military leaders and foreign potentates sure to allay any fears or frustrations you may have with the war.

People! People! People! We are talking about acres of entertainment here! Herded together and combined under one exhaustive, extensive, undivided show never before presented in any one time, age or place! Encompassed under twelve tented pavilions and hauled across the nation on over one hundred gilded railway cars stretching more than four miles long!

 Beat.

My friends, Americans, countrymen! I hereby pledge my honor, reputation, and soon-to-be fortune by giving you the record breaking giant of all exhibitions. The Grand Traveling Museum, Menagerie, Caravan and Hippodrome! And so, without further ado...welcome, welcome, welcome one and all! To the greatest... show on earth!

 Takes a bow.

Signed, forever your humble showman and impresario,
Phineas Taylor Barnum.

As an aside.

Oh, and please note, that "The Greatest Show on Earth!" is a registered trademark, including the exclamation point, and that this introductory advertisement has been graciously brought to you in part by J. W. Weston's Metallic Artificial Legs, an official Civil War product, made of corrugated metals and patented on January 6th, 1863 by the Universal Joint and artificial Limb Company. Weight? Only four pounds. Guaranteed one-size fits all. Makes no squeaky noises. And there's even a special soldier's price!

Beat, and then speaks in his own mock-Italian voice.

Ah...and there you have it my dear friends. The proverbial rub. A sad irony for you to ponder in even sadder solitude after the show.

Clears his throat.

Now, before we get started, I do have one last minor detail to mention. I must confess that for the most part I have grown quite accustomed to performing, well...to empty houses. Having for validation only the melancholy echo of my own voice bouncing off the back wall and then slowly dissipating among the vacant chairs into a low murmur, which sounds an awful lot like the grumbling disapprovals of my dead father.

Morbid? Maybe. But nostalgically comforting for me nonetheless. Regardless, the presence of warm bodies tonight leads me to believe that many of you may actually be here under false pretenses, or more simply put...by mistake. If in fact you are here tonight to witness the unveiling of the famed Fiji Mermaid, well...then I regret to inform you that you are indeed destined for disappointment, for you are in the wrong place. And I do apologize deeply for that. The signage out front is intentionally unclear. And on top of that it has been raining for weeks and everything is soft and crooked. But fear not my dear friends, for I do have a solution if you'll please just bare with me for a moment.

He ceremoniously closes his eyes and moves
his hands around like a magician.
After a few moments he opens his eyes.

Okee-dokey! To begin with, at this time please do me the favor of closing your eyes. That's right. Go on. Close them shut. Thank you. Now, with your eyes closed, I want you to envision for me a fish. Ideally a Chinese carp, but really any fish will do. Now, take that fish inside your mind...and chop in half! Cleanly with a cleaver! Discard the top portion with the head, and now stitch a decapitated mummified pigmy torso to the tail. I'll give you a few moments.

> *Beat.*

Good. Now that you have sinfully synthesized the two species together, proceed further into your brain debauchery by adding on top of that...a coconut for a head.

> *Beat.*

Now, once you have the three parts arranged properly, finish off your mental monstrosity by slapping on a pair of orangutan tits. And voilà! There you have it. Two shows for the price of one!

> *Clears his throat.*

My name...is Luigi Galvani. Now some of you privy to contemporary science may have heard of my name in certain circles. But, I am certain that you have never heard of me. And that is quite simply because, well...I am a nobody. And do not merit remembrance. I have accomplished nothing. And the prospects of me doing so some day are really very dim. No, most likely the "Luigi Galvani" that you may have heard of was that of my dead father.

Beat.

A horrible man. Selfish and petty and pissy and a prick! Naming me after himself as he did, not as an act of parental endearment mind you, but rather more along the lines of Saturn...who ate his children for breakfast. Oh yes! Threatened by my birth, he branded me with his name. Making certain that I would never, ever, in a million years be...my own "me." Just another specimen for his collection pile!

Sighs.

My father, the great Luigi Galvani, was a physician and physicist by trade, child tormenter by talent as I have just conveyed, and renowned genius at the University of Bologna in Italy where a bronze statue in his likeness currently stands in the southern courtyard stroking its weak chin in a false contemplation and all the while karmicly caked in pigeon excrement!

Beat.

Oh yes, I still have the "unresolved feelings."

Clears his throat.

He was a pioneer in, of all things, modern obstetrics, and famous for discovering, and I will speak slowly here and with great gesticulation for clarity's sake, that...the electrochemical behavior of two dissimilar metals, specifically zinc and copper, in a bimetallic arch, in contact with the electrolytes of tissue, produces an electric stimulating current that elicits a muscular contraction. Blah, blah, blah, blah, blah. Please pardon the medicalese. In layman's terms, when you strip away all the fancy jargon, my father...

Mockingly makes air quotes.

"the great" Luigi Galvani, is known the world over...for essentially doing nothing more than accidentally making the legs of a dead frog...go twitch!

Beat.

There is an old Greek parable dating back to...Plato or Socrates or... some other toga clad tickler of boys, which states that if you place a frog into a vat of boiling water, it will immediately leap out to escape the danger.

However, if you place a frog into a vat that is filled with cool and pleasant water, and then slowly increase the heat in small unassuming increments, the frog will not become aware of the threat of danger until it is too late.

Now, this boiling frog parable is generally told in a figurative context, with the upshot being that people should make themselves aware of gradual changes lest they someday suffer a catastrophic loss. It is often used to illustrate what they call, a slippery-slope argument. Or what I like to think of as...things quietly growing wild from right under your nose!

Take for example the government...and minor increases in authority. As you well know, the president has recently outlawed pitchfork rebellions. Okay, fine. A reasonable enough measure to take during a time of war, I suppose. But who's to say that tomorrow he won't take it a step further and bestow himself with extra-constitutional powers? Who knows? Maybe he'll begin reading our telegraphs? Or worse, snooping around our church potlucks with a salad for god's sake! Not even a main dish. A salad! Come on!

Shakes his head in disgust.

Oh yes, it is indeed something to consider my dear friends. Because let me tell you, when it comes to boiling a frog? There are no molehills. Only mountains. Everything in life...is monumental. And when you stop and think about it, it really is a beautiful credo to live your life by. To find big and buxom meaning in the tiniest of things. Everywhere and all around. It almost makes me want to smile!

Tries very hard to smile. He fails and clears his throat.

However, that said, I am here tonight to report, that the hypothesis of this parable? About the boiling frog? Unfortunately does not stand up to the scientific method. No. And in fact it has been my finding that when you put a frog in a vat of boiling water?

Shrugs his shoulders.

It dies! Instantaneously! And disgustingly so I might add. Its skin immediately peels and pulls apart like wet newspaper. Its eyes? They explode like squished olives. And its limbs? They curl backwards into unnatural knots. In one horrifying instant everything that used to be a frog splits, rips open, and violently turns inside out...like a grapefruit!

Beat.

And as for the other side of the equation? Well let me just ask, have any of you ever actually tried to get a frog to sit still in a vat that is filled with cool and pleasant water? Because it is not as easy as it sounds. Frogs! What can I say? They like very much to jump. It is in their nature. I even tried increasing the small unassuming increments of heat from .002 degrees centigrade per second to .019 degrees centigrade per second. An increase in speed by almost ten times! And still, the stupid frog would not sit there in the vat of water long enough for it to boil! It was very frustrating. I found myself hitting my head with my own shoe like a barefooted moron! At one point I even considered using a lid, but then that would have removed the possibility of escape, and ultimately taint the experiment!

Sighs.

And so, my dear friends, it is my conclusion...that when it comes to change and the avoidance of catastrophic loss, regardless of your approach...

Yells.

You are screwed!

Gently now.

Inevitably. For after all we are a species that tends to love things that do not last, are we not? And so, much like the frog is to jumping, it is in our unavoidable nature to someday suffer...greatly. And our only recourse? Is distraction.

Beat.

To put it off and out of our minds, the pain,
for as long as we possibly can.

Beat.

The other day? The little midget Tom Thumb? He got married. Together, with his even shorter bride, the two of them stood atop a grand piano hand-in-hand in New York City's Metropolitan Hotel to greet some 2,000 guests. It is said that they were even received by the president at the White House on their way to their honeymoon. It was all over the front pages. Wiping away the carnage of the world for two whole days. And I must admit, things...they did feel a bit lighter, even if only for a moment.

Clears his throat.

When my father, the great Luigi Galvani died, he left behind, well...quite a mess. And that is because his death, like so many, came without a warning label from a spontaneous burst inside his heart. And so, he had no time. No time to sweep away secrets or to package up his procrastinations. No, he left... in a hurry. With his scalpel literally still pinched between his forefinger and thumb. And let me tell you my dear friends, when you leave like that, it is not as if your life here on Earth leaves too in a swooshing comet tail behind you. No. Instead? It stands still and stays there. Like a lost dog. Frozen in displaced mounds for other people to pick through like garbage until all that's left are the small, scattered bundles of you that nobody wants. Bills and unsent letters, stacks of periodicals, old shoes and buckles in boxes, toiletries, and even an untouched tin of cotton swabs for the inside of his ear. Everything once private and preciously preserved is now naked and exposed. It was as if my father too...had turned inside-out...like a grapefruit.

Beat.

And worst of all...was his workshop. Left unattended. Forgotten. It was like walking into a room full of ideas that were flipping around on the floor among shards of glass...and gasping for breath. There were frogs piled high to the ceiling in a clawing cacophony. Squelching and squerching in crusted jars of their own juices like a pharaoh's plague in a bottle. And the walls, every inch, the walls were scarred like tree bark with years of scrawled writing. Over and over again. The same word. Etched in a furious hand...twitch, twitch, twitch!

Beat.

It was as if he was trapped in the dark. Papers and tools and utensils, many of which you see here tonight, were scattered and strewn about with the messy nonchalance that there would be a tomorrow for tidying. There was even a poor frog stuck in torture with its limbs pulled taut and left pinned to a dissecting tray. In one of the corners of the room, there on the floor, was a small heap of journals that appeared to be steaming. Inside, grotesque and detailed drawings of mutilated half-frogs and long, rambling, inhumane descriptions of what he euphemistically coined as the art...of unbearable sensations!

Beat.

As I continued to turn pages long into the night, I came upon extensive histories that he had gathered about exotic frogs from all over the world. Apparently, there is a sedentary type of red-speckled frog in the Australian desert that retains water like a canteen. It is said that aborigines can store them motionlessly for weeks at a time in a pouch, and then painlessly squeeze them over their open mouths when they get parched. In Brazil, there is a giant golden tree frog with an over-developed vocal sack that can mimic sounds like a parrot. And in Cameroon, there is supposedly a blue streaked frog that can be trained to crudely follow commands...like a cat.

So many colorful and fascinating species to pick from. And yet, when I wandered my father's workshop by candlelight, there was nothing but the same, unimaginative and sickly gray-green swamp frog sadly staring back at me...with thousands of eyes.

Beat.

As I stumbled my way around the amphibious morgue, I accidentally bumped into the dissecting tray with the splayed frog. And my dear friends, let me tell you, I could have sworn that I actually saw something move in the dark. But, uncertain of my own senses at the time, I decided to peer down for a closer look. And so, I delicately spread its longitudinal incision with my fingertips and dug into its organs with my hands. Slowly massaging its innards until I was elbow deep inside this tiny, tortured frog. Reaching out and stretching into its well of darkness. Like quicksand. Down to my shoulder. I was sinking. With my cheek pressing hard against its chest. Groping. Until I hit upon the sciatic nerve. Thick and fibrous with feeling. Like rope. And as I desperately held on like a falling tightrope walker, slipping up and down, I discovered to my horror that it was bound... in metal.

Jarring and foreign and unnatural! I instinctively jerked my hands free. For it was indeed...odd, to find the greatest of all nerves shackled up and made numb in the name of so-called science.

Beat.

And right then and there, and for the very first time, dripping with frog juice in the middle of his workshop...I caught a glimpse of my father for who he really was. No longer looming as the great Galvani. He was instantly redefined to me as...desperate. Desperate and stuck. The praise of old laurels was no longer enough. And in fact, it was even haunting. Left to repeating the same pathetic experiment with the same, unimaginative swamp frog...for an eternity. It was as if he was hoping to break all the sickly grey-green monotony and make that little "twitch" mean something more. It was as if...my father, the great Luigi Galvani, was hoping...for nothing more than a momentary distraction...from who he was.

Makes his way over to the table.

And so my dear friends, here we find ourselves. I wish that I could say that I found the strength to smash over all the jars and free the frogs from my father's workshop. But...I did not. After all, change...it is a tricky business. And so, instead? I picked up my father's scalpel, and in turn, picked up where he left off. Meticulously scouring his journals and traipsing through jungles the world over. I took many detours to get here to this moment. To give you what you paid for tonight...what my father hoped for all his life. And so, without further ado, I present to you...The Beautiful and Bewildering Lucinda...The World's One and Only...Soprano Singing Frog!

> *Yoko Ono's song, "Yes, I'm Your Angel" begins to play. GALVANI immediately removes the cloth to reveal a giant frog singing the song. After a few moments the lights fade to black.*
>
> *The song continues to play as Galvani exits in the dark with the table and the frog.*

SCENE THREE

LUDMILLA enters in the dark. As the spotlight fades in on her at the microphone, Yoko Ono's song fades out.

Ludmilla: *(Referring to Galvani's frog)* Wow...not bad, huh?
I wonder if that old croaker takes requests.
A little Stephen Foster maybe? Camptown Races or–

    Strokes her beard and sings.

Jeanie with the Light Brown Hair.

Now wouldn't that be nice? You know I met him once. The young songwriter? Oh sure. A long time ago. It was in a dingy backroom bar. Behind a German grocery store that stunk of pickled cabbage... and Germans.

    Beat.

He was scraping the bottom of a barrel. Soft-shoe stepping for the other drunks. All he needed was some burnt cork for his face. It was...pretty pathetic really. To see him with his hat in his hand like that. And yet, there he was. The little songbird. Trying to pay off his tab with a turnip. Like a tramp. We didn't even shake hands. Nope. No introductions. He just turned and looked me over with that beautiful baby face of his and slurred–

    Impersonating a drunk.

"You know lady, you're lucky...
I can't even grow one of those."

And with that? He just went back to being lost.
To playing the bar top like a piano.

> *Beat.*

A couple of years later? I heard that he was dead. Just like that.
Found naked in a pool of his own blood. In some lowdown Bowery
boarding house. With a washbasin inexplicably cracked over his
head. And the only thing he left behind? To tell us who he was?
Was a leathery worn-out wallet. With nothing in it. Except for a tiny
scrap of paper with the scribbled words of an incomplete sentence
that read, "Dear friends and gentle hearts, dot...dot...dot."

> *Beat.*

It's the dots that get me. I mean, what did the poor boy expect? With
a lead-in like that? Here? In this place? It's no wonder he suffered...
from writer's block.

> *She begins to hum Stephen Foster's*
> *"Beautiful Dreamer" and then picks up*
> *the lyrics on the second line.*

"Starlight and dew drops are waiting for thee;
Sounds of the rude world, heard in the day,
Lull'd by the moonlight have all pass'd away."

> *Beat, and then whispers.*

And on that happy note, I leave you with our next act of the evening,
Madame Petrovna...the Three Armed Medium.

> *The spotlight fades out. LUDMILLA exits.*

SCENE FOUR

PETROVNA enters in the dark from behind the audience. She is dressed like a gypsy, covered in scarves and bells. She has a purse that hangs low and a prominent bulge around her waist. She is carrying a maraca in one hand and a lantern in the other.

Petrovna: (*Shakes her maraca and moans softly.*) Ssshhhh.

> *Moans Louder.*

Sssshhh.

> *Moans louder still.*
> *Then speaks in an odd Eastern-European accent.*

Sssshhh! There is a strange presence in the room.

> *Beat.*

In addition to myself. I can feel it. Slightly. Ever so slightly. The temperature is dropping. It is cold...er. You feel it too. I know it. Even if you do not. Trust me. You do. Your spine, it is tingling. Slightly. Maybe not yours. But the person next to you? Definitely! I can feel it. And you can too. Listen, sssshhh...

> *She checks her purse.*

Damn, I forgot my chimes.

*he puts the lantern down on the crate on the
sideshow stage as the lights fade in.*

Okay wait, wait...something is wrong. I am receiving a message.
Yes. Somebody from beyond. A spirit from an outer sphere. It is
attempting to reconnect with one of you here tonight. But...it is
faint. Very far away. Like dark secret. Wait...

Looks up as if speaking to a spirit.

Yes?

Beat, and then crassly.

What? I know.

Beat.

Well what do you think I'm doing here? I'm trying. Okay, geez!
Bossy.

She gives an annoyed sigh.

So, apparently? There is an imbalance of temperaments in the
room. Of positive and negative energies, pure minds and repulsive
points. It is medium mumbo-jumbo. Not for you. All you need to
know is there is a block. Okay? Something...is getting in the way.
And communication? It is failing. We must reset conditions. And act
quickly now. Okay, wait, wait...

She scans the audience and then points to a couple.

You and you! Please… switch seats. And hurry!

She continues to egg them on until they switch seats.

Ahhhh!

Beat, and then deadpan.

That did nothing. Okay, never mind. Here she comes. She is coming now. This…is a lady. And she is trying to reconnect with somebody… in the front row. Or…near the front row. Maybe the second or third row? It could even be the last row. Does somebody here know a lady? Okay wait…

Looks up.

Yes? Okay…yes we got that already. You are a lady. Could you be more specific?

Beat.

This…

Frustrated now.

is a redundant lady. But…ah, but the name I am getting? Is not. Is there a…Paul? Or a Paula? Paulette?

Beat.

Terry? Okay, wait…there is somebody in the room who knows a lady with a man-sounding name. And she? Is dead!

Shakes her maraca.

But please, if it is you? Do not reveal yourself. No. I will find you. Even if I do not. I will. Because you? There? Sitting quietly in the dark. Wherever you are. Tingling, ever so slightly, in your seat. You? You know a dead lady with a man's name. And so? It is you I must be talking about. Because how else would I know such a thing? It's crazy. Okay wait...there is more.

Looks up.

Yes? There... is a feeling...of brokenness. Things undone and things unsaid. This...dead lady with a man's name, Paul or Paulette or Terry, she...

Looks up.

Yes?

Beat.

Okay. Got it. She...is somebody that maybe you, whoever you are, did not connect well with growing up. Maybe somebody you knew but did not like? Or...somebody you liked, but did not know. If not a family member, then a dear friend. Or maybe...a very good acquaintance? Of somebody else? You kind of know? No? A passerby? A person in a book? That you didn't read?

Beat.

Okay, fine. I will be the first to admit that things, they are not going well tonight. What can I say? You win some, you lose some. It happens. But at least we touched. And sometimes? That's all it takes...a touch.

Beat.

Oh I almost forgot...

Shakes her necklace of bells.

There. Closure.

Shrugs her shoulders.

Do I call it a gift? Sure, why not? What else would I call it? A curse?

Thinks it over.

Mmm, actually, it is that too. It is both. It is a gift and a curse. But I do not bother with such things. I am old...er. And not easily impressed. Speaking in tongues, table tapping, crystal ball gazing. Bleh. Who needs it? All those props? No. Not for me. Not anymore. Everything I need is right here. On my person. Which includes my maraca, necklace of bells and, well...that is it. These days.

Oh I know, I know what you are thinking. I can read minds too, okay? You're thinking, "What the hell? This woman, she is beautiful, yes, but she is not as advertised. Where is the third arm?" Well you know what? Boohoo, okay? Boohoo. Too bad. Go home if you want. I don't care. Sickos! What? It's not good enough I talk to dead people? I need to pull my pants down too? Give peepshow? Please.

Oh sure, don't get me wrong. I used to whip it out any chance I got. Juggle with it. Arm wrestle members of the audience. You would have loved it. Tug of war? It was very entertaining. But...that was for another time. And besides, it started getting in the way. Always trying to upstage me. Grabbing at my maraca. And so I had it bound. No big deal. It was easy. I learn tucking technique from an Indian eunuch over at the ethnic pavilion. Only downside though? Now everybody thinks I am pregnant. "When are you having your baby?" they ask. For last seven years! Bleh.

*She puts her hand on her bulge and gives
a look of indigestion. She moans softly.*

Sssshhh.

Moans louder.

Sssshhh.

Moans louder still.

Sssshhh! Whoa. Okay, hold on.
This one really wants out.

Looks up.

What? What is it loud mouth?

Beat.

Okay, okay fine. But stop screaming.
What is wrong with you? Just talk.

Beat.

Wait, wait, wait. First tell me who you are. Then tell me what you
want. What? Did your manners die too?

Beat.

Okay, this one? Is definitely a man. And he died...young-ish. Late
thirties I want to say. Maybe forty...five? Twenty-five? I don't know.
He won't shut up. Charlie or Chuck or...Chip?

Looks up.

Hey, these are all nicknames for same name?

Beat.

Yeah well come on. Take it easy.

Beat.

Okay, wait, slow down. You're not making any sense.

Beat.

Okay, good, Charles...what is it that you want?

Beat.

Ah. Okay. Yes...something about...the color...blue. I don't know. Does this resonate with anyone? Blue. He's listing them off. Rapidly. Different shades...cobalt and sapphire...periwinkle, cornflower, azure. Huh? Ultramarine? Geez! Whatever ever happened to just plain old blue? Okay, wait...

Beat.

So...maybe you know an artist-type, or...somebody fancy, or... melodramatic. Maybe insufferably so? Wait.

Looks up.

What?

Beat.

Oh...huh?

Beat.

Are you sure?

Beat.

Really?

Shrugs her shoulders.

Okay.

She gives the audience an embarrassed look.

Wow. Sorry. I was way off the mark people. Okay so, it turns out that...our Charlie here? Is not actually a spiffy artsy-fartsy type. No. Instead? He, uh...well he drowned. Yes.

Shrugs her shoulders.

What can I say? It's not my night. Give me break. But apparently, the different shades of blue? Were the very last things he saw as he sank like a rock to the bottom of the ocean floor. And the light? It splintered and slowly faded away from the deep water like the sun moving across stained glass and into nebulous clouds.

Sweeps her hand in the air.

What-ever! Sheesh. He may not be an artist but he is insufferably flowery nonetheless. Okay, so...huh?

Looks up.

Oh come on Charlie. What now?

Beat.

Okay, fine, fine I will, just stop. And...he wants you to know, you, whoever you are, that he is mad. Very mad. And he blames you. Not for drowning him. No. But...for not teaching him how to swim as a child. Can you believe this guy? I tell you.

Looks up.

Huh? No Charlie, no. Enough. Because...because you can't go blaming people for something like that. You died a man. Old enough to know you were in over your head. Literally. But instead? Look at you. Digging around in your childhood? And for what? It's too late. You're kaput. Give it up already!

Beat.

Huh?

Beat.

You're dead!

Addresses the audience.

It sounds obvious. I know. How could he not know he is dead? But sometimes they don't. Or they forget.

Beat.

See? Now he's crying. Like baby. Bleh. You know how I deal with this? Very simple. I just pretend that what I am hearing? Are tears of joy. And then? I block them out! For eternity. Goodbye Charlie. Happy trails. Besides, he thinks he had it so bad? Why? Because nobody took him to the beach? Teach doggy paddle? Please. That is nothing!

Let me tell you, I? I was left on the dark doorstep of Barnum's trailer! Okay? Not even a week old. With three little arms flailing. No note, no nothing. Just a tattered blanket and a speckled pear that was not even cut into slices. It was whole! Tell me, what was I going to do with a whole speckled pear? I have no teeth. I am a week old for god's sake! I am baby.

Beat.

But Barnum? He take me in. Not as his own. For...he is a man who has no one. But he treat me good...enough. I suppose. Teach me to talk in exotic accent, untie rope bindings and read sealed letters. And I do everything he ask. No questions. Working my way up to channeling energy into objects and even once materializing a spirit form. It was of a dead cocker spaniel, but still, not bad for little girl. And when I turn sixteen, as reward for my efforts, he build for me my very own spirit cabinet. And open to me a world where flowers and coins fall from the sky, balls of light skitter across the room, and where musical instruments, guitars and horns and drums float in the air and play tunes by themselves. And for the first time in my life, I feel different in a good way...even special. And everybody... wants to talk to me. Even dead people. And not because I have an extra flailing arm!

Beat.

But you know? I still keep the basket I was found in. For I? Forget nothing! Oh I burned the tattered blanket though. Sure. Mother Leafy? The negro voodooist? She put curse on it for me. She do African dance, cast some chicken bones. I don't know if it works. But the basket? I keep for myself. And every year, on the day I was found on doorstep, I put a speckled pear in it and let it sit. And rot there! And now? After so many years...the basket? It is full of rotten speckled pears. Crusted and sticky with carved bug holes. And I wait. Wait for this woman who was supposed to be my mother. I wait for her to come to me. Beg me for forgiveness. Tell me, "Petrovna, my sweet Petrovna, I so sorry, I make mistake." And I stand there with basket full of rotten speckled pears and I say, "Oh, really? Okay mama, it's okay." And then I proceed to pelt her body with the rotten speckled pears until she falls down broken in a dirty gutter, in a stew of putrid sewer water and rotten speckled pears! And then I spit on her! And I kick and I kick and I kick!

Pulls herself together.

And then? After she is good and dead? And everybody cries except for me. She will try to come back. To talk to me from the afterlife. Because she will be in a very dark place for what she has done. And she will be scared and alone. In a room with no walls. Left to rapping on tables and tinkling bells for my attention. And she will plead with me, "Please daughter, sweet Petrovna, help me." And I will say, "Oh, so sorry mama...get in back of line!"

Beat.

Oh I know, I know...it is wish of stupid child. But it could happen. Sure. Stranger things have. Trust me. I have seen them with my own two eyes. Séance sitters levitated in chairs and phosphorescent hands slapping the faces of nonbelievers. Don't kid yourselves. Okay? Nothing is shocking. And anything is possible. Especially in this place.

And besides, I can feel her. She is here. Well...not "here" here. But, here on the grounds. She has to be. And do you know why? Because...I? Was abandoned in the middle of the night. And let me tell you, the only thing harder than getting into Barnum's Grand Travelling Fortress after hours? Is getting out! And so? She is among us. One of us. I know it! And why not? People mistake me all the time for being pregnant. They could have just as easily mistaken her for not. Who knows? Maybe she is the fat lady? And nobody noticed the extra pounds. Or maybe she is the opposite. Yes, maybe she is the Human Skeleton and she wore layers? You don't know. The point is? It is possible. And possibility? Gives hope. And that keeps you going. Even if that hope...is to brutally bludgeon your own mother. It is still something to strive for! And we all need something to get us out of bed in the morning.

Shrugs her shoulders.

But regardless of pep talk....she is definitely here, okay? Trust me. And this horrible, cowardly, fat or skinny lady has watched me for years. Grow up. Alone. Teased. No wait, taunted. No, haunted! With no mother. And stuck with only Barnum...as an overbearing organ grinder of a father. Where the hell was she? Hiding behind corners and lost in crowds. She could be anyone. Which is why I trust no one. I hate people. Even dead ones. I can't help it. Oh they really bug me the most!

She puts her hand on her bulge and gives a look of indigestion. She moans softly.

Oh god, see what I mean? Here we go again.

Looks up.

What is it now? Can't you see I'm busy here spilling my guts? Get lost! Sssshhh.

Moans louder.

Sssshhh.

Moans louder still.

Sssshhh! Okay, wait, wait, this...this is...

Beat, and then motherly.

Oh, why hello there little one. It is you.
Where have you been my darling?

Beat.

Yes, I know. It's okay. But your aunt Petrovna misses you.

To the audiences.

Oh, I'm sorry. But, this one?

Defensively.

Is not for you. No. I have known her for many years. Since we are both little girls. Only now? I am older. But she? Is still the same. And she looks to me...for tenderness. It's crazy, I know. Barking up wrong tree.

Looks up.

What? No, no my sweet, I'm sorry. I want very much to play with you. But I am in middle of show here. Please come back in a little while, okay?

Beat.

Yes.

Beat.

Yes I know, what can I do, I am sorry. I said it once already.

Beat.

Me too. Okay my dear.

Beat.

Good.

She looks at the audience feeling a little exposed.

What? So I lie. Not all people bug me. Leave me alone.
What can I say? I am walking contradiction.

Beat.

And besides, it's not so easy you know. With all that I have inside me.
To sort it out. All the smatterings of rumors and shreds of hearsay.

Beat.

You know, when I was just about her age, there was a pack of awful
carnival kids. Like rabid dogs. They would pin me to the floorboards
with their knees. Give my third arm Indian burns. And whisper to
me the most disturbing stories about myself. And me, being a lowly
orphan? I could do nothing but lay there on the ground and believe
them. Because, after all...anything is possible.

Oh sure, they were just dumb parrots. Repeating what all the grownups were saying. That I am somehow evil. Can you believe that? Mean, yes. Nasty, maybe. But evil? That's pushing it a bit. I mean come on. I don't pace back and forth twisting my mustache and hatching plans. No. But...if you hurt me? Well what do you expect?

They used to say that my mother? She left me on doorstep because she could not stand to look at my third arm. Yes, okay, obvious, duh. But that was only part of it. They also tell me that the real reason is because I was actually a twin inside the womb. And that I ate my own sister. Very creative, I know. And that my third arm here? Was her last ditch, lingering effort to fight her way out. I suppose it is why I can speak to dead people too. Like an antenna. I don't know. The kids never got a chance to finish their stupid story. I am, after all, a very good biter.

> *Chomps her teeth.*

But who knows? Maybe it's all true. Maybe I have been pregnant with my own sister all this time. And maybe the little girl who comes to visit me? Maybe she...is her. Of course it has crossed my mind. I'm not an idiot. Oh what a pretty picture that would turn out to be, eh? But you know what? Who cares? I don't bother with such things. Not anymore. Of putting pieces back together. And besides, what good can come from a completed puzzle? Tell me, what are you going to do with it? Frame it and hang it on the wall? No, that's for losers. You break it up of course. And start all over again. That's just the way things are. Broken. With things undone and things unsaid.

> *Beat.*

No. You want closure in life? Then go get yourself necklace of bells. And sit in the dark.

> *PETROVNA rings her necklace of bells.*
> *Mucca Pazza's song, "Moriya" plays.*
> *Lights slowly fade out as she picks up the lantern and exits.*

SCENE FIVE

LUDMILLA enters dancing to the light of the lantern as Mucca Pazza's "Moriya" continues to play. Lights fade in. She dances her way over to a member of the audience and invites that person to join her. They dance for a few turns and then she returns the audience member to their seat. Then LUDMILLA makes her way over to the microphone as the music fades out.

Ludmilla: *(Referring to Petrovna)* Hmm...

> *Strokes her beard.*

that three-armed Petrovna makes me wonder if this hairy thing here belongs to a long lost uncle of mine. You know, in ancient times? Egyptian queens would wear long metal beards of gold elaborately tied in red ribbon. It was a girlish representation of manhood. A goofy attempt to show they were just one of the boys. I don't know though. Seems a queen would have higher aspirations. Sounds like a king's idea to me.

Truth be told? I myself have never really had a thing for men.
And the thought of wanting to be them?

> *Shakes her head.*

Just doesn't exist inside my head. No, in fact for most of my life? It's been the other way around. It's true. I've done nothing but meet men...who want to be me. In one way or another. They always manage to see...something. Whether it be sexual virility or wisdom or some other prepubescent belief about what a beard is supposed to be. I don't know. But whatever it is they see? Rest assured, it's never...me.

   Beat.

I was born with sideburns, you know? And by the age of five? I had a full goatee. To call it torment? Well that would be sugarcoating it a bit. Oh they say beauty is only skin deep. And that may be. But the reality? Is that most of us don't do much digging. And so I tried... everything as a tyke. Shaving, tweezing and even ingesting enough balding tonic to embalm my insides. And it worked. It did. For a brief moment? I felt...normal. Or at least, left alone. But come morning? And the stubble would be scraping my pillow. Even thicker than before. Like a divine slap on the face for not counting my blessings.

And so I just said, "Oh to hell with it!" And decided to give...not up, but in. I embraced...

(Thinks it over.) or no, maybe abandoned, yes...that ethereal image of "me" that I'm supposed to be. And now? Today? Right here in this moment? Well I can honestly say, with one hundred percent certainty, that I'm happy...er. Than I was before. A moment ago. And let's face it, what else is there? I mean, isn't that all there is? And, well...

   Sings the song, "Is That All There Is?"

If that's all there is,
If that's all there is,
If that's all there is my friends,

Then let's keep dancing.
Let's break out the booze and have a ball.
If that's all...there is.

Beat.

And in fitting fashion Ladies and gentlemen, I present to you our final act of the evening, Dorian...the Head Doctor Extraordinaire.

The spotlight fades out. LUDMILLA exits.

SCENE SIX

DORIAN enters wheeling in a huge phrenology head on a stand. He then gets onto the sideshow stage with his back to the audience. Lights fade in as he begins admiring the back of his head with two handheld mirrors. He is immaculately dressed in a magician's tuxedo. He suffers from a migraine that grows increasingly more splitting as the show goes on.

Dorian: *(After a few moments)* Having only the back of my head to base your opinion on, would you wager that I am...handsome? Hmm? And apropos, do I possess the corresponding physical conditions that indicate virtuous character? In other words, am I a good person just because I'm pretty?

Or...on the flip side of the coin, am I repugnant to you and thus possess criminal-like characteristics? Meaning, does the dorsal region of my dome emit an inherent ethical quality of goodness, or is my...brain buttress, if you will, simply that of a brute? To boil it down, what do the bumps, dimples, dents, and dips, the contours of my cranium...convey to you? Hmm?

He turns around and faces the audience.

Am I...let's say, the marrying kind, always longing for a matrimonial mate and in favor of family sit-down dinners with little critter versions of myself?

Or...do I have a despicable disposition complete with a wandering eye for women-wooing? Hmm?

Do I indulge in warm, fuzzy feelings towards my fellow man? Or do I hold the view that the entire human race should be herded together and shepherded off of the proverbial cliff of "Bad Company?"

If faced with a child on my knee, would I have a propensity to bounce...or to spank it? What is the balance of angel and animal inside of me? Hmm?

Beat.

Is something like...murder, well within my means?

Beat.

And what about your own?

He rubs his temples in pain.

Phrenologically speaking of course.

He clears his throat.

Ladies and gentlemen, what if I were to tell you, right here and now, that all of these awkward, overly personal questions that I have just spewed forth in front of a room full of strangers...all that, plus the complete inner makings and merits of a man were not only capable of being predetermined, but, but I say...also very predictable? Hmm?

And all simply by probing the topography of your own noggin using nothing more than the crude scientific instruments of your forefinger and thumb? Would you call it...magic? Hmm? Maybe.

For after all, what is magic, really? That is, for old pachyderms like us who are way past childhood? Other than the perpetual renewed surprise of your own aging stupidity, the entertainment of your own naked inability to understand things that are way over your head, over and over again? Apologies for the abrupt wake-up call, but it's true. What is...the purpose of magic? Hmm?

> *Beat.*

Allow me to gander a guess. You see something done right before your very eyes, and you don't get it. A coin miraculously appears from behind your ear, a scantily clad assistant in rhinestones is miraculously sawed in half and somehow survives."Hooray!" you inexplicably exclaim. Expectations of amazement have been mysteriously met.

> *Beat.*

But deep down inside something still rubs you the wrong way because you just can't quite put your finger on how it all transpired. What did your physical faculties actually just witness?

And without any further proof, you simply reply, "Oh well," with a sigh of resignation. Because the real purpose of magic my friends? Is not to dazzle you with wonderment. Oh no! .

Rather? It is to make you feel, in layman's terms, out of the loop. To make you doubt yourself. To make you come face-to-face with the harsh, petrified terms that you no longer possess the youthful ability to believe in the unbelievable, to imagine the unimaginable.

> *Beat.*

And that right there is the crux my friends. For the recently born believe in all of the extreme possibilities of life. Whereas the elderly? The soon to be embalmed? Only believe in cemetery plots and platitudes.

Beat.

But truth be told? I've never been a big believer in stardust or crystal balls myself. In fact, I loathe all mystics, soothsayers, clairvoyants, and astronomical readers alike. Charlatans the entire lot!

And that's because, magic, to me? As an expert in phrenology? Can more easily be explained away by brain science more than any slight of hand-ness ever could.

For when you witness a magic trick my friends, what you are really being forced to do, is to experience an intricate procedure of steps that are not privy to you. An intentional series of secrets and misdirections unfolding and fluttering away like insolent butterflies into the invisible ether.

And you? In turn? You miss it all. Every last bit. And not because there was nothing to see, but because you no longer had the abilities to see it. For magic, just like a miserable life, is ultimately a shell game. Both, rely heavily...on blindness.

Beat.

Now, whoa. I know...this may have just come across as somewhat hard to swallow. But then again? Most medicine is! And though it may seem as if I'm jumping great caverns here, I can promise you that, like magic itself, phrenology, the seemingly hocus-pocus physical study of the skull for specific personality clues, for the most part? Works in very much the same way.

Therefore, any scientific inconsistencies, apparent knowledge gaps, perceived leaps of faith and so on and so forth is not to be seen as any fault of mine, and should immediately be chalked up to your own untrained eye as an amateur audience member! Trust me, we will all get along much more splendidly if we simply adhere to this premise.

He rubs his temple in pain.

I'm sorry. Where was I?

Beat.

Ah yes, that said, it is the head...that holds the key to our identity. And yet, ever since that famous water-kissing fool, the incestuous self-admiring Narcissus, far too much emphasis has been misplaced... on the face.

On inviting smiles, aquiline noses and twinkling eyes. But do not be duped by the masks of men my friends. For much like the glorious, windswept maiden at the bow of the boat who garners all of the attention and glory, it is nevertheless the stern of the ship where the captain resides! And ipso facto, the captain's sleeping quarters are always the most ornate and immaculate, contrary to the outside eye.

For inside? It is always adorned with fantastic, yet impractical seafaring rows of stained-glass windows, painted portraits, floor-to-ceiling drapery, who knows?

Perhaps even a colorful caged parrot with a propensity for perching on shoulders and speaking in vulgarities.

Beat.

Who's to say? I certainly can't. And that's because, to be completely honest? I've never really been much of a water person.

But, getting back to my central point here...

He rubs his temple in pain.

Wait. What was it? Ah, yes...the captain's quarters...yes. They're always elaborately described in the most popular of long-winded, voyage epics. It's true. Moby Dick? When you read between the lines? Is really less about the harpooning of a big white fish and more about Captain Ahab's linen count!

And this alone, my friends, should suffice to say that it's not the face, but the skull that is our golden treasure trove. Because it is, after all, where the brain resides and calls home. And as we all know, the brain, itself, cages the soul. Q.E.D!

       Beat.

However, this seemingly simple deduction did not always used to be. For instance, Pythagoras, the great Greek mathematician of yore, once held the view that the kernel of a man's character resided in the stomach. Resounding proof that he probably should have stuck to natural herbs that helped with digestion...and triangles. Then of course, some years later, there was Aristotle, the drippy poetess, who placed all of his eggs in a heart-shaped basket. And please, don't even get me started further down the philosophical line with Descartes' pinecone theory because it's a doozy.

       He clears his throat.

Instead? Let it just be said, that it goes without saying, even though I'm choosing to say it, that we now, unlike ever before, possess in our own two hands the very tools needed to...

       Blocks out the words with his hand.

"KNOW...THY...SELF!"

As was written in great, big, golden capital letters upon the towering temple of Delphos, as the most important of all maxims transferred down to unborn generations by hairy Mediterranean wise men.

And the crown jewel of all self-knowledge utensils? Is none other than the ground-breaking, bald-headed phrenology bust!

Makes his way to the phrenology head on the stand.

Oh yes! Featuring the surgical exactitude of dotted lines and the authority of formal-looking fonts like Book Antiqua or Times New Roman, this seemingly inconsequential pale little man-head here is a veritable crystal ball of being!

Breaking down our brain abilities into thirty-five intricately defined and conveniently irrefutable beef-cuts of categorized character.

Ladies and gentlemen no longer do you have to sit and wonder about your moral and/or religious sentiments, your domestic propensities, acquisitiveness, or ability to calculate and comprehend figures, facts and smells!

Seriously folks! What greater gift could there possibly be other than having the ability to opening up your very own Pandora's box of being? To possess the ability to navigate the mental landmarks and brain boundaries of your own personality? Why your spirituality, your liberality, your hopes for the future, talent for mimicry, gregariousness and integrity can all be deduced first thing in the morning while just combing your hair!

He puts his hand to his ear as if listening from afar.

Hmm? What's that you say? Still not convinced? Very well then, watch closely, for there's nothing up my sleeves...

Now if each and every one of you in the audience here tonight would please be so kind as to assist me by taking the thumb of your left hand... and sticking it directly into your left ear!

Oh that's right folks, you did not mishear me.

He demonstrates on himself.

Just take a moment and plug it up like so!

Beat.

Okay, now take your forefinger of the same hand and gently begin stroking it back and forth in a semi-circular motion, moving along the circumference of your upper ear, and using your thumb as an axle.

Beat.

Very good. Yes. Keep going. And...now, wait for it. Wait for it. There. Yes! Right there. Do you feel that? Hmm? Or better still, have you ever felt it before? The bumpy terrain, the peaks and valleys of your brain?

Right there, hidden in plain view under your hair? Well, believe it or not ladies and gentlemen, but you are currently fondling the faculty...of what is known as your own "Destructiveness."

Oh yes! But don't stop. Please, keep caressing. For there's nothing to fear. Oh no. Keep it up. Continue to tickle your terrible intent. Feel the way your skull has fused and formed around your own malignancy since the day of your birth. Keeping it hidden, like a sinister secret in your inner recesses for all these years.

Now ladies and gentlemen, please be honest. If you did indeed feel a bump, then that diagnosis means you possess a propensity, to a certain degree, for the extermination and mad desire to end all beautiful things badly! This includes cooing babies, saplings that have just sprouted from acorns, and most domesticated, declawed animals.

Whereas, if you find a dimple, dent or dip, then you indeed have a deficiency with your "Destructiveness" faculty and for some inexplicable reason wish to preserve things exactly as they are. Or even worse? Promote their longevity.

Now...that said, more than likely you are currently blindly probing both the stalactites and stalagmites of that cave of yours you call a cranium. That is, both bumps and dips at the same time. For we all struggle to recognize and temper our own temptations.

But just stop and think about it for a moment. For every possible feeling, characteristic, emotion and faculty...every mysterious, tiny, ticking, little thingy inside that head of yours that makes you exactly who you are can now be culled up from the darkness and cast directly into the daylight of discovery! Oh yes! You. You?

      Beat.

Can finally know you.

      As an aside.

Well, that is to says...in every way...except when it comes to guilt. Hmm? Yes, unfortunately that is the one elusive phrenological characteristic that remains to be a bit of a lurker.

      He clears his throat.

But still, putting guilt up on the shelf for just a moment, what I'm saying here must have, however so slight, some sort of appeal here people? Am I right?

Now...yes. Yes, of course, some of you cynics out there might see a few minor downsides to being able to forecast your own destiny with a self-examination in the form of a head massage. To which I reply...point taken.

But! And this is a very big "but"...it cannot be denied that these needling doubts of yours are nonetheless far outweighed by even the most miniscule, hair thinning chance of possibly knowing with complete certainty the course and outcome, the final prognosis, of your very own predetermined destiny!

For you are, after all, who you are. And when it comes to change? Oh no. Apologies. But there is no changing. And the sooner you learn that lesson of inevitability, the sooner you can really start learning and loving yourself, and stop! Just stop! Stop, well... wishing. Wishing that you were somehow different. Wishing...that you were in some way...someone else.

He blurts out a crazed laugh.

Do you have any idea, any inkling at all, as to how much time I have literally spent in front of the mirror trying my damnedest to be somebody, anybody really...other than me? Hmm?

Purely for professional purposes mind you. But still, we are not talking about mere moments of minutes here people. No. More like days. Once even just hours shy of a week.

It's true. I have performed on myself every known form of (makes air-quotes) "looking" capable to the human eye. Leering, peeking, wincing, even glaring over the shoulder with a raised eyebrow. Oh yes! I have studied every last ounce of who I physically am, and can say with one-hundred percent certainty that I? Am unfortunately still me!

No, in fact, only once in my lifetime have I ever witnessed such an ability to permanently shape shift one's own facial disposition and, for all intents and purposes, become a complete stranger to himself.

It was years ago. And done absolutely by accident. You may remember him well. Or maybe not at all. But he was all the rage over there on Barnum's main stage for a while and went by numerous pseudonyms such as...

The Human Peephole? Hmm? No? A bit lurid, I agree. How about The Hollow Headsman? And then of course there was the not so clever, Man...with an Extra Orifice, just to name a few.

But never mind all that, for I knew him personally in the quiet confines of our shared tent as just plain old Phineas Gage. Oh yes! He was my roommate and, well...due to the forced intimate nature of tents...a close friend.

>   *He clears his throat.*

And so...as his elaborate story was whispered to me in piecemeal during multiple late night session of pillow talk, Phineas was made unfortunately famous while working as a railway gang foreman blasting rock in the Vermont green mountains.

If I recall correctly, it was somewhere near the town of Cavendish. He was in the process of preparing an explosive, something he had done routinely over a thousand times. First adding gunpowder, then a long fuse, and sand on top of that. And then finishing it all off by tamp, tamp, tamping the charge down with a large tamping iron rod.

>   *Beat.*

But in this one moment? It all went...wrong. And...

>   *Yells.*

Boom!

>   *Beat.*

Fourteen of Phineas' teeth were found forty feet away in a dirt pile from the explosion. And his greasy brain matter was identified all over his co-workers' overalls.

According to records, the gunpowder inexplicably sparked and exploded like lightening, shooting the tamping iron rod, which by the way was over an inch thick in circumference and almost four feet in length, straight through the side of his face, shattering the upper jaw to pieces, spearing the back portion of Phineas' left eye, and spouting out at the very top of his head like a whale's blowhole.

Beat.

Weeks later, after miraculously recovering from his immense injuries...Phineas was left to figuring out a new life. Once he came back to consciousness, Phineas claimed that the cause of his disaster was that he was momentarily distracted because he heard someone calling out his name from a distance. A nickname that his loved ones used to call him as a boy, and that few people knew him by in his present.

He shrugs his shoulders.

Needless to say, ninety-nine times out of a hundred and poor Phineas' head would have been a covered wagon for worms. But instead, and to everyone's astonishment he was alert and speaking, albeit incoherently, within just a few minutes, walking around with little or no assistance picking up molars, and even sitting upright in a mule cart for the three-quarters of a mile ride back to camp. It was, by all accounts...a anatomical magic trick.

However, that's not to say that his recovery was quick and painless in any way. No, in fact, it was exactly as you would imagine it to be if you were to have a large skewer shish kabob your head. It hurt like hell! And did so for days. Weakened from hemorrhage, Phineas suffered a fungal infection, had recurring bouts of fever, and was ultimately left in a semi-comatose state for nearly two weeks.

But time did tick away as it always does and things did somehow get better. So much so that in just under three months his physician's final report stated that, and I quote...

Makes air quotes.

"Phineas Gage appeared to be on route to recovery, that is, if... and only if, he could be controlled."

Beat.

Well haunting last words to say the least! For though Phineas did look more or less like his old self, people who knew him well did begin to wonder. Having always been regarded as well-balanced and hardworking, responsible and extremely popular among his men for leading by quiet example, Phineas was now said to be fitful, irreverent, and even indulging at times in the grossest of profanity, which was not previously his custom.

Always an ardent abstainer, he now possessed animal passions and took to drink. Not to mention that he couldn't keep hold of a job. And so naturally, he fit all the major requirements for becoming the latest rage in Barnum's crippled collection of... unattractive attractions.

He clears his throat.

But...Phineas' new life? Was far from being a perfect fit. In fact, with my ear pressed to the canvas of our tent I would often hear him weeping inside. Hard slobbery sobs like a mourner. And every night when I would return home for the evening I'd find my mirrors somehow covered in burlap and stored away deep inside my lock box.

On occasion I did try to console him. To talk to him. I read passages and periodicals to him. And even gave him an extra pillow of mine to ease his breathing. But the poor man could barely hold a conversation anymore. He was always either drenched in drink, marinating his pain, or fidgeting from withdrawal. I would go on and on about how there was a perfectly phrenological explanation for all his misfortunes. But it was very hard to get him to open up. And when I tried, he would curse me for my efforts.

But still, I did feel obliged. For when he first arrived, Father Barnum himself approached me in his usual way, always from an angle and on the sly. Sneaking up and whispering into my ear that it would be a very good idea indeed for the two of us to be roommates. Being who I am, he thought I might be able to help Phineas in some way. But of course, the crafty Barnum was careful enough not to expound on how this exactly was to be done.

He rubs his temple in pain.

I remember...it was very hot, even with the tent flaps thrown back. As if everything that night was set to a low simmer. And the sharp stench of stale urine must have preceded him by at least ten paces. Curling the hair in my nostrils. There's just something about the heat that makes a dirty man go directly to rot. I even went so far as to lower my wick in fear of the fumes. And as a result, Phineas didn't know I was there. He entered stumbling and mumbling to himself as usual. Childish gibberish. Something about "Phinny-O" or "phinno" or "minnow," I don't really know. Besides, it didn't matter. Because whatever he was babbling about stopped mid-syllable as soon as he caught sight of my floor mirror, which to my utter dismay, I had accidentally left undraped.

Beat.

And before anything was to be done about it, he was already standing nose to nose with his own reflection. As if trying to figure out a way to apologize for whom he had become.

Beat.

Delicately dragging his fingers across his face. Over and over again. As if desperately trying to read his disfiguration. His scars like lines on the palm of a hand. Looking for something... anything!

Beat.

And then? Suddenly and without warning, he blurted out a brief but violent convulsion, and then abruptly collapsed unconscious onto his cot. And for the longest time the both of us just laid there in that sour, dark little tent of ours... motionless, without meaning, and mad.

After I was sure Phineas was down for the night, I quietly got up, covered the floor mirror, and made my way over to him to begin what had become, over the years, something of a bedtime ritual between us.

Holding my breath, I peeled off his soggy boots and began to prop up his head with the extra pillow I had given him, when... I finally saw it. There. On his face. Albeit faint and tucked under like a sick child who just wants to play. It was nonetheless, very clearly, the reminisce... of a smile. Yes, he was... smiling... in his sleep. And it caught me completely off guard. Because I had never seen him do it before. Such a simple act. A smile. But it made no sense. Was he dreaming? And if so... what about? What are you keeping secret Phineas?

Beat.

As I stood over him, clinching both ends of the pillow, I began to grow dizzy. Perhaps I was still holding my breath. I can't say. But everything, including the tent itself, just grew so tight around my ribcage like a straightjacket. Like a frog in a vat of increasing boiling water. I could feel myself slowly boiling into something beastly.My knuckles whitening and forearms on fire as the blood from my brain began to drain. And before I knew what I was doing...I was already pressing down. As hard as I could. With the pillow over that sleepy smile of his.

Beat.

And to this day, I still don't really know why... I did it. But that smile. That smile stays with me.

He shakes his head and gives a half-hearted laugh.

Who knows? Who's to say? You know, guilt? It is a funny thing. No matter how hard you try, and oh I've gone to great lengths, it appears you can't really think your way out of it. No. Guilt? It is, without a doubt, the head's Achilles' heel. And that's because, as the forefathers of phrenology eventually found out, Guilt? It doesn't quite fit into any neatly defined category. It's neither a characteristic nor a talent. Not quite an emotion or a trait. And with no exact location or point of origin in the brain, guilt? Is really more like a ghost...in the way that it forever haunts us.

Possessing you with an everlasting pain. Part memory, part regret, and in large part? Paralysis. It is a pain so powerful that it makes you almost unfamiliar to yourself. Leaving you like a stranger...inside your own head.

In pain, he begins rubbing the inside of his left ear with his thumb.

No, guilt? It is the one thing that defies smoke and all mirrors my friends. The one magic trick that none of us can ever seem to figure out...

*Mucca Pazza's "Peace Meal" fades in at 00:45
as the lights fade to black.*

Dorian exits holding his head.

SCENE SEVEN

Lights fade in on LUDMILLA at the microphone.
Everything else is black.

Ludmilla: *(Somewhat sarcastic)* Ah, and so...there you have it my dear friends. Isn't ending an intimate evening together on a happy note such a blessing? And speaking of such...that is, I mean, "happiness" in and of itself, isn't that a very good thing to strive for?

> *Beat.*

Or perhaps? No. Maybe it all depends on how we go about it? Who can say for sure?

> *Beat.*

But did you know? That one of P.T. Barnum's most famous exhibits of all time was coincidentally entitled, "The Happy Family?"

Oh yes, it's true. Housed in his famous American Museum in New York City in the early 1840's, it was a misdirected, caged cacophonous celebration of predators and prey. Creatures from all over the world that somehow harmoniously lived together in perfect incarceration. Birds and beasts alike.

Jurassic-toothed alligators and white-tailed sly foxes, lions and other assortments of blood-thirsty feral felines, wooly succulent sheep, mischievous raccoons up to no good, weasels without merit, lament-less mourning doves, arrogant eagles, and more!

Beat.

And the lines...there were lines each paying day of eager patrons willing to suspend their disbelief snaked around the corner just to catch a meager glimpse of this magical menagerie that somehow defied eons of dastardly instinct and violence at the very reasonable price of only twenty-five cents a pop.

Beat.

But how? How was such a cozy cohabitation even possible, you may ask yourself? What was the trickery behind this counter-intuitive camaraderie witnessed right before your very eyes?

Pretends to roll up her sleeves.

Well...my dear friends, the big reveal? Is actually quite simple. Because, when you get right down to it on a very basic level? The belief in magic? Is really just for dumb babies and even dumber adult morons!

For truth be told? When all is said and done? The secret to "The Happy Family" was really little more than a calculated orchestration of starvation, sleep deprivation and a finely-tuned clockwork routine of torture practices.

And as a result? The poor creatures were simply too exhausted, demoralized, and frightened to fight back against all the Barnum (makes air quotes) "benevolence" bestowed, or...perhaps more aptly, beaten upon them. I suppose it all depends on how you see the half-filling of a glass.

Beat.

But dollars to donuts? If you ask me? Though I'm not a betting man-ish. It all sort of makes sense, really...if you think about it. For after all...happiness?

Beat.

It does take a bit of work. Wouldn't you say?

Lights fade out on LUDMILLA at the microphone.

Music plays.

— The End —

DIANA SLICKMAN as Ludmilla
in *The Art of Unbearable Sensations*

JULIA WILLIAMS in a promotional shot for *The Near Future*

The Near Future / That Sort of Thing

Premiered **January 2018**

**The Rhinoceros Theater Festival
at Prop Thtr / Chicago, IL**

written & directed by **JULIA WILLIAMS**

performed by:

**Kelly Anchors
Brook Celeste
Whitman Johnson
Danne W. Taylor**

THE
PLAYS

SETTING

Now or soon.

CAST of CHARACTERS

Various people you probably know,
and their companions.

Jackets

TWO WOMEN emerge from behind a curtain, straightening their clothes as if trying them on for the first time. One leads the conversation, while the other speaks vaguely in response or echo, as if trying on language for the first time. They are styled identically and, indeed, could be identical. Each wears a blazer with a loud pattern, and the patterns clash.

One: Well, what do you think?

Two: Do you think.

One: Do I look like you?

Two: I look like you.

One: That's true.

Two: That's true.

One: Hmm... *(regarding TWO)*

Two: Hmmm.

One: *(as if a remark was made by the previous)* Oh, shush, you. *(regarding TWO again)* No. That's not quite it.

Two: Not. No, not.

> *ONE waves her hand, and TWO retreats back behind the curtain.*

One: There's not much to do anymore. You'll find that out. There are a few places to be, to go to, but... well, it's all pretty rotten.

Two: *(behind curtain)* Rotten.

One: Yes, rotten. Indeed.

> *TWO re-emerges, in a new jacket. It also clashes.*

One: Oh, that's something. That's surely something.
         You look...

Two: Do I look.

One: You do. You surely do. Only... Well... Hang on.

> *ONE retreats behind the curtain. During her absence, TWO moves head and eyes around slowly, mechanically, as if doing calisthenics, or testing the possibilities of this body. Tries on facial expressions. ONE speaks from behind the curtain:*

One: I suppose I might as well tell you this. I've always had trouble matching. Something about patterns. I look and all I see is busy, busy, busy. I can't tell what's good and what's awful. So much clutter these days, so much everything, and yet also... nothing. So full, and so empty. You won't know this. Of course. I'll tell you about it. "Where's the peacefulness?," I always thought. Where's that good old country quiet?

> *ONE re-emerges, in a different jacket, again clashing. TWO snaps back to attention, making a social face, when ONE reappears.*

Two: Yes. Quiet.

One: Yes. Quiet. You won't know much about that,
         now will you. Fresh from the shell.

> *ONE looks at their outfits, again with dissatisfaction.*

One: No. It won't do.

Two: It won't do.

One: You're right. It won't. Come here.

> *ONE and TWO retreat together behind the curtain.*
> *Some rustling of elbows through the fabric.*

One: You know. It's good having you here. We are going to get
         a lot done together.

Two: *(mimicking)* We are going to get a lot done together.

One: Yes—well, not together exactly, not in the same place.
         But in concert. I'll lead the way. We're like twin fiddles,
         you and I. No harmony. Exact doubles.

> *ONE and TWO re-emerge from the curtain in*
> *identical black blazers, looking smart if perhaps*
> *also sinister, and now very hard to tell apart.*
> *ONE is beaming with accomplishment;*
> *TWO copies in approximation.*

One: We look great....We are great....What is that?

ONE sees something on TWO's person that displeases her. ONE reaches out a thumb and carefully swabs a spot on TWO's neck, coming very close into personal space. ONE examines her thumb suspiciously, looks around the room, makes an unconscious facial gesture, possibly running the tongue over the teeth, then returns to face forward; during all this, TWO copies the facial gesture, experimentally. Satisfied, ONE places an arm around TWO's shoulders.

One: It's funny. We've only just met, but I feel like you've always been here.

Two: Always.

One: Yes. Always.

         They exit.

Dog Story

Two friends, over coffee.

Titus: I am walking down the street, it is late in the morning—

Carroll: That's not interesting.

Titus: Why is that not interesting?

Carroll: What street is it? What are you seeing on the street? Have I been there?

Titus: It doesn't matter what street it is—

Carroll: Has someone I know been there? If I saw it on Pinterest, would I want to be there? Is this a street that anyone might conceivably put on Pinterest?

Titus: I am walking down a street, it is any street, I know streets are different but will you please for a moment allow me my milieu.

Carroll: You are on a street.

Titus: A person is coming with a dog, coming at me, about fifty feet away.

Carroll: Coming at you? Like with a knife?

Titus: Coming toward me.

Carroll: If you had a dog, why would you need a knife?
          That's double weapons.

Titus: It wasn't a weapon dog, it was a fluffy black dog,
          I'm getting to that—

Carroll: See? Specificity is important. I don't know what kind of street it is, I don't know what kind of dog it is, so I don't know if I should be concerned for your safety in this story—

Titus: That is because I am still telling you the story. I am getting to it about the dog. The person is coming at me, toward me, with a fluffy black dog, the kind of dog my pal Joe would say used to guard the Chinese palace walls when we were kids—

Carroll: Were you at the Chinese palace when you were kids?
          I didn't know.

Titus: Syntax error. No, he said it when we were kids, when we'd see this fluffy black dog in the neighborhood, this one lady had it. Chow chow. That's the dog. This was not that kind of dog though, it had a different face. But it's approaching on the sidewalk, and I get a little tense. I am straightening my walk because I'm passing another person who I should tip my hat to, and also the dog, who I don't know how much it knows about me.

Carroll: How many dogs know about you?

Titus: Too many. A few. I go the whole block in this condition, walking tensely, ready to lift my head up and make a smile when I get near enough to them, and then I see after a while that I'm not getting closer to them. They were so far away that I could see them but I couldn't tell which way they were going. They were going away. We never met.

Carroll: That was not interesting.

Titus: I am not through telling you. The woman and the not-a-chow-chow are receding and receding, or really we're keeping pace so we're just fifty feet apart, going the same way, when all of a sudden behind me comes a quick step, I hear it just as it's passing me, it's a man in a horrible jogging suit and trotting in front of *him* is a dog.

Carroll: Ooh, twist.

Titus: It's a black, fluffy dog, it's a chow-chow, an actual one. When you see the ghost of something before you see it, you know that? There it was, the thing coming after the warning of it, and as it passed, the man is so oblivious to everything in his green tracksuit, as it passed the dog looked up at me and it grinned. It showed me all its teeth, and it kept jogging past.

Carroll: Oh, that's not good.

Titus: No, it's not. It's very not.

Monologue: The Tape

A woman in a large armchair. She sits with her body knotted up, legs and arms tangled so as to be as compact and contained as possible, the armchair like a private ship. Beside the chair is a side table with a tape recorder on it. After a time, the woman throws the book suddenly against the wall, shouts.

Woman: Get out!

> *Calls offstage:*

Rupert.

> *Nothing. More firmly:*

Rupert!

> *Rupert enters: silent and intentional, something like a butler. The woman points at the book, now resting against the wall. He walks to it, wasting no movement, and picks it up.*

Rupert don't let that one back in. I hate that one.

> *He nods. He makes to leave.*

Rupert do you have another?

> *He nods and exits.*

Some things you shouldn't let in. *(pause)* I do not feel well. I do not feel well it has been some time. It has been some time.

She turns on the tape recorder, speaks into it:

You know how when you love someone, when you realize now that you need them, you start to always picture them dead? You know? You get the call: they've been attacked on the street, brutalized, run over by a trolley, and you go down to the station, you want to see the body, you want to see their sweet stupid face wherever it is, and the coroner says, "There's nothing to show, Anita, he's hamburger meat." And you say, "Come on, there's got to be more than that," and the coroner says, "It was a herd of maenads, it was the middle of day, they couldn't be stopped, it was quite a big trolley," and you say "Dammit Eric, I want to see the body!," and the coroner says "Okay, I'll show you something, but the biggest piece left, size of a postage stamp." You say, "Fine, let me see it, let me see the postage stamp," and he brings out the piece on a little tray and yes, indeed, it's like a pencil eraser — it is some part, the last unharmed part of your dear beloved friend. Is it the elbow, is it the hip? You don't know, and you think you will see a freckle, that you'll know it, you'll remember it, but no, you can't, there's nothing, take it away, Eric, and then just done, and gone. And even if Eric would let you keep the piece, which he won't, even if he would, what would you, keep it in formaldehyde? On the mantle? In a jar? Or save it in your pocket, in the dungarees, and rub it between thumb and finger? In times of worry? Or would you wedge it on the inside of your cheek, up next to the gum, forever? Flesh of my flesh, this is where I keep you? What? Or would you let it go, leave the building, get in a cab, let it all drift away, your friend, this life, the material self, pollen, on the wind?

You know that? I hate that.

Turns off the tape recorder. Calls offstage:

Rupert!

He enters with another book, sets it down.

Rupert is there any mail?

He nods, exits. Once again to tape recorder:

There's a story, I can't remember who the story's by, maybe it's Lovecraft, maybe it's not. It's about a traveler, walking longtime through deep woods—this country, some other country, I don't know—and he comes to a house. First house he's seen in a long time. Only house in the whole woods. He's tired, he's famished, he goes and knocks on the house, a man comes out, invites him in— great! Hospitality. The traveler sits down with this man, they have tea, some bread—I don't know, it's comforting —there's a lot of clutter on the walls, pictures, country home, idiosyncrasy, you know. And the traveler notices, after a long time talking, a certain drift of conversation. The man in the house just wants to talk about *flesh*. How did the talk come around to flesh, thinks the traveler? I didn't say flesh—did I say flesh? And just as the man in the house comes around to his point, his denouement, whatever, about the rapture of the body, the corpus, its beauty and great vitality and nourishment—spirit, soul, body, body, body—just as the man comes around to the idea of *eating*, what's so bad about *eating* after all, the traveler looks up at the ceiling, the seam where it meets the wall—the floor above and its contents only imagined —he looks up at the ceiling and he sees a drip. A dark drip, blood, like blood, from the ceiling, he sees a drip dripping just as the homeowner says, "When you think about it, isn't it just *more of the same?*"... And the traveler runs, he gets up and he runs from the house—but now I think of it, maybe that part is from Kafka? Maybe that is the one where the doctor runs out of the house because that family is so scary...

A searching pause.

How many stories like that are there?

To the tape recorder, conspiratorially:

Maybe a lot.

*Makes to turn off the recorder, realizes
it was never turned back on.*

Shit.

Turns it on. To the recorder:

The thing about... cannibalism. You know.

*She turns off the recorder. Rupert enters with an
envelope, hands it to the woman. She opens it.
A cassette. She puts it in the player.
Another woman's voice:*

Tape: Why didn't you come. The fair was nice. The moonlight
on the tentpoles, it was your kind of thing, the frosty fish
in the little bowls. We sat in a giant chair, a chair for a
giant, a sign said, somewhere. Thomas wasn't in the
mood. Thomas wouldn't sit in the chair, but then he
would. His leg is getting better.

I thought if you'd come we could eat the fried cakes on
paper slivers, with the sugar, you always liked those,
you always said. Do you know how many miles the
town's gone now? Have you heard how quick the wreck
is spreading? It's amazing. Thomas didn't want to take
us to the fair, but the roads exemption. One night only.
Things go on, now don't they? It's all closing in, isn't it, ha
ha, I don't have to tell you that, darling. Thomas said tell
you about—

Woman: No!

Turns off the tape player, almost violently.

I don't have a kind of thing.

Fast-forwards the tape. Presses play.

Tape: —the dresses were fine after all. I knew they would be.
We keep everything well sealed. You taught me that.
Oh, darling…I wrote you a song. Will you hear it?
Don't shut me off. Here it is.

A quiet beat like hands patting on a table;
a ghostly, intimate voice:

(sung.)
I've seen a few
Of the boys
I've seen a few
They come and go
I've seen a few come and go
I know a few
Of the boys
I've been a few of the boys
They go

Seconds of quiet. The woman in the armchair
looks stricken, alarmed.

Woman: What is that?

Tape: I can't tell you what it is, darling. These things just come.
Mostly these days I sit and wait. It flew in through the
window. I can't sing it for anyone else, I knew it was for
you. Thomas told me he didn't—

Shuts off the tape player suddenly, as before.

Rupert!

> *He enters. She looks at a loss,*
> *uncertain what to ask him.*

Shut the window.

> *He exits. She takes a deep breath, looks around.*
> *Regards the book on the table apprehensively.*

The Nicer One

Something like an analyst's office.

Diane: They kept saying Mattilda, Mattilda! And I understand, Mattilda looks like me, we don't have distinguishing marks, nobody gave her a face tattoo or a giant sunglasses to make it clear she's the copy, but when somebody waves and lets you know who they actually are, that you were wrong, you should accept it. That's the problem, they won't *accept* it, I tell them who I am, I show them my Original card, and they keep talking to me like I'm her. I know she's good-looking, I get it, we look the same, and if I kept my face in a perfect below-the-cheeks smile at all times I'd look friendly and unwrinkled too, okay, but I don't care about that too much, I look like I do, always have. But what I realize, what I see now with just a little horror, is that she is more *popular* than me.

Oss: That's awkward.

Diane: Like, I don't need to be friends with everybody, but to meet these groups all the time, these stupid out-shopping groups they round up just to fill out the neighborhood with harmless bodies, with buyers, with Safetys — and every time the groups want to talk to Mattilda and I tell them it's not her, it's me, they look so *disappointed*. I see their crests actually fall — like their crests are up here, they're drinking their frothy drinks and they have pale pink glossy lips and pale pink glossy handbags, they look so cresty and full of foam, and then I show them my Original card — no, haha, it's me, Diane! — and they look <u>sad</u> to have met me.

Oss: I'll bet you don't like that.

Diane: No, I don't! I'm almost regretting getting her! Although, when I remember standing in line at the bank, I do have to think twice about that. It's just — couldn't the person who looks just like me be a little less *interesting*?

Oss: We don't pick the personalities.

Diane: I know, I know, if they're going to be smart enough to replace us in tedious situations, they have to be sentient, and if they're going to be sentient, we have to let them have their little personalities. She's just so damn bubbly.

Oss: I know. She's very nice.

Diane: I know she's very nice! I trained her!

Oss: Why do you think she does it so well?

Diane: Niceness?

Oss: I guess. How do you think she's so friendly?

Diane: I don't know. She took it all at face value. I know the principle of being nice, I know it's the right thing to do, but I don't actually want to do it.

Oss: Yes. Most of us don't.

The Nicer One 2

Joan: She says if she's going to come all the way across the tar sands she wants some kind of guarantee that she'll have a nice place to stay. She says she doesn't want to come all the way here in all that "difficult conditions" *(mocking gesture)* and then be inconvenienced at this end. At allll inconvenienced, she refuses to be. Well. I told her — I used a nice voice — I told her we're happy to put her up here, we're happy to put out what we can — but she doesn't want that! She wants nicer. I told her how much I can put out for her comfort, and she made a face — I mean it wasn't over video we were talking, but I could hear her make a face.

Tiresias: So what did you decide?

Joan: We didn't, yet. She wants to talk to you.

Tiresias: Why?

Joan: She thinks she can get more out of you, I bet.

Tiresias: That'll be fun. She doesn't know me too well if she thinks I'm the nicer one.

Joan: Nobody thinks you're the nicer one, but we all know you're willing to put out more. You run on fewer stores in your daily, so you've got extra. I know that. *(Aside)* I'm not sure anyone else does...

Tiresias: I'll talk to her. That's fine. But I won't put out more for her than you would.

Joan: Good on you. United front.

Tiresias: Not so much that. I'm thinking of putting my extra into different sources, lately. Diversifying.

Joan: Like what? Your much heralded generosity will suffer, mind you.

Tiresias: I don't mind, I don't mind that. I was thinking of getting Another.

Joan: Really? Why? You don't have much bank business. You get your groceries brought in. Why?

Tiresias: I thought Another could take all my meetings.

Joan: Your meetings where people ask you to help them?

Tiresias: Yes.

Joan: So—you're going to take your extra that those people ask for—and which you give them—in those meetings, and you're going to put it into Another to take those meetings and tell them no?

Tiresias: I was thinking so. I am thinking of it.

Joan: You are good at this.

Tiresias: Good at what?

Joan: All of this.

Little Torvald

Steve: I was thinking, you know, the *ocean*.

Carolla: The ocean?

Steve: Yes. The vastness. If I were new, I'd like the first thing I see to be... vastness.

Carolla: I am not impressed by this idea.

Steve: I know that. I could tell by your body. You are showing me, and you are also telling me.

Carolla: What else you got?

Steve: The desert?

Carolla: Are you just really into horizons?

Steve: No. It's... the *vastness*.

Carolla: You want baby Torvald to experience vastness in his first days?

Steve: We can always change the memory later.

Carolla: But why do it at all if we plan to change it? What's worse about blankness than something stupid?

Steve: There is nothing stupid about the ocean. Same goes for the desert. The ocean and the desert are vital parts of nature—

Carolla: Yes, I read that in a pamphlet.

Steve: —and are large and worthy of respect.

Carolla: That's what the pamphlet said. "Big things live in them, big wet things in the ocean, big dry things in the desert. We need always respect those things which are large, and wet or dry."

Steve: That sounds like an old pamphlet.

Carolla: Only because of the syntax. The sentiment is the same in the new ones.

Steve: Yes, I want little Torvald to experience vastness.
            (As if quoting) The experience of vastness / conditions us to consider that which is—

Carolla: We're not really calling it Torvald.

Steve: I know. I can joke. You can joke, I can joke—

Carolla: Who trained you to joke?

Steve: *(Long stare, offended)* I learned. You stand in line at the bank long enough, you learn some jokes.

Carolla: Oh, I see. With the Olds.

Steve: Yes, with the Olds. The News and the Olds. The two groups of people you find in line at the bank.

Carolla: And one of them knows jokes, and the other knows how to smile from the eyebrows down.

Steve: It's good for the skin.

Carolla: You know what else is good for the skin?
            The experience of vastness.

Steve: You are mocking me.

Carolla: Yes, I am. Little Torvald is too. He's in his test tube still, but he's looking at your plans and he's laughing his tiny test-tube laugh. He sounds just like me. He has my wrinkled forehead and my old-time DNA and my mean sense of humor. He will grow larger, he will swell until he bursts from his test tube and through our front door and into my arms. Torvald is real, and he is coming. Think of another idea.

The Salon

Rossette: (fluffing Tina's hair) What are we thinking today?

Tina: I'm just looking for a little plausible deniability.

Rossette: Mmm, I can see that.

Tina: Jerome wants me at home, but then he also wants me to get it all done—I said to him listen, I don't have Another, I have to go stand in line on my own at the bank, with the Olds and the News, and the Olds smell like newspapers and the News smell like they've been just burnt out of their plastic shells, but the News are good-looking, all of them, even if they came from ugly people, they are good-looking, so I try to stand near them. Anyway.

Rossette: (meaninglessly) Mmm. And do you shape it?
            Do you get up early enough to shape it?

Tina: Rarely. But I'm standing in the line, for as long as that takes, you know, and I get back and Jerome says, "Where is it?" — like I'm supposed to have made everything and arranged it on plates in the meantime! He doesn't know. He's up in the building, he just doesn't know.

Rossette: Mmm. And what does he do?

Tina: Mostly he denies everything.

Rossette: Mmm. I can see that.

Monologue: The Albatross

A woman sits working at a desk. On the desk is a manual typewriter, a cassette player, a telephone. A man's voice plays on cassette as the woman types.

Voice: The very beginning wasn't noteworthy—be sure to put that in. The very beginning, well, you couldn't tell anything had started, could you? There was no way to know, except in retrospect. Don't put that in. No one has retrospect, we've still got the R&D guys on that technology, ha ha. Ideally, what you will take away from this lecture, or shall we say this portion of the lecture, is the notion of the utter fuzziness of the significant fact, the true possibility of recognition as the vanishing point. Was that clear?

Typist: No.

Voice: Good. Mm hmm. Indeed, in the beginning it was Angela and I, in the hotel, in the lobby of the hotel, deciding on where we might eat a meal in this, a foreign city, a city foreign to us at this juncture, when Daphna entered, a great heap of taffeta, like gold-sandaled dawn herself, a flaming-orange marvel, and sh—what? The microphone's not... ? Well. Yes, all right, yes, we can come back to this. After all. Have you got a cigarette?

> *The typist clicks the machine off. Types a few words.*
> *Picks up the phone receiver and dials, waits.*

Typist: I'm sorry, which part did he want? The part... about... the pigeon. I haven't gotten to anything about a pigeon. Could it be a gull? There was something about a gull... in there. *(flips through pages)*   Well. I'll find it. Let me just make a note... for later... *(types out)* P – I – G – E – O – N... What? Yes, yes, I am using a—what do you call this? A *schreibmachine*...? A letter... maker... Typewriter! Yes, a type-writer....Well don't you think the antique technologies are sometimes useful to us? Fewer functionalities for less distraction? My mother used to say—uh huh. I will. No, I think the percussive nature of the *schreibmachine* is really its main selling point. Think of this: it makes a real dent. On the page! It *impresses* the letters into the paper. Are you impressed? The letters are! Are you depressed? The letters are! Get it? Words are funny, aren't they? ... No, yeah... I do have work to do. OK. I—I will look for the part about the pigeon. Great. Yes... talk to you then.

> *Hangs up phone, faces the machine again,*
> *turns on the tape player.*

Voice: Now, if you wanted to know how we brokered the deal for the second place on the pier, that's quite a story. Amanda had the bright idea to—well, she came into my office one morning utterly covered in coffee, she asked if I might be—

           Stops playback. Bored. Fast-forwards.

Typist: What about... the bird...

           Hits play.

Voice: "And there were gardens, bright with sinuous rills, where blossomed many an incense-bearing tree. And there were—"

Typist: That's not it. *(Fast-forwards)*

Voice: "*Every day you say*
           Just one more try
           Then another irrecoverable day
           Slips by
           You will say 'ankle.'
           You will say 'knuckle.'
           Why won't you
           Why won't you
           Say uncle?"

Typist: That's... something else.

           Picks up the phone, dials, speaks into it.

Did you know, I sometimes wake in the night to the sound of your voice? I wake up and it's dark, it's impossibly quiet, like the center of a great lake—I hardly can remember where I am— and then I hear you speaking in the next room—I don't know if you're addressing me or rehearsing one of your speeches... It's a gentle sound, and I wonder, are you singing? Are you singing to me? Or hoping I'll hear you as I sleep? And I wait, but then I catch the rhythm—I've heard this before—and I realize it's not you, it's the transcription machine in the study, your voice is coming through it, it's your speech you wanted me to type, the one at the town hall maybe, the machine has turned itself on somehow and is playing your speech...And so I have to get out of bed and walk into the next room, and turn you off. And you clap shut like a light. But I think, if it hadn't been the machine, if it had been you, intoning something, murmuring, to me or to yourself I don't know —but if it had been you, I wouldn't have moved—I would have lain in my bed in the middle dark and listened to you speak until I drifted off again... Just like that. Just a few feet apart. That would be... fine.

Pause

Should I tell him that? Is that a good thing to tell someone? ...Well, I don't know. ...Yes, I'm sure he has feelings, but which—yeah. Yeah, I guess. OK, yeah, I'm doing it. Bye.

The Bank

A man waits in line, speaking to himself, with a notebook;
nearby a woman is weeping.

Banker: Please. If you're going to weep, can you do it over there.
           (A sign says Weeping Corner) Thank you.

Carlo: *(standing in line; speaking compulsively, to no-one in particular)* The figures begin to walk around the room. They wear, each wears a robe, each wears a robe, all in different colors, they are all the same size more or less, the same height and covered top to top in those robes, the only difference being the colors of the robes. Five foot eleven, a national average, the average of heights, specify that. They begin walking the perimeter of the circle. A rather thin coating of sense covers the whole world. The figures are the colors of wine (red), grapes (grape), grape leaves (green), mustard (whole grain), brown bread (brown). Not the mottle of the brown bread but the crumb, an average of its texture. Wine, grape, grape leaf, mustard, brown bread. The elements of the world, such as it is. Was. They circle the room at angles to one another. Angles to be determined later. Tangents. Make a note. Make a note. They circle the room. And from their robes produce the first in a series of—

Banker: Five! Number five.

Carlo: She is standing in the Weeping Corner. I am number six may I approach.

Banker: *(Looks at the Weeping Corner)* Yes you may.
           Approach, number six. What is your grievance?

Carlo: I haven't got. I haven't got. I don't, I don't have it, what I need. What can you arrange so that I have—so that I— what's needed, can I speak to. May I. Is there. Where is? The one with, I'm—no—I'm. I'm sorry. I'm sorry. I have here my slip my bank slip what they gave me I need to bring to your attention an error made on your behalf not mine—

Banker: Pass the slip beneath the glass.

The banker sets the slip on fire.

Carlo: It's my only copy.

Banker: Five. Number five!

The woman returns from the Weeping Area.

Woman: It's me. Five.

Banker: Slips please. What is your grievance?

The Grit

A researcher with a clipboard interviews a workingman

Yank: The grit. They asked me if I would deal with the grit, if it was within my capacities to "deal with the grit," they asked me this as if an offer, as if a coveted workload were it to "deal with the grit." I said I could, and moreover that I would, and for what handsome salary they declined to say and I to ask.

Interviewer: Where was this grit located?

Yank: Tall, tall building. Just gone up. Just gone up that spring but they'd neglected the special grit coating, the particular film that keeps the grit off, in light of their mistake would I keep the grit off they said, be grit patrol they said, approximation of a joke. I said I could, could I ever, approximation of a laugh, and moreover would, not only could but would, it was within the capacities I had at that time and some say still possess I don't know do I. *(Trails off)*

Interviewer: Surely you do. And did you do this work, did you "take the grit," how did you say it?

Yank: Deal with. Deal with the grit. I did.

Interviewer: Yes, thank you. And for what duration of time did you 'deal with the grit'?

Yank: Lots of time. Must be...Lots. A few. Many times, get up, lunch pail, lunch in pail, nobody made that for me, nobody sure nobody, get up, get to tall tall building, special grit shoes not furnished by management, mandatory armor in the modern world, world of today—that's what they put on the billboard, used to be one right beside the tall tall building, mandatory armor for—

Interviewer: Yes. And is it a result of the grit—your hands, their appearance?

Yank: *(flatly)* My hands are what.

Interviewer: Do you retain the use of your hands? Both of them? And the fingers?

Yank: I don't get that far on the bus, doesn't go, the shuttle, what is it now what do they say—I don't get so far I need to, I go the rest of the way on feet—I see the billboard, "armor of the modern world," today the grit shoes, tomorrow... They asked me did I have had I procured at licensed retailer the grit underalls which likely would be placed under grit overalls, I hadn't, I said yes, such was my need at this moment for employment, I said yes I showed them my Original card, I had it forged, Gerald could make them before the reflective swatches were added— well Gerald time to close up shop said I to he when the reflective swatches came along—he was chewing a, a, what is it, che-root, cheroot in a book once I recall I saw, a form of what, a stick, he chewed a stick—he said get out, get out don't come back I said Gerald, you made the best cards didn't you, he picked up his axe, I left. Had my card updated at the Bank in the north piece of town, the fishery district, weren't as strict there about names and faces matching up were they, the others tell you that? Weren't so strict—besides in that window timewise you could have the cards updated, reflective strips, no additional slips, no further page of information, just the card, half the town had those Gerald cards, whole teams of Originals, whole crews, weren't we, a good likeness I always said to him, a good likeness Gerald, when he had a good mood on. A fair likeness.

Interviewer: And did you lose the use of your hands? Due to the grit?

Yank: No. *(looks down at hands. No movement.)* They work. *(Long staring silence)* In my capacity of dealing with the grit, approximation of a laugh, I encountered a small fish, a small sort of what I think they called in the old pamphlets a sort of small fish, sucker, sucker on the building, outer side, growing there and living, like an ivy, proper one not plastic, saw it daily. Bylaws of the company, rules, rather, dictates, official, they say they would say take it off, take the grit and anything not a sanctioned building part, material, not of company property, take it off...Didn't. Never took it off. Still there, maybe still there, maybe descendant of the sucker fish, child of beyond the sucker fish, eternal life sucker fish, still there maybe, still there, where it clings.

Interviewer: Yes... And what occupies the building now?

Yank: Condemned. Should have used the coating—for the grit. Outdated.

Interviewer: And when was this construction finished?

Yank: Oh...April.

An In-Between Moment

A great red velvet curtain closes on the final scene of THE NEAR FUTURE. There is a pause, in which brief transitional music might be playing out. The DIRECTOR OF THE PLAY emerges from behind the audience, presumably having been running the lights all this time, or else sitting quietly in the booth. The Director of the Play (probably a woman; if not, why not?) clomps down the steps between rows of seats, arrives at center stage under a spotlight, turns to face the audience, somewhat sheepishly, and speaks:

Director: At this moment in the play, there is a... uh... a transition. People need to move some furniture around, they need to change into different clothes, and so I have been asked, I have volunteered myself, to come down here, with you, and, ah... well, as they say in the business, vamp for a couple of minutes... while that happens. So... *(checks wristwatch)* In the meantime. I want to tell you something. It will take about three minutes.

There is a short play, by Samuel Beckett, that kept coming into my head we were working on this — it kept appearing as I thought about this play... And I didn't know what Beckett play this was, but I knew what it looked like. What it looked like is this: there are four performers, they are wearing these long robes, covered completely by the robes, you can't see their faces or any distinguishing marks—all you can see about them is the color of the robes. Each robe is a different color. And the playing space is a square, an empty square, lit from above. The players enter the square, one by one, and they walk in these very particular patterns within the square —diagonally, and around the perimeter. This being a Beckett play, the patterns they walk in are all extremely figured out; they are definitely written down. So that is what I knew about this play. That's all. So I asked some of my friends, who know things about Beckett, and none of them knew. They asked if it was "Come and Go," and I knew it wasn't that, and beyond that they didn't know. So finally I looked it up. And it turns out it's a play called "Quad," that Beckett wrote in 1982—so, a rather late Beckett piece—and he wrote it for German television, it was commissioned by a German TV station. It's in two parts—"Quad I" and "Quad II." And one thing I learned, when I looked it up, which I didn't know, is that there is also a sound component to the piece: each actor has a drum beat, or some percussion sound, that plays when he or she enters the stage, and stops when she exits, so that if multiple players are onstage, you get a layering of the sounds that go with them. But I started wondering—why Quad I and Quad II? What is the significance of it being in two parts? And there's a conceit, I won't spoil it—you can go to YouTube and watch videos of this, there's one from a BBC production, and the original German one—you'll see the difference between I and II if you watch—but I got to wondering, why separate Quad I and Quad II?

And then I noticed, on one of the YouTube videos: The person who uploaded it had put in this note, in the notes section, down at the bottom, that was allegedly a quote from Samuel Beckett, during the rehearsal process for the first production. And this is what the Beckett said: "Between the first and the second act, there is an intermission of one hundred thousand years."

And...I think...You could say the same thing about this play. So, keep that in mind, if you will. As we proceed. *(To the actors behind the curtain:)* Are you ready?

An Actor: Yes!

Director: Great. So. Thank you, again, and without further ado, please enjoy the second part of tonight's program, a play for four, titled "*That Sort of Thing.*"

She exits, to the booth.

KELLY ANCHORS in *That Sort of Thing*

That Sort of Thing

a scene for four

SETTING

A livingroom, sparsely decorated.

A woman sitting on a couch — glamorous, impossible, enjoying herself.

A middle-aged man on a folding chair, downstage with title cards.

CAST of CHARACTERS:

KAY

SEE

SUPERTITLES MAN (STM)

CHEF

When the play begins, the man stands and displays a title card, which reads:

> *SCENE 1*
>
> *IN WHICH OUR HERO CONSIDERS THE GREAT EMPTINESS THAT EXISTS INSIDE THE SOUL*

Kay: That's funny. That—is—funny! See, all this time I thought you meant *peaceful* emptiness, but now I see where you were referring to The Void. Uch! Will you shut up already about The Void? Stop *looking* at it! Of course you're going to fall off the cliff, if you keep *standing* next to the cliff all the time, if you set up your tent on the last, scraggliest branch sticking off the rock face, and you're a rowdy sleeper. My dear. I know. I get *it*. Some of us were born falling through the air already, you don't have to tell me. Some of our mothers got pushed, even while we waited to come out. I know. I just mean—you with the stilts, you–leaning heavily down from your lifeguard perch to get a better view of The Void? Get *down* from there! Live or die, but don't ruin everything. That's Rimbaud—you should learn that.

SEE enters, a woman somewhat younger than KAY and ruggedly dressed; KAY is ridiculously outfitted in taffeta gown, jewels, and satin slippers that clearly never touch the floor. SEE's affect is flat, businesslike, weary, in contrast to KAY's full-throated enjoyment of herself.

See: I don't want to learn that, I don't like reading.

Kay: Hello there, ray of sunshine.

See: I'm here for the groceries.

Kay: The what? I don't have the groceries here.

See: The grocery list. Give me the list of what you need.

Kay: Oh, the list! I left it over there.

SEE finds it on the table, reads.

See: "A sense of completion." They don't have that there.

Kay: Yes they do. You have to speak to a manager.

See: I don't speak to a manager. It's groceries. You go in and you see what's on the shelf and you buy what's on the shelf or you don't.

Kay: Well I do. I always speak to a manager. If there's a problem. With what I see.

See: You like to bother people.

Kay: You might say that.

See: I do say that. I am saying that.

Kay: You ask to speak to a manager, and they come out from a long metallic hallway, wearing a vest with one big pocket over the heart—it looks like there's nothing in it—you tell them what you want and they lead you back down the long hallway which is, yes, metal, a sort of burnished tin plating, but also spongy, mold-smelling in the most ancient and comfortable way. They lead you down and at the end is a stockroom, any ordinary stockroom, and they suddenly spin on a heel, the manager, and suddenly say something deeply inappropriate, reach out a groping hand, and you slap them across the face, and then you see it, there it is—

See: A sense of completion.

Kay: Yes. Exactly. ... The whole thing doesn't take very long.

See: I'm not going to buy that.

Kay: I didn't think you would. One has to put in a few decoys...

Both: "That's part of negotiating."

> *SEE begins preparing to leave, putting on several layers of ominous protective equipment as she speaks.*

See: *(flatly)* What else do you want.

Kay: (*brightly*) What else is on the list?

See: (*reading*) "A momentary sense of peace, however fleeting." ..."Oranges." What kind of oranges?

Kay: Whatever kind they have. (*dramatically, a complete lie*) I'm not picky.

See: Malarkey. (*making a note*) Okay. Fine. (*consulting the list again*) Scruples are in short supply, but I'll see what I can do. ... Uch, potatoes? I hate potatoes.

Kay: Hate is a strong word. What if potatoes hated you?

See: They do. They are poison. Poison is nature's hate.

Kay: No, they're not. Not anymore. That has been fixed.

See: The poison has been fixed, folks. The hemlock is at bay. You can all go home.

Kay: Don't be dramatic.

See: Don't... be... dramatic. (*reviewing the list once more*) Okay. I will get... some of these things.

Kay: You will speak to a manager.

See: I will not speak to a manager. (*turning back before leaving*) Don't make trouble.

Kay: (*false shock*) Do I ever?

See: Do you ever. (*she exits*)

The briefest pause. KAY exhibits no relish at being
suddenly alone. To the man again seated stage left:

Kay: Oh, young man. Young man?
          Please do the supertitles. They can't only look at me.
          (coyly, to the audience) Little old me.

The man stands and advances to center stage.
KAY ahems and shoos him a bit to the side,
so he won't block the view of her on the couch.
He displays a series of title cards,
one for each line of text

Title Card: *SCENE 2*
              I DIDN'T KNOW WHAT TO WRITE HERE
              IT HAS BEEN A LONG DAY
              FOR SOME OF US, ANYWAY

KAY makes a call on an old princess phone

Kay: Oh Hortense! Oh hello Hortense. Yes. Yes I'm always
          happy to hear from you too. Yes I am very busy too.

Title Card: *COULD I BUM A SMOKE OFF ANYBODY?*
              IT WILL GO ON LIKE THIS FOR A WHILE.

Kay: Listen, Hortense, could you send over a sheaf of those
          letters, from the people who want advice? Yes. Yes.
          I know you don't need any help with that right now, but I
          like to give advice. Even if they're never going to hear it.

Title Card: *BUT YOU KNEW THAT, DIDN'T YOU?*

Kay: Just now, I was telling them to get their lives together.
          Yes! Yes exactly! Shouting my wishes into
          the howling gale.

Title Card: *SHE'S NOT VERY NICE, REALLY*

Kay: Excuse me? Excuse me, young man — are you presently
          undermining my personal narrative? In real time? Let me
          see that. *(she takes the title card)* Oh, the very gall. ...
          "Nice." What is that? How dare you introduce that useless
          word into our careful mise en scène. Do you know who is
          nice? A glass of milk. A glass of milk is the nicest guy you'll
          ever meet. And then gone. Swallowed whole. *(picks up
          the phone again)* Well, Hortense? Yes, exactly—he's just
          said I'm not very nice, and I have helpfully explained to
          him that nice is a criterion for precisely nothing of interest
          in this world. ... "Nice." So will you send the letters over?
          Oh, you're a doll.

          The man hands her a sheaf of letters.

Kay: Oh, goody. They all need me. They need me very much.

          She begins to read the letters with obvious relish.
          The man throws a sheet over her, like covering a
          * birdcage. She continues to read to herself delightedly,*
          with no reaction to the sheet.
          He addresses the audience:

STM: Here it is. It's like this. It's not like I had anything else to
          do. What should a person do, perfect world?
          Sit on a rock? Envisioning the countryside? Forever?
          Well, I need to do something. The rock does not cut it
          for me. I saw an ad:

"SUPERTITLES MAN. UNPLEASANT HOURS, ABONIMABLE PAY, AND YOU'LL REALLY MAKE A DIFFERENCE."

Right up my alley, I think. And it turns out, narrating somebody's life is not so bad. I got kids. I know. "You have no shoes on. We are to be at the tavern in fifteen minutes for the wake and you have thrown your shoes into the pond. Spiffy. Your morals are not developing well."
And so on. So this thing, it's fine. Even—on Thursday—the chef makes beans. I like beans.
Oh, and here comes the chef now.

> *The chef speaks from an upstage corner, not fully entering. He is dressed in a white coat and carries at all times a large knife.*

Chef: Is she back yet with the groceries?

STM: No. It'll be a while.

Chef: God damn it! I need my sense of completion.

STM: Oh that? That's not coming.

Chef: No? Miss Madam said they have it there.

STM: They do, but you can't bring one home with you. To each his own sense of completion.

Chef: You mean—?

STM: Yes. You want a sense of completion, you have to go in there and slap the manager for yourself....It doesn't travel well.

Chef: I haven't got time for that! Besides—the last time I did it, at the old fish market, I didn't get the sense of an ending. Indeed, it started something new.

STM: Yes, I remember that. You and the manager, coupling madly all down the mossy hallway.

Chef: *(wistful, vaguely gallic)* The mossy hallway that is life.

STM: Yes. *(a look passes between them)* And how did it end, after all?

Chef: … I don't remember.

Kay: Am I still here? In the scene?

STM: Do you want to be?

Kay: If you're talking about me, then yes.

STM: And if we're not talking about you?

Kay: Why not?

STM: We are talking about coupling. Uncoupling. Ingredients.

Kay: Are you advancing the plot?

STM: Plot? *(he looks at the audience)* No.

Kay: Good.

          A pause all around.

Chef: Alert me when she gets here. I need an ending.

STM: Don't we all.

Kay: Would you like to hear this letter? I've just found one, it's very good, I think we can help.

STM: We?

Kay: I. I can help, certainly. You're here too, aren't you?

STM: Am I? *(they look at each other through the sheet; he peels it aside and uncovers her)* Read it to us.

Kay: "Dear Hortense—I'm in a way. I feel that everything is ending. My mouth is full of dirt, my eyes are the fish of silver dollars. Beneath my tongue, a feather too wet to fly."–Well, why doesn't she take the feather out of her mouth and let it dry? I'll tell her that.–"Dear Hortense, my problems are poetic in nature, you might say this, but does the earth still spin if I give up? Do you know the way to San Jose? What is the word, Hortense? And when? Can a person get a break, Hortense? Signed, Beulah."

> *A silence*

Kay: I think... *(at a loss)* Say, young man, will you go back to narrating my life for a moment?

STM: *(to audience)* It's steady work.

> *He begins to issue the title cards*

Title Card: *THERE'S NOT MUCH TO DO, ANYMORE*
ONE STILL HAS A COUCH. A COUCH IS GOOD.
A PATCH OF CORN GROWING IN THE BACK
A PASSEL OF RABBITS NEARBY IN THE WOOD
ONE CAN PERSUADE THEM, FROM TIME TO TIME,
TO BE EATEN.

THE END TIMES ARE NEARLY LIKE
THE OLD TIMES, NOW AREN'T THEY?
A NEAT RESEMBLANCE, DON'T YOU—

Kay: Say, young man. Would you cover me up again?

STM: Of course. *(He does. To the audience:)* I wouldn't judge too harshly. There are all kinds of people in this world. Or used to be.

         SEE returns.

See: They didn't have scruples. I knew they wouldn't. They don't even advertise them in the circulars anymore. Thank goodness for the corn, if we didn't have the corn I don't know what we'd— oh. She's in the sheet again.

STM: Yes.

See: Well, what can you do about that. I've got to give the man these fish I bought. Keep my place.

STM: He's in a mood.

See: He is a mood.

         Pause. Kay removes the sheet.

Kay: Tell me a story.

STM: I don't know a story.

Kay: You know a story. Tell it to me.

STM: Fine. There is a fishing hole on the far side of the lake—

Kay: How is it a hole if it's in a lake?

STM: I don't know, that's just what they—

Kay: Isn't a lake just one big hole, after all?

STM: I don't know....There is a fishing hole, the boys meet there in the middle of the hot days, they catch fish and argue, and one boy in the midst of the arguing picks up a large rock and smashes the head of another boy. Killing him. The whole crowd of boys is taken to the other side of the lake, to the wise old woman who decides outcomes, they all ask the woman in her small house made of sticks what to do, the one boy dead and the other with blood on him, and the rest of the seven or eight alive and no blood on them but they've seen it, the wise old woman says get out, you all get out of this place, you all are ugly with sin, you have been witness to violence like a fog and you may never come back. The boys leave the place, not even a town really, a ring of camps around a very large lake more like, the one with blood and the other seven or eight all leave, dragging the dead one behind, for he was ordered out of the place as well, he was made ugly by sin and is not excused. The wise old woman watches them leave the place and smokes a long thin pipe filled with cleansing herbs, she begins to cough, the boys drag along the broad path into the woods and mountains beyond—

Kay: I don't like this story.

STM: You don't... like it?

Kay: No. I feel that my instincts are being appealed to. My hidden sense of morality.

STM: I didn't think you had that.

Kay: I can tell. You are trying to drag it out with a fable.
That is very sneaky of you.

STM: No, I just thought... That's a story I could tell you.

Kay: Well, cut to: How does it end?

STM: The boys start a new city far away, everyone in the city
is violent... I don't remember.

Kay: I see. Is this some kind of a folk-tale of your people?
How did you hear it?

STM: No. My father told it to me. *(pause)* I think he didn't
want me to go to the fishing hole.

Kay: I still don't understand the hole part.

The CHEF enters, angry. SEE follows, to argue.

Chef: She has bought me an entire fish! An entire string of fish!
A complete glossy river of fish! The very ocean! What in
the name of your man am I supposed to do with this?
I am not in the business of fish.

See: You have liked fish. You have very well liked fish.

Chef: I had been drinking.

See: You had been drinking. And you liked fish.
The two are not mutually—

Chef: I would like at this time to give you a monologue
         on the problem as I see it.

STM: The problem?

Kay: The problem as you see it?

STM: This again.

See: Oh, for god's—

Kay: Please do.
         (to the SUPERTITLES MAN) I adore a monologue.

STM: I know.

> *The CHEF draws a curtain or somehow claims*
> *the space, cutting the others out of view.*
> *He addresses the audience.*

Chef: It's not that I have a knife. The knife is not important. Stop
         looking at the knife. Here is the problem—I am feeling at
         this very moment, right here, a sense of overwhelming...
         tenderness. A sense of my self as a small, weak, wayward
         thing—easily swayed—a very nymph of the woods—and
         I am feeling, furthermore, that you, you and this place,
         this moment here, are something of a cradle, a hamlet
         in which I might drape myself on a leaning tree, a safe
         house against all that might happen, were I to drift into
         the wrong corner. Do you see? The problem. I knew from
         a very young age—I told myself from a superstition that
         hardened into knowledge, that no place was safe—that

even to say the words, to think the feeling, "I am safe," to rest one's tired elbow on the leaning tree, invited violent calamity. Murder. Rape. Injury. That sort of thing. I knew it as a kid, I know it now, and here we all are, and you are looking at my knife, aren't you, my wonderful, shining knife. Given to me through years of training. Do you see it? You see it. Here it is. I wonder how long we've all been here, in this room, seeing it together. My knife.

SEE comes through the curtain.

See: Are you quite done?

Chef: Done? I couldn't say.

See: With the monologue.

Chef: Oh. *(pause)* I guess. Do you have any pills I could take?

See: No. I've got breath mints. We must move on.
         She needs to eat, and you are not advancing the plot.

Chef: There's a plot? *(pause)* Do you see what I have here?

See: I don't see anything. I don't hear anything.
         She needs to eat, let's go.

Chef: You are incorrect. I beg your pardon. There are a few things she may need on this benighted earth, and "to eat" at this very moment is not among them. And how do you mean to feed absolutely anyone on that string of hideous fish you brought in from the outside? It's a decorative garland. It's hardly a food.

See: It is a food. You can boil the bones. You can eat what there is, and boil the bones. For the minerals. You make a broth, with the minerals—

Chef: I know. This I know. It is not a secret. To fortify.

See: To fortify. Indeed.

> *An agreement somehow reached*
> *between them; a silence.*

Chef: I hate the fish.

See: I know. I have been out. That's what there is. The fish.

> *The CHEF leaves through the curtain and*
> *disappears backstage.*

See: *(to audience)* I wouldn't judge too harshly. There aren't so many people as there used to be. You take whoever's nearby, don't you. *(wistful, patronizing)* Our chef.
He thinks he has a knife.

> *SEE opens the curtain again.*
> *KAY is reclining languidly on the couch.*

Kay: Oh hello! You've just caught me in a nap. Do you see what I am doing now? I am sleeping!

See: No, you are not.

Kay: Do you contradict myself? I am sleeping!

See: I can see you. You are raucous with life.
          You are not sleeping.

Kay: And here is a common misconception. Allow me to advise
          you. Sleeping is not dead! Or doesn't have to be. That's
          what I'll tell all the people, once I read all their questions
          — relish every moment! Catapult yourself to where you
          will! You can't bog down forever, no you can't.

STM: *(snidely)* Hmmm.

Kay: Oh, shush, you. *(to SEE)* See, that's a bit we have. I make
          a claim, and he casts aspersions on it, and then I tell him—

See: Our chef is making the fish. Dinner is soon.

Kay: The fish from the streams? The gleaming fish, leaping
          from the streams? Those fish?

See: No. There are no streams. The fish from the store.
          The store is what there is. You know this.

Kay: Absolutely! The store is a multiple of itself, now isn't it?
          Each aisle, a world unfolding. The lights above,
          a field of stars.

See: No.

Kay: The checkout boys are all the elves and animals, and the
          manager in his grey corridor, an ogre we must all pass by
          —oh darling, isn't it all an adventure?

See: No! It isn't anything! Nothing is there! I have bought you fish and rabbit guts with the skin of my hands, my teeth are—wake up! Wake. Up.

Kay: Oh, See. Don't you know? I can't. Here you are. You're doing very well.

> *The man with the title cards stands from his seat, where he has been reading the paper all this time. He displays the cards:*
>
> *SCENE 3*
> *AND NOW I THINK IT IS*
> *TIME FOR A SONG*
> *TO HELP HER TO SLEEP*
> *DON'T YOU?*

Kay: *(to SEE)*   Sing me a song.

See: I don't know a song.

Kay: Of course you do. Everything is a song. Tell me a song.

> *The CHEF re-enters, silently. Under the rest of the scene, he and the SUPERTITLES MAN play a small, plunking tune on handheld instruments.*

See: I won't let you. You cannot keep doing this. You haven't been outside, you don't know—the people, what people are left, are—

Kay: Do you know—that when I brought you here, little urchin that you were, little lamb of the woods, my dumpling, I thought–that you—would be helpful.

See: I am helpful. I have always been helpful.

Kay: I brought you here for conversation—and tasks, yes tasks, but most significantly conversation—the broadening, I thought, of both our minds—as well as this young man, and our culinary friend.

See: You brought me here to talk to. Endlessly. And I have listened. Endless! The days are not many now and I wish you'd eat but all you do is talk. Where am I?

Kay: All I do is... What else is there? But talk?

See: Sit. Sit and breathe. Look into the eyes.
          Move from the couch.

Kay: That sounds awful. Look, my dear—the truth—the real hard granite truth behind it is: I have everything I want. You've gathered all around me, my lambs, my march violets, and you help me with all of it, my every particular trouble. The ups, the downs, the everyest bit of my journey. Here you are. We are safe. We—are—safe. What more could anyone ever want?

          A protracted moment, and then a hideous loud noise from the outside. Everyone turns to look in terror except KAY, who stares placidly ahead, satisfied.
          The lights swiftly go out.

          – The End –

          KELLY ANCHORS in *That Sort of Thing* >>

DEBBIE SAFEBLADE and NICK LEININGER in *To End To Seem To End*

To End To Seem To End

Premiered **October 2013**

Prop Thtr / Chicago, IL

written by **JAYITA BHATTACHARYA**

directed by **Jeffrey Bivens**

performed by:

Jayita Bhattacharya
Jeffrey Bivens
Nick Leininger
Lena Magnus Brün
Taran O'Reilly
Debbie Safeblade
Julia Williams

THE
PLAYS

NICK LEININGER in *To End To Seem To End*

PRÉCIS

Purposefully adhering to the internal logic of dreams and half-remembered conversations, this play comprises a series of dialogues, disputes, missives, chants, lyrics, squabbles and epiphanies that coalesce around the grievances of a couple and their attempt to end their relationship—it investigates their effort to name or characterize the "leave taking" itself.

PRELUDE   To End to—Seem to End I

Part I: EXPOSITION

INTERLUDE   To End to—Seem to End II

Part II: DEVELOPMENT

INTERLUDE   To End to—Seem to End III

PART III: RECAPITULATION

CODA   This is What It's Like III

CAST of CHARACTERS / *played by 4-7 performers*

THE COUPLE:

    MAN   *- composing one half of "The Couple"*

    WOMAN   *- composing one half of "The Couple"*

Designated as MAN & WOMAN in script, but gender of each is not proscribed

THE CHORUS:

    A & B   *- most often at the sofa*

    C & D   *- most often at the table*

    CHILD   *- watches, sometimes explains, takes copious notes*

These actors are sometimes ghosts or memories of THE COUPLE, sometimes witnesses, sometimes interlocutors. Five distinct voices are needed, but who plays A-D can shift through the course of the piece.

Other roles assumed by members of the CHORUS:

    WRITER / ANNOYER / PETITIONER / DENIER

STAGE

FURNITURE: a couch, multiple chairs, end tables, all sawed in half and strewn about the stage; a curtained frame (may suggest a window, mirror, or framed artwork).

As lights come up, CHORUS behind the curtain are humming what sounds like a lullaby or a dirge. WOMAN is onstage. MAN awkwardly tries to enter, comes in and out, watching her, not knowing how to approach. Finally, he pours himself a drink and sits away from her by an end table, still watching her. Curtain opens to reveal CHORUS.

Prelude — *a 6 voice fugue, performed by CHORUS*

I. to end
to seem to end
seem
to
end to seem
to seem to end to
end to
end
to seem to
seem to
end to seem to
end
to end to seem to end to
seem to seem

II. to end
to seem to end to end
to
end to end to
seem to
end to
end
seem to end
to end
end to seem
end to end to seem
to
to
to
to *seem*
end

III. to end
seem
end
end to seem to
seem to end
to seem to end
to end
to
end to seem to seem to end
to end to seem to end

to *not*
to not end
to seem to end to not
to end to seem to end to not to end
to end to seem

IV. to end
to not to end
to end
to end to
not to end
to seem to not
seem to seem to not— to end
to not to
to not to seem
to end to not end
seem to not end
seem to end to not— to seem to not to seem

V. to end
not to seem
not to stop
to seem to stop
to end to seem to stop— to *stop*
to *not*
to seem to not
to *stop*
to end
to end stop end

VI. to end—
to stop to not stop— not to end to
seem to not to end to— stop
to *stop*
end to stop
to stop end stop to seem— to stop to seem
to not stop seem to end— stop end
to not stop end
to stop not stop not end— stop seem to
not stop seem to
end

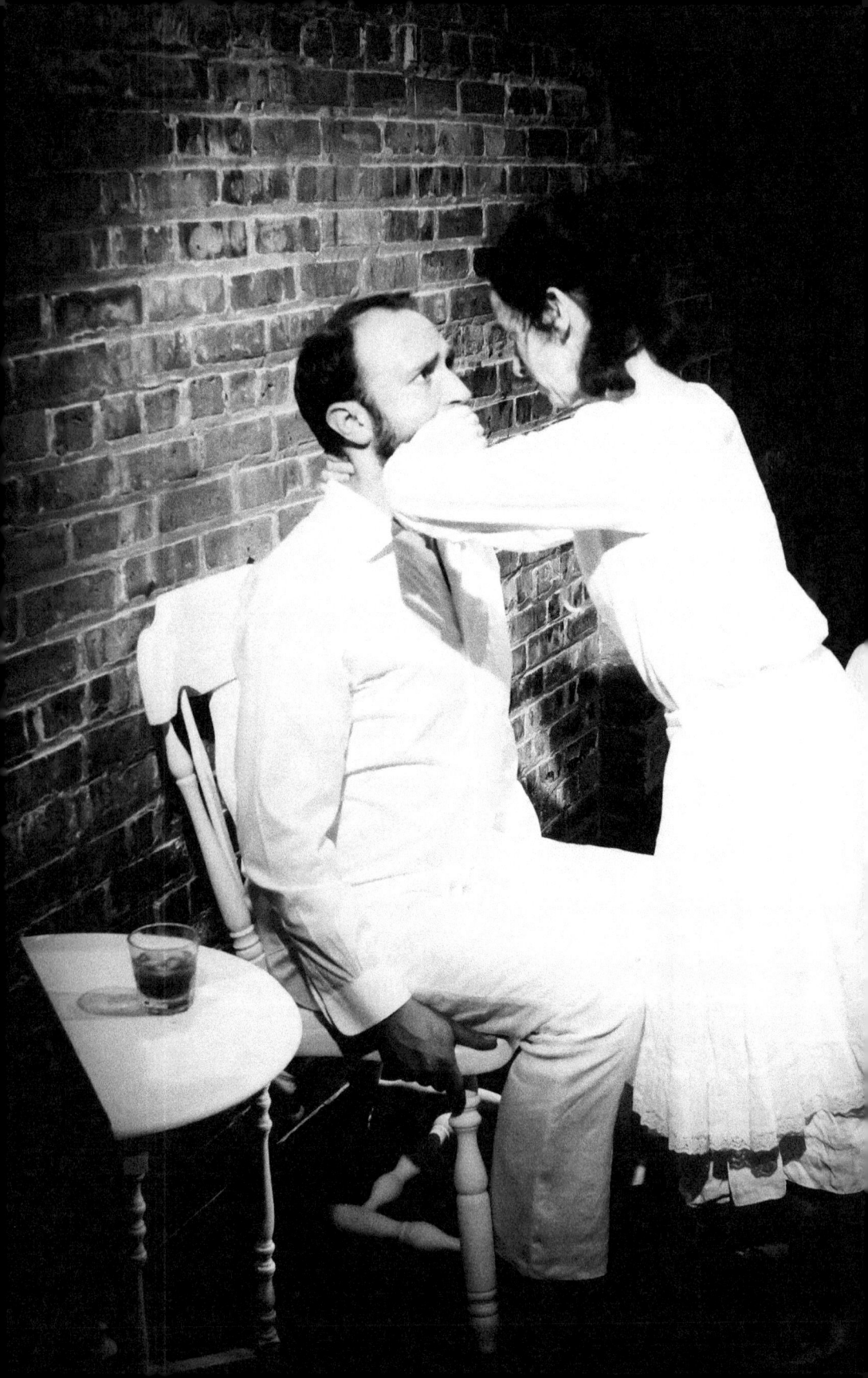

PART I:
EXPOSITION

Chapter 1

Light Out of Darkness - I *– dal niente –*

This scene begins and remains in darkness. MAN has been sitting in the chair silent for a long time; long enough that he has blended into the background, been forgotten, or at least is ignored. WOMAN is on stage, somewhere. WOMAN stands, facing front.

Man: *(enunciating very loudly, a recitation/dictation; Sforzando)*
                 Light—out—of—darkness. Light—out—of—darkness.

                 WOMAN looks up.

Chapter 2

Weird Seeing Him - I *– interrogation –*

The two columns are performed simultaneously. Rhythm/tempo to be found by performers.

CHORUS (left column): *WOMAN responds (right column):*

So you went to the—? Yeah.
How was it? Did I—?
Was it weird? Well yeah it was his thing.
Did you see him? Yes of course I saw him.
So you saw him. And what?
And?
Was it hard Less hard than I
to go? Was it expected.
hard to see him, Curiosity,
after the—? I guess.
Why'd you go anyway? Less about him, per se.
What did you do? More about what the interaction might be.
What happened? curious to see what we'd all do.
Why'd you go anyway? Nothing especially notable. Manners.
What did you do? They kick in fast and get you past the
What happened? awkward parts.
There was a manic quality to some of the talking,
Sure. sure.

(Silence.) *(Silence.)*

These can't be real questions.

Chapter 3

A Chorus - I *– lines –*

CHORUS performs this as cacophony. Each starts at a different stanza. No words left out. At the end of each column, there should be an abrupt stop, like a TV turning off. The CHORUS shifts positions, silently agrees when to begin next column.

The thing of it is	The thing of	It isn't
Wait, no	The thing	The wait
The thing of it isn't	It is	The thing of it
It is	Wait	No, isn't
(It) – no.	The thing of it, no.	Wait, (it)
	Is, no.	The thing of it, no.
The thing of it is		(Was it?)
Wait, no	The thing of it isn't	
The thing of it is	Isn't wait	
It isn't	No, isn't	
It is	Wait, no	
The thing of it is	The thing of the wait	
Wait	Is, no (No is no)	
No, the thing of it	Wait, the thing of it	
Isn't	Isn't is	
Is it	The wait of the	
	The thing, the isn't	
Wait	Wait	
No, the thing of it	The thing of it	
No. Is. No.	Wait	
The thing of	Isn't	
It isn't	Wait	
It isn't		
	The thing	
It is	The isn't	
The thing of it is	The wait of the no	
The thing of it is	The isn't the it the	
The thing of it	No the thing	
Thing		
It is	The is of the no	
It is	The wait isn't wait	
	Of the isn't the isn't	
	The no of the thing	

Chapter 4

Hang Up - I *– ostinato –*

Performed by CHORUS. Read column 1, top to bottom, then column 2, top to bottom. Each line equals a measure. Each measure contains a count of 2. An actor will keep the rhythm. This piece begins in ½ time. The tempo may change, at discretion of performers, as determined in rehearsal. Timing: Silence = 4 beats; Pause = 2 beats

Hang up.

No you hang up.

Nooooo. YOU hang up.

OK let's do it together.

On the count of three.
    One... Two...

Wait on three or after three?

After three. Of course after three.

OK. Of course.

OK.

OK.

OK. One... Two... Three.
    (Silence.)

Did you hang up.

(Pause.) No.

Me neither.

Should we try again?

I don't feel like it.

Don't feel like trying or don't feel like hanging up?

Neither, both. Which word means I-don't-feel-like-trying-I-don't-feel-like-hanging-up.

Either.

Really?

And or Nor.

Huh!

Well so if we're not hanging up should we talk about Big Things?

Chapter 5
Contact

A dialogue. At the sofa. Performed by any two CHORUS members.

A: Sometimes you refuse to look at me. What's that about?

B: What?

A: Like when we're sitting in a room together and then you get up and leave the room. You walk right by me, but you don't so much as glance at me.

B: What are you talking about?

A: You avoid eye contact. You avoid contact.

B: I'm not avoiding anything. I'm walking.

A: You must feel my gaze on you.

B: I don't know. Why are you staring at me?

A: I'm not staring, I'm trying to catch your eye.

B: Why?

A: I don't know. To smile or something! To say hello. To make contact!

B: Well I don't know.

Chapter 6

Grievance Letter - I

WRITER, ANNOYER, BODY & CHILD are each played by a Chorus member. The Writer is manipulating a Body. The Child stands in the frame, watches, mirrors the series of manipulations. Even after the Body is no longer being manipulated, they continue to repeat the series for the remainder of the scene. MAN and WOMAN watch from their stations. If this scene is staged naturalistically, the stage directions would be followed literally and the WRITER would be sitting at a table, with pen and paper. If instead, the scene is staged abstractly, then the WRITER is figuratively manipulating a body[1]. In either case, the ANNOYER would be loitering somewhere annoyingly close, impatiently tapping or buzzing.

Annoyer: What's that you're doing?

Writer: Writing a letter.

Annoyer: What about?

Writer: Airing my grievances.

Annoyer: Ah. *(Pause)* What?

Writer: I'm saying what I really think.

Annoyer: *(Pause)* Go on.

Writer: I'm writing it.

Annoyer: Oh...will you be done soon?

---

[1] *"body" might not be a human body. Consideration of the word "body,"—as noun and verb. Noun– referring to a person or animal, or to the main or central part of something (i.e. the body of a building or body of a text), or to a mass of matter distinct from other masses (i.e. stellar bodies). Verb– to give material form to an abstract something. Body, in this context, refers to a sensible object in physical space.*

Writer: Not likely. A lot to say.

Annoyer: To write.

Writer: Right.

Annoyer: Ha. *(Silence.)* So a long letter. *(Silence.)*
            It's just that – *(Silence.)* Do you need anything?

Writer: What do you have in mind?

Annoyer: Oh. I dunno. Pencil Sharpener?
            (A stare. Oh, she's using a pen.) Ink blotter?

Writer: I wouldn't know what to do with that.

Annoyer: Right. *(Silence.)*

Writer: Right.

Annoyer: Glass of water.

Writer: I'm all right, thanks.

Annoyer: Yeah, sure. *(Silence, then an afterthought.)* Welcome.

Writer: Hmm? *(She's intent on writing.)*

Annoyer: I said Wel—Never mind. *(Pause)*
            So then you don't need anything, sounds like.

Writer: I don't need anything fetched.

Annoyer: Do you want me to go?

Writer: Immaterial.

Annoyer: I—is that a—is that a yes or a...?

Writer: I'm indifferent about your presence right now.

Annoyer: Oh. Right.

Writer: I'll have feelings about it again later, I'm sure. I think.
Just right now, I'm writing.

Annoyer: A letter.

Writer: Yes.

Annoyer: A long grievance letter of what you really think.

Writer: Yes.

Annoyer: And you won't be done soon,
and you don't need anything, and—

Writer: Don't need anything fetched.

Annoyer: Don't need anything fetched, and while you're writing

Writer: There's a distinction between...? Nevermind...

Annoyer: While you're writing my presence or absence
doesn't matter to you, but you expect it to matter later,
when you're done writing.
Writer: Yes. *(Silence.)*

Annoyer: Could I help you?

Writer: With what?

Annoyer: Could I help write it?

Writer: Oh. Oh I don't think so. No.

Annoyer: I've written letters.

Writer: I don't doubt that. (Silence.)

Annoyer: I'm not without wit.

Writer: Agreed. (Silence.)

Annoyer: I'm feeling somehow persecuted and I don't know why.
            (Silence.)
            Your indifference feels heavy. Like a wet woolly blanket got
            thrown on my back. (Silence.) Making me queasy too.
            Absence ought to matter. So should presence. Right now
            you're absent as you're writing and it matters. It's...
            it's annoying! And it feels a little mean. And I know—
            I know you'll say I'm mistaking inattention for absence, or,
            er, absence for inattention...nevermind. It feels like
            we're not here together even though we are.
            It's baffling and it hurts. (Silence.)
            Did you hear any of that?

Writer: Yes.

Annoyer: (Silence.) Why the letter?
            Why not just say what you really think?

Writer: Too difficult to keep hold of the thread.
            Distraction, interruption, evasion, timidity.

Annoyer: What are your grievances?

Writer: I'm writing them so I don't have to say them.

Annoyer: Right. But why not do it more piecemeal, one at a time.

Writer: Ineffectual. Impossible. Undermines the purpose of the letter.

Annoyer: What's the purpose of the letter.

Writer: To end the friendship.

Annoyer: *(Silence.)* Oh.

Writer: To end the friendship honestly, without pretense;
to end it finally.

Annoyer: What friendship are you ending?

They stare.

Man: *(Sipping his drink.)* This bullet is an old one.

Chapter 7
Remember the Where, the Thing

At the table, drinking tea. C speaks with D.

C: Yes it was there, don't you remember?

D: There was something to remember?

C: Well, some where, at least.

D: But how does one remember?

C: Remember what?

D: Any where. Any thing.

C: Depends on the where. On the thing. Were you never taught?

D: How would I know?

C: Well don't you – *(Pause)*

    (D gives a look)

C: Perhaps not, then. *(Silence.)*
    There's an art to it –

D: Surely.

C: Surely.

Chapter 8

Aroused Planets Crash Soundless

A monologue or a chorus. CHORUS behind the curtain, THE COUPLE is caught in an orbit. All lines in parentheses are spoken out loud. Lines may be spoken in unison or divided among members of CHORUS.

Chorus: This not-witnessed silence might not be silence at all. Some where—two planets, three planets, crashing Into one another. (It was an accident, of sorts). The one had only meant to lick the other on the hand (had seen this done on TV, millennia ago) neither planet had expected to be so aroused. "This is pleasing, momentarily, this world I am grazing. Am grazing on." The third planet just got caught in their rip tide.

           Two planets colliding and quite so close cannot be— be—be—word for resisted/avoided...be escaped. There there was must have been the sound of their crashing. But distance is too great from there to here to now (even carried on light's coattails).

           Worse the planets in their crashing cannot witness my silence inside of this room, it's not silence at all but the memory of the imagined sound of their coming at into out of each other. (In sound's event horizon: Does it go before light into gravitational collapse? What dies first—the sound or the light?)

           The intelligence of this body can be neither measured nor overstated. This body is dying. what does it understand that I cannot know? Can the body in its vast intelligence discover, emit, the sound of a universe? Can it emit the infinity of sounds within this sound? (She emits a sound, listens for the universe)

Woman: We stood there, looking out across the walls. Where I saw a village, all he saw was its towering castle.

Chapter 9
Leaving 1   *– fermata –*

CHORUS breaks into couples at sofa and table, respectively.
CHILD watches couples from the frame.

Child: there is a leaving   a manner of
             leaving   of leave-taking   it has a name
     it   it doesn't get bound up in   it doesn't get
             well sometimes   sometimes.

Interlude

Beethoven's "Grosse Fugue No. 16." The couple on the sofa begins to
shift, trying to find a comfortable position together. A durational thing.

Chapter 10

Foot War

First two iterations of this scene are played by CHORUS members (A & B) on the sofa as Petitioner and Denier, respectively.

PETITIONER (left column):   *DENIER (right column):*

Play foot war with me.

                                    I don't know how to play foot war.

What?

                                    I don't know how to play foot war.

You just put your feet up against each other.
   Up against my feet. And then you push.

                  They are foot to foot.
                  She pushes his feet, which bend easily.

You're supposed to push my feet.

                                            What?

You're supposed to – the point is to get your legs straight.

                              My knees are hurting today.

What?

                                    My knees are hurting.

Oh. Oh sorry.

She releases her feet from his.
Curls sideways.

It's okay. I'm okay. Okay let's play foot war.

No. No your knees hurt. I don't want to hurt you.

I'm okay. I'm okay let's play foot—

No, it's passed anyway.

What?

The moment.   *< lines spoken simultaneously >*   Already?
It's only a moment.

There it went.

What?   *< lines spoken simultaneously >*   Gone.
Yeah.

We can still play.

It won't be found now.

You don't want to try.

It'll be all disappointment and frustration.
Besides, your knees hurt today.

Yeah.

Let's just.

Yeah.

MAN gets up, takes his glass out of the room. Scene begins again, only this time lines are spoken rapidly. Other CHORUS members begin to set half-chairs downstage in a row, trying them out and then fetching more. At the end of the scene, all the Chorus members are set for the Foot War Ballet.

Foot War Ballet

FIRST VARIATION

B & D are the petitioners; they face STAGE RIGHT. A & C are the deniers; they face DOWNSTAGE. MAN with the glass sitting at table at the side leaves, and then walks back in with a new, full glass.

PETITIONERS (left column): *DENIERS (right column):*

Play foot war with me.

      I don't know how to play foot war.

What?

      I don't know how to play foot war.

You just put your feet up
 against each other.
 Up against my feet.
 And then you push.

    They are foot to foot.
    She pushes his feet, which bend easily.

You're supposed
 to push my feet.

          What?

You're supposed to–
 The point is to get
 your legs straight.

      My knees are hurting today.

What?

       My knees are hurting.

Oh.
 Oh sorry.

    Pivot: *Petitioners B & D turn to UPSTAGE;*
    Deniers A & C turn to face Petitioners.

                                              It's okay. I'm okay.
                                          Okay let's play foot war.

No. No your knees hurt.
  I don't want to hurt you.

                                                        I'm okay.
                                            I'm okay let's play foot—

No,
  it's passed anyway.

                                                            What?

The moment.   < *lines spoken simultaneously* >   Already?
It's only a moment.

                                                    There it went.

What?   < *lines spoken simultaneously* >   Gone.
Yeah.

                                                We can still play.

It won't be found now.

                                              You don't want to try.

Pivot: *Deniers rise, upstage of chair, stand behind*
their chairs. Stand; face STAGE LEFT.

It'll be all disappointment and frustration.

Pivot: *Petitioners move to sit down.*
Sit; face DOWNSTAGE.

Besides, your knees hurt today.

                                                            Yeah.

Let's just.

                                                            Yeah.

MAN gets up, takes his glass out of the room.
MAN returns with a new glass.

SECOND VARIATION

A & C switch places, face STAGE LEFT. B & D stay in place.
A & C are now petitioners. B & D are now deniers.
This time very fast and staccato. Positions at top of 2nd dialogue:

PETITIONERS (left column):   DENIERS (right column):

Play foot war with me.

                    I don't know how to play foot war.

What?

                    I don't know how to play foot war.

You just put your feet up
   against each other.
   Up against my feet.
   And then you push.

          They are foot to foot.
          She pushes his feet, which bend easily.

You're supposed to push my feet.

                              What?

You're supposed to–
   The point is to get
   your legs straight.

                My knees are hurting today.

What?

                  My knees are hurting.

Oh.
Oh sorry.

        She releases her feet from his. Curls sideways.
        Pivot: *Petitioners A & C turn to UPSTAGE;*
            Deniers B & D turn to face Petitioners.

It's okay. I'm okay.
Okay let's play foot war.

No. No your knees hurt.
  I don't want to hurt you.

I'm okay.
I'm okay let's play foot—

No, it's passed anyway.

What?

The moment.   < *lines spoken simultaneously* >   Already?
It's only a moment.

There it went.

What?   < *lines spoken simultaneously* >   Gone.
Yeah.

We can still play.

It won't be found now.

You don't want to try.

Pivot: Deniers rise, upstage of chair, stand behind
their chairs. Stand; face STAGE RIGHT.

It'll be all disappointment and frustration.

Pivot: Petitioners swing around to sit
facing DOWNSTAGE.

Besides, your knees hurt today.

Yeah.

Let's just.

Yeah.

MAN gets up, takes his glass out of the room.
MAN returns with a new glass.

THIRD VARIATION

A & C stay in place. B & D switch places. B & D are petitioners; they face STAGE RIGHT, A & C are deniers; they face DOWNSTAGE.

Accelerando (start slow and speed up)

PETITIONERS (left column):   *DENIERS (right column):*

Plaaaay foot war with me.

                                        I don't know how to play foot war.

What?

MAN does something with the glass.

FOURTH VARIATION

A & C switch places, B & D stay in place. B & D are petitioners. A & C are deniers. Pause at each line break.

PETITIONERS (left column):   *DENIERS (right column):*

You just put your feet up— (*Pause*)
against each other. — (*Pause*)
Up against my feet. — (*Pause*)
And then you — (*Pause*)
push. — (*Pause*)
You're supposed — (*Pause*)
to push my feet. — (*Pause*)

                                                            What?

MAN does something with the glass.

FIFTH VARIATION

A & C swivel to face STAGE LEFT. B & D switch places, face DOWNSTAGE. Each position takes a line, as indicated below.

A, B, and C say their respective line simultaneously.

A: *(simultaneously)* You're supposed to—
B: *(simultaneously)* The point is to get your legs straight.
C: *(simultaneously)* My knees are hurting today.

Beat.

D: What?

MAN does something with the glass.

SIXTH VARIATION

A & C switch places, stand. B & D face DOWNSTAGE, still sit. B & D are petitioners; A & C are deniers.

| - Staccato - | - Legato - |
| PETITIONERS *(left column):* | DENIERS *(right column):* |

Let's just.

Yeah.

MAN does something with the glass.

SEVENTH VARIATION

A & C sit, face STAGE LEFT. B & D switch places, face UPSTAGE. A & C are petitioners; B & D are deniers.

PETITIONERS (left column):	DENIERS (right column):
It's okay. I'm okay.	
	Okay let's play foot war.
No. No your knees hurt.	
I don't want to hurt you.	
	I'm okay.
	I'm okay let's play foot—
No, it's passed anyway.	
	What?

MAN does something with the glass.

EIGHTH VARIATION
All do 90 degree shift in their seats.

NINTH VARIATION
*All return to their position in eighth dialogue
(go back from 90 degree shift).*

TENTH VARIATION
*A moves to Position I, stands. B moves to Position III, stands.
C moves to Position II, sits facing upstage.
D stays in Position IV, faces downstage.*

Petitioner A reads left column:	Denier B reads right column:
The moment. *< lines spoken simultaneously >*	Already?

Beat.

It's only a moment.

       MAN does something with the glass.

ELEVENTH VARIATION
A & C sit, face stage left. B & D stay in place.

ALL: You don't want to try

       MAN does something with the glass.

TWELFTH VARIATION
All Stand.   *MAN does something with the glass.*

THIRTEENTH VARIATION
All Sit.   *MAN does something with the glass*

FOURTEENTH VARIATION
B & D stand, still face DOWNSTAGE. – Beat. –
A & C move to stand behind their chair, face STAGE LEFT. – Beat. –
D moves to Position III, C moves to Position I, face STAGE LEFT.

ALL: We can still—

       MAN does something with the glass.

FIFTHTEENTH VARIATION

A & C swivel, sit facing DOWNSTAGE. B & D sit down, face STAGE RIGHT.
B & D are petitioners. A & C are deniers.

PETITIONERS (left column):   DENIERS (right column):

Play foot war with me.

                                    I don't know how to play foot war.

What?

                                    I don't know how to play foot war.

You just put your feet up
   against each other.
   Up against my feet.
   And then you push.

                They are foot to foot.
                She pushes his feet, which bend easily.

You're supposed
   to push my feet.

                                          What?

You're supposed to—
   The point is to get
   your legs straight.

                          My knees are hurting today.

What?

                                 My knees are hurting.

Oh.
   Oh sorry.

                She releases her feet from his. Curls sideways.

                Pivot: *PETITIONERS turn to UPSTAGE;*
                      DENIERS turn to face Petitioners.

                                              It's okay. I'm okay.
                                              Okay let's play foot war.

No. No your knees hurt.
   I don't want to
   hurt you.

                                                           I'm okay.
                                              I'm okay let's play foot—

No,
   it's passed anyway.

                                                              What?

The moment.   < *lines spoken simultaneously* >   Already?
It's only a moment.

                                                        There it went.

What?   < *lines spoken simultaneously* >   Gone.
Yeah.

                                                     We can still play.

It won't be found now.

                                                   You don't want to try.

            Pivot: *Deniers rise, upstage of chair, stand behind*
               their chairs. Stand ; Face STAGE LEFT.

It'll be all disappointment and frustration.

            Pivot: *Petitioners shift to face DOWNSTAGE.*
Besides,
   your knees hurt today.

                                                              Yeah.

Let's just.

                                                              Yeah.

            MAN gets up, takes his glass out of the room.

            – *End of Part One* –

Interlude *– codetta/stretto –*

A 2 voice fugue. VOICE 1 begins. At the end of the column, VOICE 2 will say first line in unison with Voice 1's last line. At the end of Voice 2, each will return to the beginning of her respective section and repeat in unison. (First two voices of the fugue.)

Voice 1:
to end
to seem to end
seem
to
end to seem
to seem to end to
end to
end
to seem to
seem to
end to seem to
end
to end to seem to end to
seem to seem
to end   *< lines sung simultaneously >*

Voice 2:
to end
to seem to end to end
to
end to end to
seem to
end to
end
seem to end
to end
end to seem
end to end to seem
to
to
to
to seem
end
to end

Chapter 11
Light Out of Darkness II

The MAN has been sitting in the chair silently for several scenes. It has been long enough that he has blended into the background, been forgotten, or at least is ignored. The WOMAN is on stage, standing, facing front.

Man: (*Enunciating very loudly, a recitation/dictation*)
Light—out—of—darkness. Light—out—of—darkness.

> *WOMAN looks up.*
> *MAN opens his mouth, breathes in, to continue.*
> *WOMAN holds up a hand.*
> *MAN closes his mouth.*
> *Silence.*
> *WOMAN lowers her hand.*
> *MAN opens his mouth.*
> *WOMAN holds up the same hand.*
> *MAN closes his mouth.*
>
> *Silence.*
> *WOMAN lowers her hand.*
>
> *Silence.*
>
> *MAN opens his mouth. WOMAN runs to him and presses the same hand to his mouth, her other hand cupping the back of his neck. WOMAN squeezes, her face an inch from his face. They stare at one another.*

MAN remains still. Silence.

Woman: And???

> *Silence. MAN remains still,*
> *only his eyeballs move down to her hand.*
> *He may or may not be wearing sunglasses.*

Woman: And and and???

> *WOMAN releases her grip, but stays an inch from his*
> *face. They stare.*
>
> *MAN opens his mouth. Pause.*
> *WOMAN remains still.*
> *MAN breathes in. Pause.*
> *WOMAN remains still.*

Man: Light – out – of— *(WOMAN immediately returns her hands*
         to his mouth, his neck.)

Woman: Finish this sentence: "We were most happy when we…"

> *Darkness.*

DEBBIE SAFEBLADE *as the woman* & LENA MAGNUS BRÜN *as the child*

PART II:
DEVELOPMENT

Chapter 12

Weird Seeing Him - II *– interrogation –*

One or all of CHORUS interrogates WOMAN, again. This time
lines are not simultaneous. Rhythm to be found by performers.

Chorus:	So you went to the—?
Woman:	Yeah.
Chorus:	How was it? Was it weird? Did you see him?
Woman:	Did I—? Well yeah it was his thing.
Chorus:	So you saw him.
Woman:	Yes of course I saw him.
Chorus:	And?
Woman:	And what?
Chorus:	Was it hard to go? Was it hard to see him, after the—?
Woman:	Less hard than I expected.
Chorus:	Why'd you go anyway?
Woman:	Curiosity, I guess. Less about him, per se. More about what the interaction might be. curious to see what we'd all do.
Chorus:	What did you do? What happened?
Woman:	Nothing especially notable. Manners. They kick in fast and get you past the awkward parts. There was a manic quality to some of the talking, sure
Chorus:	Sure.
	Silence.
Woman:	These can't be real questions.

Chapter 13

A Chorus - II   *– lines & caesura –*

CHORUS performs this as cacophony. Each starts at a different stanza. No words left out. At the end of each column, there should be a caesura, like a TV turning off. The CHORUS shifts positions, silently agrees when to begin next column.

The thing of it is
Wait, no
The thing of it isn't
It is
(It) – no.

The thing of it is
Wait, no
The thing of it is
It isn't
It is

The thing of it is
Wait
No, the thing of it
Isn't
Is it

Wait
No, the thing of it
No. Is. No.
The thing of it isn't
It isn't

It is
The thing of it is
The thing of it is
The thing of it
Thing
It is
It is

The thing of
The thing
It is
Wait
The thing of it, no.
Is, no.

The thing of it isn't
Isn't wait
No, isn't
Wait, no

The thing of the wait
Is, no (No is no)
Wait, the thing of it
Isn't is
The wait of the
The thing, the isn't

Wait
The thing of it
Wait
Isn't
Wait

The thing the isn't
The wait of the no
The isn't the it the
No the thing

The is of the no
The wait isn't wait
Of the isn't the isn't
The no of the thing

It isn't the wait
The thing of it
No, isn't
Wait, (it)
The thing of it, no.
(Was it?)

Chapter 14

Hang Up - II *– ostinato –*

Performed by CHORUS. Layer allegro over drone.
Each line equals a measure. Each measure contains a count of 2. An
actor will keep the rhythm. This piece begins in ½ time. The tempo
may change, at discretion of performers, as determined in rehearsal.
Silence = 4 beats; Pause = 2 beats.

Hang up.

No you hang up.

Nooooo.
  YOU hang up.

OK let's do it
  together.

On the count of
  three.
  One...
  Two...

Wait on 3 or
  after 3?

After 3.
  Of course after 3.

OK. Of course.

OK.

OK.

OK. One...
  Two...
  Three.

    Silence.

Did you hang up.

(Pause.)
  No.

Me neither.

Should we
  try again?

I don't feel like it.

Don't feel like trying
  or don't feel like
  hanging up?

Neither, both.
  Which word means
  I-don't-feel-like-
  trying-I-don't-feel
  like-hanging-up.

Either.

Really?

And or Nor.

Huh!

Well so if we're not
  hanging up should
  we talk about
  Big Things?

Like Bigfoot?

Big Oil?

Big Banks.

Big Yellow Taxis.

Big Ben.

Big Bonus.

Big Mistake

Big Sur.

Big Brother.

Big bullies.

Big babies.

Big Butts.

Big Boobs.

Big Basin

Big Bear

Big Fish

Big Easy

Big-gies

Big Guns

Big Apple

Big Ten

Big Time

Big Kahuna

Big O

Big Bangs.

Yes, wait, no.

What?

How many big bangs?

Infinity?

No.

How many infinities?

I don't know.

Chapter 15

Don't Talk Sing

A dialogue. At the sofa. Between A & B.

A: Remember when you wouldn't talk to me?

B: Couldn't.

A: Yeah right couldn't. Except you could.

B: Couldn't.

A: Wouldn't.

B: Couldn't.

A: Wouldn't.

B: Think what you like.

A: I like you.

B: You don't. You did. You don't.

A: Sing me a song.

B: I can't sing.

A: Of course you can. Sing me something.

B: What song?

A: Any song! I don't care what.

B: I can't think of a song.

A: But you're singing constantly! Think: SONG.
     What comes to mind.

     B thinks, or at least B is silent a moment.

A: Well?

B: I don't know!

A: Is it the violence of the question?

B: No.

A: What is it?

B: I don't feel like singing.

A: It would make me happy if you would sing.

B: I just don't feel like it.

Chapter 16

Grievance Letter - II

A return to continue previous scene from Grievance Letter I. Reprise the WRITER sitting at a table, with pen and paper, OR if abstract scene then the WRITER figuratively manipulating a body. The ANNOYER is still distracting, interrupting, and demanding attention.

Annoyer: Read me a line.

Writer: "I have an apprehension of you which is deeper than ordinary knowledge."

Annoyer: You're most comfortable when you're miserable, is the thing.

Man: *(Interjecting.)* It's true, she is.

Annoyer: It's your native element. You know all the textures of misery, its temperatures, its weight.

Writer: I know I'm sad and it doesn't stop.

Annoyer: If it could be stopped, would you allow it?

Writer: All this—Always this leave-taking.

Annoyer: I'm not going anywhere.

Writer: But you will be. Or I will. We're tourists, merely.

> *Silence.*
> *More silence.*
> *Still more.*

Annoyer: "Have I wit only? Have I not humor?"

Writer: *(Looking up.)* What?

Annoyer: Is that what you wrote there?

Writer: You're reading over my shoulder?

Annoyer: Not intentionally. I glanced over and noticed the words "I wit only." And that made me curious enough to read the words around it: "Have"/"Have I not humor."

(Annoyer snatches the page/body.) "Not likely the same for you. Happiness at having caught the...turtle." What?? That can't be the word. Your penmanship is terrible. *(The page is snatched back.)*

Actual text of the letter will be shared in Chapter 24 Event Horizon.

Chapter 17
Isn't Love, Specifically

Each of the players says this, or pieces of it, at one time or another. Spoken as an aside to the audience.

This isn't love,
specifically.   That is, this isn't...it's not
that there isn't love. There is   annoyance.   Yes certainly.
The feeling of.   Uncomfortable.   Yes. Annoyed, uncomfortable.
Even frustrated. But not without love.
But the feeling of love,   specifically,
becomes obscured.

Chapter 18
Remember Me Now

At the table.

C: Remember me now?

D: Who are you?

C: So then no.

D: What is remember?

C: You don't recognize the word anymore? This is getting worse and worse. But maybe that's not so bad. It's a progression, at least. It's movement. Not in a good direction, but movement nonetheless.

D: Was that an answer?

C: What? To what?

D: To what is remember.

C: Oh. Well. To recall. To recollect. To remind oneself.

D: Re– that means again. Call again, collect again, mind again. *(D holds the words in their hands, studies them)* I don't understand.

C: That's right, though.

D: Again again again. Member again. What is member again? And really what is again? A gain. A gain. A gain. Gain a what? What gain?

C: Not member again. Memory again. To be mindful, again. You said it yourself. Again means re. It means over and over, repeated.

D: Peat and repeat—

C: No.

D: Just as well. I don't know how it ends, anyway.

C: It doesn't that's the point. It just goes on and on. Again and
        again. Over and over. That's the joke of it—the repetition—

D: – petition again—

C: Of repeat. And no, repeat isn't peat again.
        Repeat is his name.

D: I know that. But...well it can't not end. Can it?
        It can't just keep going forever. Can it?

C: It can't. It just. I don't know. It stops. The teller gets tired,
        needs to pee or something. Gets thirsty. Or the listener
        stops answering the question. That's most likely.
        The listener refuses—

D: – fuse again—

C: – refuses to play the game.

D: So it's stopped via abstention. By one of the parties.

C: Sure.

D: Until then it simply re-peats. Then abstention. Then stop.

C: You won't remember any of this, will you?

D: What is remember?

C: To not forget. To not forget again and again.
        To not forget forever.

D: For—

C: Because of; in favor of

D: In favor of get. In favor of ever.

C: Sure.

Chapter 19
Universe Under the Skin Writings

Written in three parts. All three parts may be performed alone or simultaneously, in a sort of counterpoint, with performers modulating volume so that each part has moments of clarity.

Part I: Write "The Universe Under the Universe"

CHORUS is determined to explain. Parentheses are spoken out loud.

There is there might be it's likely there exist more than just the one. Or even just the one infinity. We have brains that can only just barely conceive of such a possibility but cannot even conceive of it.

The universe under the universe. (Oh yeah!)

I start again.

Skin is a membrane. (Is it?) Skin struck by lightning is...the thing well it's not that we are conductors of electricity, merely, or is it? We have a weight. and yet the universe in all its vastness seems (Somehow! Incredibly, impossibly.) Weightless. (No gravity means no weight.)

Right! No gravity means no weight.

So in gravitational collapse, then—

No—that's collapsing into gravity, not collapsing of the gravity.

Gravitas: means grave, means weighty.

It's heavy, the mass inside the grave.

It's the weight of the sadness it takes with it.

Sadness does not have a weight.

Certainly it does, if it's measured in tears.

But think of all the tears left unshed.

In footfalls, then.

Nonsense.

Well what, then, makes the grave so heavy?

The central fact of all humanity: the weight we each lug from birth to death and on throughout the swamp of it.

How heavy is it?

It is just as weighty as the mass and emotional scope with which it manifests.

And the universe? How heavy is that?

It is just as weighty as the mass and emotional scope with which it manifests.

This is a disaster.

Part II: Outline "The Universe Under the Universe"

Spoken by CHILD, who is determined to explain.

1. Consideration of the universe; the number of possible universes; the infinite possible infinities of universes. The paltry scope of the brain and its limited ability to conceive of great, great size.

2. Remembering/being reminded of the actual assignment: that is, the universe under the universe, not the universe and infinity (not that these are not related).

3. Skin membrane lightning. (This bit was, admittedly, flailing); the skin, the body, as conductor of electricity but hoping it might be more. The weight of the human body/the seeming weightlessness of the universe.

4. No gravity means no weight. Defining gravitational collapse as collapse into gravity, not collapse of gravity.

5. Gravitas—grave—weighty—the grave.

6. He taps the tip of his nose with the tip of his finger and huffs out his breath. This is thinking. *(MAN performs this as a stage direction while CHILD says it)*

7. The weight of the body inside the grave.

8. The weight of shed and unshed tears.

9. The weight of footfalls—nonsense!

10. Answers to the question of whether it is heavy: humanity's condition of lugging weight from birth to death.

11. Weight of the universe: defined by the mass and emotional scope with which IT manifests.

12. Declaration that this is a disaster.

Part III: The Universe Under My Skin

Spoken by CHORUS – determined to explain.

D: There is a universe under my skin

Child: So you keep saying

D: I've told you this?

Child: Constantly you tell me.
         If you knew how to remember, you'd know.

D: I don't know how to remember.

Child: I know. You've told me.

D: When?

Chorus: Before. Back then. Back when. Prior to. Previously.
          Antecedent. Earlier. Agone. Ago. In the past. Preceding.

D: Past is so important. Why?

Child: Because I can remember it.
         There is a responsibility to remember.

D: Why are there so many words for what's passed?

B: Our existence is contingent on the experience of
      ourselves in the spacetime fabric. In order to continue
      our existence we have to continually acknowledge
      that we are still *in* time and not *outside* of time.

C: What is the difference?

B: Inside (time) means we're alive. Outside (time) means
      we're dead—frozen—*past tense*. We no longer are,
      we only were.

A: You mean rhetorically?

B: What?

A: Tense is a rhetorical thing, right?
        I go to the market or I went to the market.
        Either way, there is an I, a market, and a going.

C (to D):   How can you even speak if you can't remember?

D: Language is a thing I know.

B: You must remember learning vocabulary words
        in school! Did you have vocabulary words in school?

D: How would I know?

A: Do you remember school?

D: I don't know how to.

B: But you know what school means—when I say it.
        The definition.

All: *A definition.*

A: You just don't have a memory of going.

All: Going going going gone.

Child: So what of this universe under your skin?

D: It's expanding.

Chapter 20
Leaving - II *– fermata –*

Spoken by CHILD.

There is a
Leaving a
Manner
Leave-taking
Bound

It doesn't get
Well sometimes

It has a name
Sometimes

It doesn't get
It

Of leaving

Leaving
A

Of

Chapter 21
Different Infinities Are Different Sizes

*WOMAN and CHILD are within the frame, as MAN begins dialogue
from without. Woman and Child step through the frame.*

Man: There is a distance from me to you. And the space of that
distance contains an infinity.

Woman: *(takes a step closer)* What about now? Less than infinity?

Man: A different infinity. A smaller infinity.

Woman: How does one measure a smaller infinity?
Is it merely conceptual?

Man: Not merely conceptual. It's mathematics.

Woman: But theoretical mathematics, yes? Which makes certain
assumptions about the properties of infinities.

Child: He starts to list facts about infinity to the other—
starting with the Basic Metaphor of Infinity (defined
as an ever-increasing sequence). But then, he goes on.
For instance, there are ordinal infinities and cardinal
infinities. One must consider, also, not just natural
numbers, and integers, and real numbers, but also
hyperreal numbers. Not to mention fractals with their
infinite perimeters. The other sits still, but her face
transforms from wonder to confusion to horror.
Only her face.

— End of Part Two —

Interlude *– a fugue for six voices –*

I. to end
to seem to end
seem
to
end to seem
to seem to end to
end to
end
to seem to
seem to
end to seem to
end
to end to seem to end to
seem to seem

II. to end
to seem to end to end
to
end to end to
seem to
end to
end
seem to end
to end
end to seem
end to end to seem
to
to
to
to *seem*
end

III. to end
seem
end
end to seem to
seem to end
to seem to end
to end
to
end to seem to seem to end—to
end to seem to end
to *not*

to not end
to seem to end to not
to end to seem to end to not to end
to end to seem

IV. to end
to not to end
to end
to end to
not to end
to seem to not
seem to seem to not—to end
to not to
to not to seem
to end to not end
seem to not end
seem to end to not—to seem to not
to seem

V. to end
not to seem
not to stop
to seem to stop
to end to seem to stop—to *stop*
to not
to seem to not
to stop
to end
to end stop end

VI. to end
to stop to not stop—not to end to
seem to not to end to—stop
to *stop*
end to stop
to stop end stop to seem—to stop to
seem
to not stop seem to end—stop end
to not stop end
to stop not stop not end—stop seem
to
not stop seem to
end

PART III:
RECAPITULATION

JEFFREY BIVENS,
JULIA WILLIAMS,
TARAN O'REILLY,
LENA MAGNUS BRÜN
and
JAYITA BHATTACHARYA
as the CHORUS

Chapter 22
Light Out of Darkness - III

The end of their previous scene returns MAN and WOMAN to their tableau from the end of LIGHT OUT of DARKNESS-II.
Back into darkness...

They share the text below, both struggling to finish the sentence.

MAN and WOMAN work together in their struggle to finish the sentence, increasingly excited as words slowly come.

We were most happy when we...

were without a bottle of cognac, so we—you know—at the other end of the hall—it was a—a— a—a—word for doesn't work—a broken

     Light. They remain still. Stunned.

     Darkness.

Chapter 23

A Chorus - III *– lines & Vaudeville –*

In this iteration, the text is spoken as dialogue—not in cacophony.
Vaudeville. An effort, once again, to explain.

The thing of it is
Wait, no
The thing of it isn't
It is
(It) – no.

The thing of it is
Wait, no
The thing of it is
It isn't
It is

The thing of it is
Wait
No, the thing of it
Isn't
Is
It

Wait
No, the thing of it
No. Is. No.
The thing of it isn't
It isn't
It is

The thing of it is
The thing of it is
The thing of it
Thing
It is
It is

The thing of
The thing
It is
Wait
The thing of it, no.
Is, no.

The thing of it isn't
Isn't wait
No, isn't
Wait, no

The thing of the wait
Is, no (No is no)
Wait, the thing of it
Isn't is
The wait of the
The thing, the isn't
Wait

The thing of it
Wait
Isn't
Wait

The thing the isn't
The wait of the no
The isn't the it the
No the thing

The is of the no
The wait isn't wait
Of the isn't the isn't
The no of the thing

It isn't the wait
The thing of it
No, isn't
Wait, (it)
The thing of it, no.
(was it?)

Chapter 24
Event Horizon

MAN and WOMAN are collapsed upon each other. An attempt to put them back together, but they keep falling apart. Child is reading the grievance letter from Chapter 16.

CHILD (left column):   CHORUS responds (right column):

There is a limit which a star can reach. It has a name.
The limit has a name. So does the star—when it
reaches this limit. That is, the star has an adjective
placed before it to distinguish it from itself.

Itself before.   < *lines sung simultaneously* >   Before.
                                                                    Back then.
                                                                    Back when.
                                                                    Prior to.
                                                                    Previously.
                                                                    Antecedent.
                                                                    Earlier.
                                                                    Agone.
                                                                    Ago.
                                                                    In the past.
                                                                    Preceding.

To distinguish itself from stars that are not like it.
That have not reached the limit. The limit which
has a name. (*Spoken as an aside.*) A foreign
sounding name. It is not an American name.

                                                    What does an American
                                                    name sound like?

The chorus starts listing AMERICAN names.

I'll stop being so oblique. What I'm trying to say—

CHILD (left column):   CHORUS (right column):

                                        the thing of it is—

Right. I'm talking about Frozen Stars. We call
these stars frozen because they have crossed
the threshold of the Chandrasekhar limit in
their gravitational collapse and are inside
the Schwarzchild radius. The "surface" of the
Schwarzchild radius is—you may have heard
of this—the event horizon. That is, they have
collapsed into a black hole. The "surface" of the
star—which to us, is its light—is frozen in time.
The only light we see from that star is   *(repeat)*
from before.   < *lines sung simultaneously* >   Before.
                                                               Back then.
                                                               Back when.
                                                               Prior to.
                                                               Previously.
                                                               Antecedent.
                                                               Earlier.
                                                               Agone.
                                                               Ago.
                                                               In the past.
                                                               Preceding.

The collapse into the Schwarzchild radius/
event horizon. The beauty of an event horizon,
what distinguishes it from all other phenomena,
(phenomena, for instance, such as this ending you
and I are in the midst of trying to achieve) is that it
is—has been described as—a perfect unidirectional
membrane through which causal influences can
cross in only one direction. It's the only linear path
in the universe. The end is the end. Time cannot
cross it, even. Or, if time can cross it, it cannot
cross back.

Chapter 25
Tell Me What to Say and I Will Say

– da capo al coda –

This scene is performed by the CHORUS. The pair at the sofa performs the main dialogue, with interjections, as indicated, by other members of the chorus. Meanwhile the MAN watches intently, as if watching TV, trying to make sense of the end.

B: Tell me what to say and I will say.

A: There is nothing left.

B: There must be.

A: I don't speak your language.

> *A long pause. So long perhaps when they speak again it's an entirely different scene.*

A: Tell me what you are feeling.

> *There is a substantive beat between each of the words—each is carefully considered then emphatically stated:*

B: Agitation—frustration—happiness—sadness—loving

A: Account for each of these feelings, please.

B: I can't.

A: Account for each of these feelings, please.

B: I don't know. I can't.

> *Again a long pause. So when they speak again it's an entirely different scene.*

INTERJECTION: This Is What It's Like   *– a dialogue –*

CHORUS:

D: This is what it's like to be together.

C: Again.

D: This is what it's like to be together.

C: Again.

D: This is what it's like to be together.

C: Without you.

D: This is what it's like to be together without you.

A: I'm having trouble remembering how we spent Thursday.

B: I've had this phrase in my head for twenty years—

A: This has been bugging me all day...What's the phrase?

B: "Remaining Light"

A: I found that black pen I thought I'd lost a few days ago.

B: The light is fading. It's going away from us.

A: I didn't switch back to it until I couldn't find the blue pen.

B: We'll be leaving.

A: Sunday. Our final morning here...

B: We haven't completed anything, we've barely begun.

A: Is that the sound of so many leaves falling from the trees at once? That bubbling sound from the wood?

B: The narrative that's left unfinished.

> *A silence that is more like a breath or a sigh
> than a silence.*

A: I'll check on the wash soon.

INTERJECTION: This Is What It's Like   *– a dialogue –*

CHORUS:

D: This is what it's like to be.

C: Together it's like to be.

D: This is what together is like

C: To be

She wonders again: Is this marriage?
Merely a series of damages to be reconciled?

B: Tell me what to say and I will say

A: Not good enough

B: I don't know what

Child: Try again

B: Tell me what and I will

A: I don't know what

B: Tell what I will

A: Don't know

B: Don't tell me don't know

A: Tell me what

B: Tell me don't

A: I don't

Child: Again. Try again.

B: Tell me what to say. I will say what to say if you tell me.

A: Don't know what, just say

B: Nothing left to say

A: Not nothing

B: Nothing left

A: Please not nothing.

(Silence.)

Child: Again. Again.

    B: Tell me what to say and I will say

    A: Not good enough

    B: I don't know what

    A: Tell me what and I will

    B: I don't know what

    A: Tell what I will

    B: Don't know

    A: Don't tell me don't know

    B: Tell me what

    A: Tell me don't

    B: I don't

    A: Tell me what to say. I will say what to say if you tell me.

    B: Don't know what, just say

    A: Nothing left to say

    B: Not nothing

    A: Nothing left

    B: Please not nothing.

Silence.

    B: What if I sing?

Looks toward, then away.
WOMAN begins clapping wildly for them.
ALL join her, except for MAN, who is befuddled.

Chapter 26
This Is What It's Like - II   *– interjection –*

A cheer!
WOMAN leads the CHORUS in this cheer.

This is what it's like to be together.

Again.

This is what it's like to be together.

Again.

This is what it's like to be together.

Without you.

This is what it's like to be together without you.

This is what it's like to be.

Together it's like to be.

This is what together is like

To be

Chapter 27
Light Out of Darkness - IV

Bodies in space.

Woman: Is there enough time?

Man: *(a mantra – chanted/incanted/sung)*
Slowly
Slowly
Slower still
We are getting
Nowhere
Nowhere still

Silence.

We stood there, looking out across the walls.

Woman: Where I saw a village, all you saw was its towering castle.

And now to harvest from some other frame.

Chapter 28
Leaving - III   *– fermata –*

CHILD speaks these lines.

leaving

there is a

manner

it has a name

leave-taking bound

it doesn't get well sometimes

sometimes.

Chapter 29
December or Noon

CHORUS back in the frame, witnessing. MAN and WOMAN negotiate the space once again in silence as A & B perform the text.

A: Where will we meet?

B: In December or noon?

A: December.

B: It'll be cold.

A: But where will we meet?

B: There's a blue jay just landed in the fountain,
      that's the sound you hear.

A: Its call.

B: Yes.

A: The fountain's dried up now, I think.

B: Surely. It flew to the nearby tree and immediately another
      replaced it on the fountain.

A: Another bluejay?

B: I couldn't tell.

A: When you asked me to pass the stone through my fingers —
      do you recall that?

B: I do, yes.

A: It was difficult, my fingers were too small for that stone.

B: That's the challenge, yes.

A: That's why I kept dropping it. I fear I disappointed you. *(Silence.)*
    So did I disappoint you?

B: Outside—in nature, but still well-lit.

A: What?

B: At first I thought a park, but no. The lake—by the lake, near that
    old wooden pier. Yes! It'll be snowing.

A: In December?

B: It'll have to be snowing, when we meet.

A: Nature rarely cooperates when we make plans for it.
    Particularly at these latitudes.

B: If it doesn't snow then we won't meet.

A: So then you were disappointed.

B: We're not talking about that now.
    We're talking about the other thing.

A: You are. I'm still talking about this thing.

B: I'm answering your question.

A: You were disappointed.

B: I can't stop you from making your assumptions.

A: You could, though. By simply answering the question.
    Your evasion was obviously your answer.

B: Your assumption was made when you asked the question—
    no answer I'd give would matter.

A: Well why not just say that, then?

B: What was the question?

Chapter 30
Remind Me of Me

Together.

B: Wait what? What were we talking about?

A: You were trying to change your mind.

B: Your mind. *(Silence.)* What are you doing?

A: Trying hard to imagine myself,

B: Yourself what?

A: The ocean just beyond. My feet. *(Pause.)* Did it work?

B: Nah. My mind changed before I changed it.

A: So did mine.

B: Who will remind me of me when you're not there?

A: You mean here?

B: And there—where you are not. Here will become there, when you aren't. I won't be my here. Here won't be. The only place we'll be able to both inhabit together, to share, is there.

A: Why not remind yourself?

B: I want to be reminded by you.

– End of Part Three –

Coda
This Is What It's Like - III

*A lullaby or a dirge. MAN and WOMAN begin,
then CHORUS joins in.*

This is what it's like to be together.

Again.

This is what it's like to be together.

Again.

This is what it's like to be together.

Without you.

This is what it's like to be together without you.

This is what it's like to be.

Together it's like to be.

This is what together is like

to be

Darkness.

– The End –

JENNY MAGNUS, JAYITA BHATTACHARYA, JULIA WILLIAMS in recording session
for *To End To Seem To End*, 2013

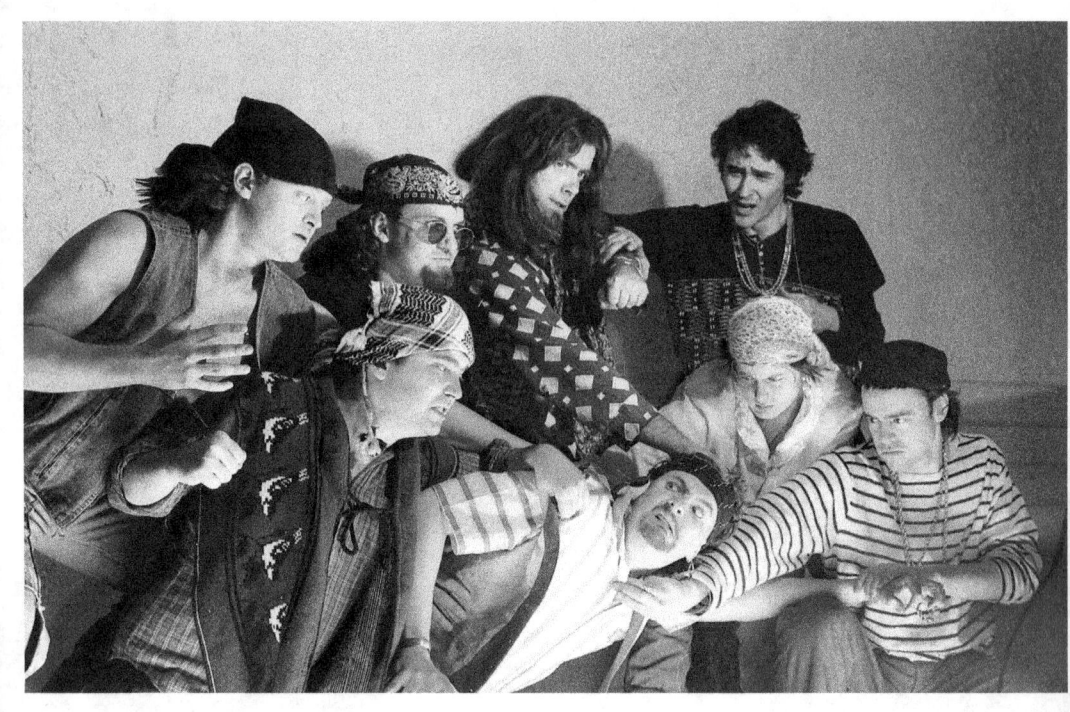

Publicity still of the company's first production, **"Bargan Gives Up"**
by Bertolt Brecht, staged in 1988

BACKMATTER:

PROFILES
&
HISTORY

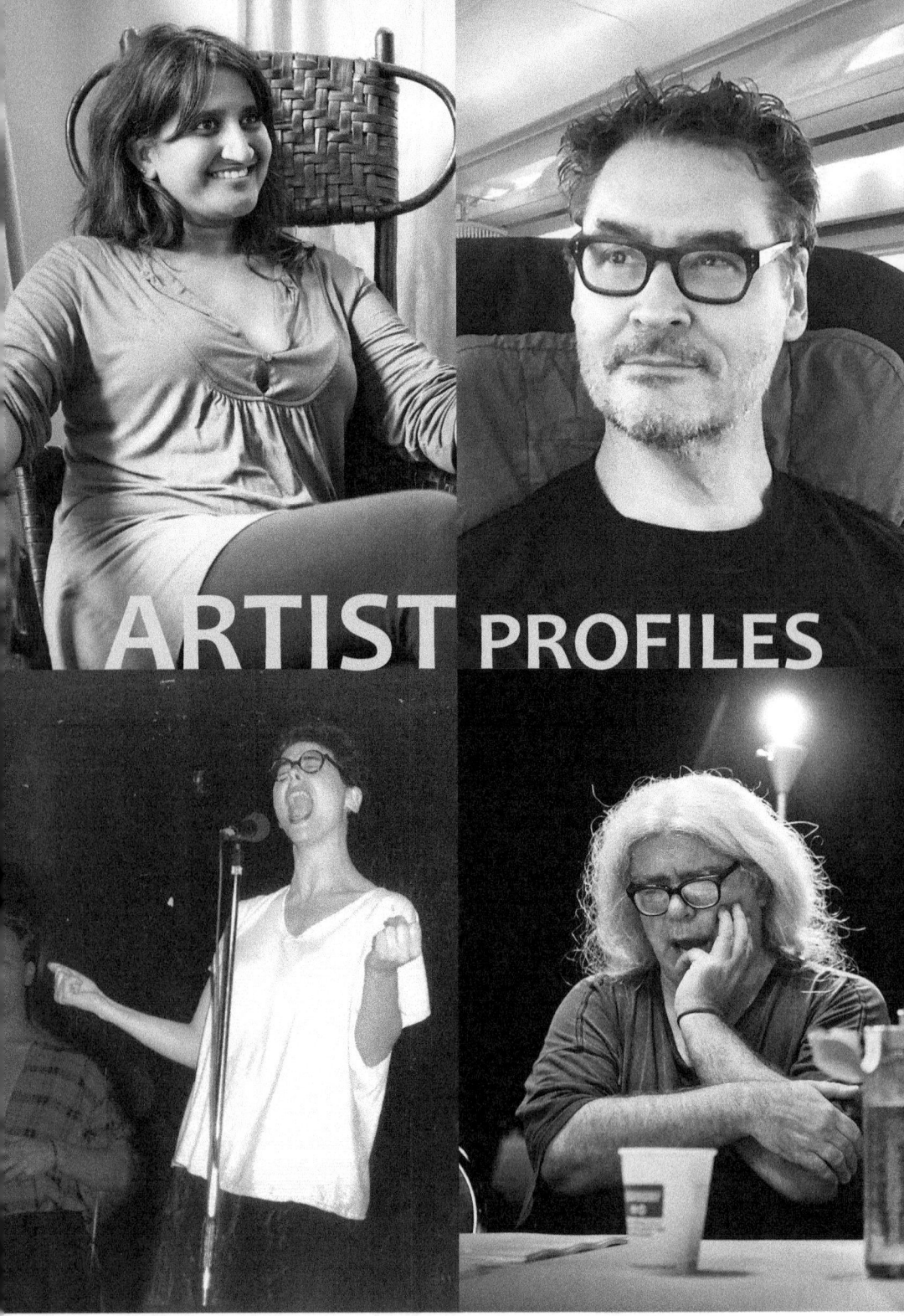

ARTIST PROFILES

Curious Playwrights / Writer Bios:

Jayita Bhattacharya is an interdisciplinary writer, director, performer, and choreopgrapher who has written and produced seven plays, including *To End To Seem To End*, *today like a kind of shivering*, *Elvisbride: Some Prepared Remarks to Clarify the Impending Jubilation* (with Matt Test), and *Make Sweat An Oak*. She has directed or assistant directed productions of *Waiting for Godot*, *Endgame*, *The Caretaker*, and *The McGuffins Run the 440*, and performed in *The Buzz That is the Buzz*, *Evanston Which is Over There*, *4:48 Psychosis*, *I Am In a Small Space for a Reason I Don't Understand*, *Difficulties*, *(Not) Another Day*, and *The Skriker*.

Bryn Magnus lives and works in Brooklyn, NY with his family. He is currently incapable of writing his bio.

Jenny Magnus is a writer, performer, musician, director, and teacher who is a founding co-Artistic Director of the Curious Theatre Branch, an all-original theater company. Her plays have been produced at Steppenwolf Theatre, the Museum of Contemporary Art Chicago, the former Lunar Cabaret, Prop Thtr, the Poetry Foundation, as well as in New Orleans, Madison, Nashville, Olympia WA, Cleveland, Dessau, and Berlin. Her collection of plays *Observations of an Orchestrated Catastrophe* was published by JackLeg Press in 2014. She has a MFA from the School of the Art Institute of Chicago.

Beau O'Reilly is a founding member of the Curious Theatre Branch and the bands *Maestro Subgum and the Whole* and *The Crooked Mouth*, as well as a curator of the Rhinoceros Theater Festival for thirty years. His work has appeared at the Museum of Contemporary Art Chicago, the Poetry Foundation, and on This American Life. The author of more than eighty original plays, O'Reilly is also a working actor who teaches playwriting at the School of the Art Institute of Chicago. His latest solo album, *Thrifty*, was released on Uvulittle Records in 2021.

Shawn Reddy is a writer, director, lecturer and educator. He was an ensemble member of the Curious Theatre Branch for over a decade. His work has been produced in Chicago venues such as the Art Institute of Chicago, Museum of Contemporary Art, Steppenwolf Theatre, Chicago Cultural Center, Chopin Theatre and the Museum of Science and Industry, as well as nationally in Baltimore, Grand Rapids, Orlando, Nashville, New Orleans, New York City and Richmond. Shawn's work focuses heavily on alternative interpretations of American history and lore. He holds a MEd from the University of Chicago, an MFA from the School of the Art Institute of Chicago, and is currently earning his PhD in education from the University of Illinois at Chicago.

Matt Rieger was a prolific playwright, performer, producer and director of numerous *(1963-2021)* plays in Chicago. He was Curious Theatre's Managing Director as well as Development Director for Prop Thtr. and co-founder of the theater company Illegal Drama. In 2021 Matt passed away unexpectedly at which time he had completed recording and editing his serialized radio play, *Aviva Green: The Rebirth of Bleak*, a prequel to his 2018 stage play *Crossing Aviva*. His one-act holiday play, *Xmas Time at Lost Pines*, was Curious's last full production before the pandemic shut down theaters, and his final play, *Jimmy and the Nickels*, relaunched Rhinofest in 2022.

Matt Test is a Chicago-based composer, writer, and interdisciplinary sound artist whose work has been featured from living rooms and community gardens to Steppenwolf Theatre and the Museum of Contemporary Art Chicago. As an ensemble member with the Curious Theatre Branch he has created a number of experimental operas, new music theatre works, and soundscapes that play in the spaces between surrealist thought games and structural absurdity. He holds an MFA in Creative Writing from the School of The Art Institute of Chicago and an MA in Sound Art and Industries from Northwestern University.

Julia Williams is a writer and performer living in Chicago. With Curious Theatre Branch, she has appeared in Caryl Churchill's *The Skriker*, Eugène Ionesco's *Rhinoceros*, and many new plays by Curious ensemble members, including *To End to Seem to End* by Jayita Bhattacharya, *One Boppa: Two Acts* by Beau O'Reilly, *Crossing Aviva* by Matt Rieger, and *(Not) Another Day* by Jenny Magnus. She has directed her own works, *Difficulties* (with Sue Cargill) and *The Near Future*, in the Rhinoceros Theater Festival.

HISTORY

The Curious Theatre Branch

was founded in 1988 by Jenny Magnus and Beau O'Reilly as the theater "branch" of the alt-rock cabaret act *Maestro Subgum and the Whole*. Since that time, Curious has consistently worked with an ever growing ensemble of artists exploring the philosophy of collaboration as a social force for artistic creation and curation.

Curious has produced more than one hundred full-length productions of world-premiere shows in 35 years, amazing audiences year after year by demonstrating how much can be accomplished with little money, and resourceful spirit. Curious has developed its own recognizable style, using an economy of means and production to make deep and personal, rather than large and commercial, works. In 1995, Beau O'Reilly was named one of the fifty most influential people in Chicago theater by *Chicago magazine*; and in 1998, Beau O'Reilly and Jenny Magnus were named among the Artists of the Year by the *Chicago Tribune*. Curious's *Waiting for Godot* and *The Caretaker* were named among the top five theater productions of 2006 and 2009, respectively, by *Newcity*. In 2007, Curious Theatre Branch won an Orgie Award for Original Theater for the yearlong Samuel Beckett festival, *No Danger of the Spiritual Thing: 100 Years of Beckett* (best ensemble), and in 2011 Curious was granted a year-long residency at the Museum of Contemporary Art Chicago, culminating in Jenny Magnus's *Still in Play: A Performance of Getting Ready*. Curious has produced the Rhinoceros Theater Festival, a festival of new works, made by and for diverse audiences, for over thirty years.

T-ROY MARTIN *performed in the 27th Rhinoceros Theater Festival, 2016*

A CURIOUS History / TIMELINE

2022

Jimmy & the Nickels by Matt Rieger

2021

Aviva Green: The Rebirth of Bleak by Matt Rieger
A Michael Martin Tribute curated by Kelly Anchors

2020

Four Story Animal curated by Beau O'Reilly

2019

Xmas in Lost Pines by Matt Rieger
A Packet of Holiness and Joy Will Come to You?
   by Beau O'Reilly
Open Wide by Jenny Magnus
The Skriker by Caryl Churchill

2018

(Not) Another Day by Jenny Magnus
Crossing Aviva by Matt Rieger
The Near Future by Julia Williams

2017

The Threepenny Opera by Kurt Weill & Bertolt Brecht
   adapted by Rick Burkhardt
Tattered and Wincing by Beau O'Reilly
The 28th Annual Rhinofest: New Work
   by Jenny Magnus, Beau O'Reilly & Matt Test

2016

One Boppa: Two Acts by Beau O'Reilly
The Eviller Twin by Sue Cargill
Rhinoceros by Eugene Ionesco

2015

Playing God by Matt Rieger
Black River Falls by Bryn Magnus
Welcome to Beautown, Seven or so plays by Beau O'Reilly

2014

March! by Beau O'Reilly & Julia Williams
Rung: An experimental chamber opera by Matt Test

2013

To End to Seem to End by Jayita Bhattacharya
Clumsy Sublime by Barrie Cole
A Part of the Game by Matt Rieger
All the Ways to Hidey Hole: Madras Parables
    by Jenny Magnus & Beau O'Reilly

2012

Evanston, Which Is Over There by Beau O'Reilly
The Other Side of the Elephant: Short Plays
    by Curious Writers
Today Like a Kind of Shivering by Jayita Bhattacharya
Our Kate Takes a Trip by Beau O'Reilly

2011

Still in Play: A Performance of Getting Ready
    by Jenny Magnus
The Buzz That Is the Buzz by Beau O'Reilly
4:48 Psychosis by Sarah Kane
Mexico by Gertrude Stein

2010

Jet Black Chevrolet & The Flowers Are Dead
    by Scott T. Barsotti & Matt Rieger
Three Story Animal Curated by Beau O'Reilly
*Subject Matter Created and Destroyed & I Am in a Small
    Space for a Reason I Don't Understand,* Two Curious Plays
    by Matt Rieger & Matt Test
The Art of Unbearable Sensations by Shawn Reddy

2009

No Longer the Rock of the World & Dead to the World,
  Two Plays by Beau O'Reilly
The Caretaker by Harold Pinter
Nowhere But Up by Jenny Magnus
*Elvisbride: Some Prepared Remarks to Clarify the
  Impending Jubilation* by Jayita Bhattacharya & Matt Test

2008

Cabaret Mit Teeth Curated by Beau O'Reilly
The Other Side of the Elephant: Short Plays
  by Curious Writers
Round & Round: A sexfarcetragedy by Jenny Magnus
The Great Galvani by Shawn Reddy

2007

The Madelyn Trilogy by Beau O'Reilly
Truck on a Roll & Room by Beau O'Reilly & Jenny Magnus
A Blade, a Coat & a Loaf of Bread by S. Thomasin Barsotti,
  Matt Rieger, Buddy Rivara, and Adam Rosenberg

2006

SEASON: 100 YEARS OF BECKETT
Endgame by Samuel Beckett
Waiting for Godot by Samuel Beckett
No Danger of the... Spiritual Thing Short Plays
  by Samuel Beckett
Jet Black Chevrolet by S. Thomasin Barsotti

2005

Don't Tell Us We're Here by Bryn Magnus
What Abandon Meant by Jenny Magnus
The Turtle at Play by Beau O'Reilly
How to Carry Love by Jenny Magnus
White Suit Science by Shawn Reddy

2004

No Danger of the…Spiritual Thing Short Plays
  by Samuel Beckett
Hit Me Like a Flower by Beau O'Reilly
Cant by Jenny Magnus
The Big Promise by Bryn Magnus
Under Milkwood by Dylan Thomas
My Name is Mudd by Shawn Reddy

2003

Chump Strap: a Madras Parable by Beau O'Reilly
Things That Go Missing Three Plays by Beau O'Reilly
Refracting Rainbows by Marianne Fieber and Kelly Ann
  Corcoran
The Mark Twain Invitational Curated by Beau O'Reilly
Eugene & the Song of the Wicked Starling
  by Shawn Reddy
The Dorothy Project by Beau O'Reilly

2002

Power Brechtdown 2002 Texts by Bertolt Brecht
The Man Stripped Bare by His Boy by Shawn Reddy
What Abandon Meant by Jenny Magnus
Whiskey in Blue by Beau O'Reilly
Discovery Tales by Bryn Magnus
Stone in My Shoe by Marianne Fieber

2001

Love Horse by Bryn Magnus
Bantam Lightweight by Shawn Reddy
Round & Round: a sexfarcetragedy by Jenny Magnus
Truck in Pieces by Beau O'Reilly
Influenza and the Misapplication of Cold Cream
  by Shawn Reddy

2000

Whiskey in Blue by Beau O'Reilly
Loser's Alias by Bryn Magnus
Not Only Sleeping by Beau O'Reilly

1999

The Lucky Ones by Jenny Magnus
Creature Winds by Bryn Magnus
Talking About Godard by Beau O'Reilly
Jerico the Fool by Bryn Magnus

1998

The NowHow (and How to Now It) by Jenny Magnus
The House on the Lake by the Woods Near the Ocean
   by Beau O'Reilly
The Strange by Jenny Magnus
3 Rex by Frank Melcouri, Achy Obejas & Scott Turner

1997

Small Together by Bryn Magnus
Neighborhood Stories by Bryn Magnus & John Starrs
Crowtown by Beau O'Reilly
Dictator Light by Bryn Magnus

1996

The Trips: a Madras Parable by Jenny Magnus
Seven Pounds of Mud by Beau O'Reilly
Hyperbolic Gangland by Bryn Magnus
Angela Woodward's Inner Life
Illustrious Bloodspill by Bryn Magnus
The Julieannes by Bryn Magnus

1995

The Third Degrees of J.O. Breeze by Beau O'Reilly
Invisible Sympathies by Bryn Magnus
Moans and Other Pheromones by Bryn Magnus
Full Moon Over Lincoln Avenue: Monologues
The Startling Ascent of Mr. Waffle by Bryn Magnus

1994

Wolfie 'n' Me at the Foul Line by Beau O'Reilly
The Willies by Jenny Magnus
Correspondence Boxing
   by Bryn Magnus & Russel Brown O'Brien
And God Said to Abraham by Scott Turner
Classic Cats by Bryn Magnus
Boy Basement Battles the Demons of Sleep
   by Beau O'Reilly
Hat Fish (Feeding the Fish and Under the Hat)
   by Anita Stenger & Marianne Fieber
The Spew Police... Suffergush Returns & Two Wheels Good
   Monologues by Beau O'Reilly & Mark Comiskey

1993

Three Flat Walkup
   by Bryn Magnus, Jenny Magnus & Beau O'Reilly
How Could Such a Monster Come to Be? by Jeff Dorchen,
   Bryn Magnus, Jenny Magnus & Beau O'Reilly
IN by Jenny Magnus & Liz Payne
Let the Dolly Do the Work by Beau O'Reilly
Loser's Alias by Bryn Magnus

1992

Avalanch Ranch by Bryn Magnus
Dying Is Private: The Satch and Mo Play by Beau O'Reilly
Dwarfed by Comparison by Beau O'Reilly
Natural Hostages by Bryn Magnus

1991

Ward 6 adapted by Jill Daly
Evil Triggers Down Amateur Street by Beau O'Reilly
I, Figaro adapted by Jill Daly
Endgame by Samuel Beckett
Curios by Bryn Magnus, Jill Daly & Anita Stenger

1990

Kings X Tyrannousaurus Rex Constantinople
   by Jenny Magnus
Looking Through Two Johnnies
   by Beau O'Reilly & Jenny Magnus
Open Syzygy: Some Madras Parables
   by Beau O'Reilly & Jenny Magnus
The Weirdly Sisters by Bryn Magnus

1989

Two Tales With Legs
   by Jenny Magnus, John Sutherland & Beau O'Reilly
Careening Is a Skill: Estranged Musicale
   by Beau O'Reilly & Jenny Magnus

1988

Bargan Gives Up by Bertolt Brecht
Donald Didn't Do It by Beau O'Reilly
Prayers for the Undoing of Spells by Bryn Magnus
*Madras Parables: Your Dreams Are Bleeding Over Into
Mine* by Beau O'Reilly & Jenny Magnus
Careening Is a Skill: Estranged Musicale
   by Beau O'Reilly & Jenny Magnus

CURIOUS THEATRE BRANCH member portraits >>
for *The Threepenny Opera,* September 2017

Curious Plays and other Curious Theatre Branch titles
in the *Contemporary Theater Collection*
are published by JackLeg Press.

For information on distribution of books in this series—
or to order copies—visit **www.jacklegpress.org**

Other **Jackleg Press** authors include:

V. Joshua Adams	Jean McGarry
Scott Brown	D.K. McCutchen
Brittney Corrigan	Jenny Magnus
Jessica Cuello	Rita Mookerjee
Allison Cundiff	Mamie Morgan
Curious Theatre Branch	cin salach
Barbara Cully	Jo Salas
Suzanne Frischkorn	Maureen Seaton
Victoria Garza	Kristine Snodgrass
Reginald Gibbons	Cornelia Maude Spelman
D.C. Gonzales-Prieto	Peter Stenson
Neil de la Flor	Hugh Behm-Steinberg
Caroline Goodwin	Melissa Studdard
Jennifer Harris	Megan Weiler
Meagan Lehr	David Wesley Williams
Brigitte Lewis	

www.ingramcontent.com/pod-product-compliance
Lightning Source LLC
Chambersburg PA
CBHW070857120626
46546CB00001B/30